I0822204

CENTER FOR ORIGINS RESEARCH

# Issues

IN CREATION

# *CORE Issues in Creation*

## Series Introduction

A complete model. For my entire professional career this has been my dream for young-age creationism. We have long had a need for a scholarly presentation of not only the discipline-specific implications of young-age creationism, but also a scholarly presentation of our field's epistemology and of the foundational philosophies of all the disciplines – from biblical studies, to philosophy, to the pure sciences, and to the applied sciences beyond. This is a huge task which requires the intentional, concerted, effort of a world-wide community of scholars across all the disciplines. And, as we build that community we will need outlets for the research results, including outlets for the extensive monographs which will be involved. *CORE Issues* has been created for the publication of young-age creation model-building monographs. This monograph series is not for the publication of scholarly critiques of alternative positions (other venues exist for that kind of publication). Rather, *CORE Issues* has been created to publish any monograph in any discipline (philosophy, theology, physics, geology, biology, archaeology, linguistics, *etc.*, *etc.*) which substantially contributes to the systematic development of a positive, young age creation model. Such monographs will be required to thoroughly review the creationist literature on the subject, offer a constructive interpretation of the subject's data, integrate well with other disciplines as the model is constructed, and advance creation model development. *CORE Issues* is peer-reviewed and will strive for the very highest scholarship standards.

I am very pleased to introduce the *CORE Issues* with a monograph by Todd Wood which offers a preliminary creationist interpretation of the Galápagos Islands. Not only does Dr. Wood offer some intriguing suggestions on the Islands' geology and climate from a young-age creationist perspective, he substantially advances the entire discipline of creation biology with his application of baraminological techniques to the Islands' flora and fauna. This monograph is exemplary of the works we anticipate in this series. He fully reviews previous work by creationists, offers a positve model for the Galápagos Islands which integrates with the most recent creationist research, substantially advances the creation model, and opens up exciting opportunities for future research. It has also survived a rather rigorous peer-review process (more than 12 professionals are to be thanked for their services in this regard).

*CORE Issues* does not accept unsolicited manuscripts, but researchers with ideas for future monographs should contact '*CORE Issues* editor' at **info@bryancore.org** (or *CORE Issues* editor; Bryan College, Box 7802; Dayton, TN 37321-7000).

Kurt Wise
Bryan College
Dayton, Tennessee
8 April 2005

# A Creationist Review and Preliminary Analysis of the History, Geology, Climate, and Biology of the Galápagos Islands

TODD CHARLES WOOD
Assistant Professor, Center for Origins Research
Bryan College

Center for Origins Research Issues in Creation
Number 1
June15, 2005

Wipf and Stock Publishers
199 W 8th Ave, Suite 3
Eugene, OR 97401

A Creationist Review and Preliminary Analysis
of the History, Geology, Climate, and Biology
of the Galápagos Islands
By Wood, Todd Charles

ISBN: 1-59752-180-9
First printing June, 2005.

## Abstract

The Galápagos Islands have long served as an example of, and apologetic for, evolution. In this review, I summarize and evaluate the history, geology, climate, and biology of the Galápagos from a creationist perspective. I find that the relationship of Darwin's intellectual development to the islands has been overstated. Darwin's visit to the Galápagos was an important factor in his acceptance of species transmutation but not in his development of natural selection. Geologically, the islands are both simple and complex. They are simple in that they are all remnants of basaltic hotspot volcanoes. The Galápagos is complex in that the tectonic history of the region and the source of the hotspot magma remain controversial. I conclude that the extant islands are entirely post-Flood. The climate of the islands is dry, but irregularly devastated by recurring El Niños. Due to a lack of comprehensive chronological tools for creationist researchers, it is difficult to evaluate evidence of past climate. I make an argument that rainfall in the Galápagos was consistently higher during the post-Flood ice advance. The biological sections address baraminological status of ten different organismal groups found in the islands: the giant tortoises, iguanids (including the iguanas and lava lizards), weevils, Darwin's finches, pelecaniforms (including the flightless cormorant), the Galápagos penguin, the Galápagos hawk, endemic composites (*Scalesia*, *Darwiniothamnus*, and *Lecocarpus*), *Opuntia* cacti, and *Mollugo*. Aside from the ongoing studies of Darwin's finches, I find little evidence for natural selection. Instead, the marine iguanas, giant tortoises, penguins, and flightless cormorants exhibit signs of pre-adaptation. Even variation and selection in the finches has not produced new species. My primary conclusion is that the Galápagos offers numerous opportunities to field test creationist theories, and rather than being good examples of evolution, the biology and geology of the islands are consistent with a young-earth creationist model of earth and life history.

## Contents

## Acknowledgements

I would like to thank Kurt Wise for many helpful discussions "around the table," as I worked to synthesize information about Galápagos geology into the creation model. Without his insight and assistance, the geological and climatological sections of this work would be much poorer. Many thanks also to Vonnie Johnson at the Bryan College library for deciphering my handwritten interlibrary loan requests (especially those crazy journal titles). Thanks to Stephanie Mace for assistance in creating figures, scanning datasets, and ordering the many materials that I studied while researching this work. Thanks to Andrew Snelling, Joe Francis, and anonymous reviewers for their helpful editorial comments on earlier versions of this work. This research was supported by donations to the Center for Origins Research at Bryan College.

# I. Introduction and Historical Overview

## 1.1 Introduction

Mention of the Galápagos Islands immediately evokes images of a young Darwin discovering evolution while voyaging on the H.M.S. *Beagle*. Even though this popular impression contradicts the historical record, the myth of Darwin's activities in the Galápagos continues. Although Darwin credited his speculations on the origin of species to his visit to the Galápagos, the islands appear only rarely in *Origin*, figuring most prominently in his discussion of evolutionary biogeography (Darwin 1859, chap. 12). Despite this apparent ambiguity in Darwin's thought, Julian Huxley wrote, "It was on the Galápagos ... that Darwin took the first step out of the fairyland of creationism into the coherent and comprehensible world of modern biology" (Huxley 1966).

What are we to make of Huxley's claim, aside from objecting to his unflattering characterization of creationism? More importantly, just how important are the Galápagos to the growth and endurance of evolutionary theory? Does the modern myth of the Galápagos as a catalyst to the "discovery" of evolution preclude even the possibility of creationist interpretations? The answers to these questions depend on who does the answering. In discussing the biogeography of the Galápagos, Ernst Mayr (2001, p. 34) wrote, "For a creationist there is no rational explanation for distributional irregularities, but they are completely compatible with a historical evolutionary explanation." Creationists Henry Morris and Gary Parker (1987, p. 89) wrote of the Galápagos, "How did Darwin explain the 'origin' of these various finches? Exactly the same way a creationist would." Because the Morris and Parker passage antedates Mayr's by at least 13 years, these writers obviously must disagree on the very definition of "creationist explanation." Such basic disagreements reveal the importance of the Galápagos as an emblem of evolution: Despite the ongoing progress of creationism and the rise of reasonable creationist explanations, evolutionary icons persist. Before discussing the ongoing creation/evolution argument as it applies to the Galápagos, it is helpful to review their geographical and historical setting.

The Galápagos Islands comprise 121 volcanic islands and islets 600 miles west of Ecuador (Snell *et al.* 1995) (Plate 1). The archipelago straddles the equator, with most of the major islands in the southern hemisphere. Europeans accidentally discovered the archipelago in 1535, as the fourth Bishop of Panama Tomás de Berlanga sailed from Panama to Peru on a mission to mediate dissension between the conquistadores Pizzaro and de Almagro (Markham 1892; Slevin 1959). His ship became caught in the Doldrums and drifted 500 miles off course, bringing them in six days to the yet-unnamed Galápagos Islands. He reported his voyage to Emperor Carlos V in a letter dated April 26, 1535 (reproduced in Slevin 1959). In the letter, the bishop recounted the barrenness of the archipelago and the difficulty of finding sufficient water. The men of the ship were reduced to chewing cactus for moisture until they finally found a pool that contained enough drinking water for the crew. Two men and ten horses died of thirst before the ship reached port in Peru a month after leaving the Galápagos (Slevin 1959). Though he was the first to discover them, Berlanga did not bother to name these islands. The first reference to the *Galápagos* islands appears on a map of the world published in 1570, 35 years after Berlanga's visit (Slevin 1959; McEwen 1988).

During the seventeenth and eighteenth centuries, the British used the archipelago as a base to attack Spanish ships and settlements in South America. Significant descriptions of the Galápagos of this period come from the journals of buccaneers Ambrose Cowley and Edward Davis (Slevin 1959). In the late 1790s, the islands became a regular port of call for whalers looking to stock their ships with tortoises for fresh meat. The first permanent human inhabitant came to the islands in 1807 but abandoned his solitary existence for the mainland after only a few years (Slevin 1959). In 1832, Ecuador claimed sovereignty over the islands and sent settlers to Isla Floreana (Larson 2001, p. 52). When Darwin visited in 1835, about 200 people lived on the islands, primarily criminals and "undesirables" (Darwin 1839, p. 456). This colony was abandoned a few years after Darwin's visit, and numerous other attempts to colonize the islands during the 1800s also failed (Thornton 1971). Later colonization efforts by Ecuador proved more successful, resulting in an estimated population of 600 permanent residents by 1900. By 1995, nearly 14,000 people lived on the islands (McFarland and Cifuentes 1996).

After World War II, scientific attitudes towards the Galápagos changed dramatically. Previous scientific expeditions, such as the California Academy of Sciences expedition of 1905-1906, emphasized the collection of vast numbers of specimens during their brief visits to the islands. These collecting efforts were motivated by a perceived urgency to preserve organismal remains in museums before they became extinct in the wild. In 1935, however, an Ecuadorian corporation proposed for the first time that the Galápagos be protected by the establishment of a research station (Smith 1990), a project that languished until the 1950s. In 1954, German scientist Irenäus Eibl-Eibesfeldt visited the islands and became a key European supporter of Galápagos conservation (Larson 2001, p. 177-178). In the U.S., ornithologist Robert I. Bowman joined the cause after a 1952-1953 visit (Larson 2001, p. 182). Finally, Julian Huxley's influence in creating the United Nations Educational, Scientific and Cultural Organization (UNESCO) provided needed funding for the establishment of a permanent research and conservation organization, the Charles Darwin Foundation for the Galápagos Islands (CDF) (Smith 1990).

The CDF was organized under Belgian law in July, 1959, with Julian Huxley as honorary president of the executive council. That same year, the government of Ecuador created a national park covering the undeveloped lands in the Galápagos (97% of the archipelago) and negotiated an agreement with the CDF to build and maintain a permanent research station at Academy Bay, Isla Santa Cruz. Construction began in 1960, and the official dedication took place in 1964. In attendance were members of the Galápagos International Scientific Project, a 66-member interdisciplinary team that spent five weeks in the Galápagos to expand scientific research in the archipelago (Cohen and Bowman 1964; Bowman 1966). Joining them were many Ecuadorean governmental and military dignitaries. After the dedication, the Ecuadorean government and CDF officials signed an agreement allowing the CDF to own and operate the Charles Darwin Research Station for the next 25 years (Smith 1990). The agreement was extended in 1988 (Smith 1990) and renewed for an additional 25 years in 1991 (Evans 1992).

Despite the importance of the Galápagos to the history and mythology of evolution, creationists have rarely commented on the islands. In one of the earliest references to Galápagos in creationist literature, Byron Nelson (1927, p. 78) wrote, "The theory of creation does not require, as Darwin and his cohorts have supposed, that the plants and animals of the Galapagos Islands ... were created there." Later, Clark (1940, p. 52) argued that the variety of Galápagos species supports their origin by natural selection, a radical suggestion for a creationist at the time. Other early references appear in Frank Lewis Marsh's 1944 book, *Evolution, Creation and Science* (p. 243) and in a later review of Dobzhansky's *Genetics and the Origin of Species* (1945). Given Marsh's general acceptance of evolutionary mechanisms within the "kind," it should come as no surprise that his comments on Galápagos are decidedly neutral. He mentions only the strong affinity between Galápagos species and those found on mainland Central and South America.

Several creationists visited the islands during the twentieth century and beyond, the most notable being the 2003 tour offered by the Institute for Creation Research (Anonymous 2003). The most extensive creationist account of the Galápagos is Lester Harris's book *Galapagos: A Creationist Visits Darwin's Islands*, published in 1976. At the time, Harris was a herpetologist at Loma Linda University (LLU) who initiated purchase of property for LLU in the Galápagos and supervised a course in Galápagos biology during the summers (L. Brand, personal communication, 2003). Harris's book presents the flora and fauna of the islands with a very popular tone, peppered with anecdotes of Harris's own visits. In the book, Harris expresses the most common creationist opinion of the islands, that Darwin correctly deduced that species on the islands had evolved by natural selection but that he improperly extrapolated beyond this to assume that all species evolved from a common ancestor over a long period of time. Harris wrote, "Didn't Darwin draw bigger conclusions from what he saw than he should have? Didn't he stick his neck out and guess that a lot more happened in nature than really took place? I think so." (Harris 1976, p. 13).

At about the same time as Harris worked at the Galápagos, John Klotz, a member of the Creation Research Society Board of Directors, also visited the islands and published an account in the

*Creation Research Society Quarterly* (Klotz 1972). He covered much of the same information as Harris but does so with a more professional tone. He also agreed with Harris's basic premise: Darwin was "right in his explanation of the origin of the unusual plant and animal forms he observed on the Galápagos, but wrong in his conclusion that when he demonstrated change and even the origin of new species he had proven macroevolution" (Klotz 1972).

Though Harris's and Klotz's position of accommodation is common among creationists (e.g. Morris and Parker 1987, p. 89), it has not been critically examined. Based on the statements of Harris, Klotz, and Morris and Parker, we might describe creationist opinions of Galápagos as "Darwinian with a limit," which would explain the general desire to determine the "limits of variation" (Marsh 1976; Lester and Bohlin 1989). The position is easily taken when confronted with the compelling evidence of speciation and apparent evidence of natural selection in the Galápagos. The question remains, however: How much did Darwin correctly infer about the nature of speciation? Recent advances in creation biology would suggest that much of the modern neodarwinian synthesis is inadequate for understanding speciation (Wood 2002a). Wood's concept of mediated design would change speciation from a random, selection-induced process to a pre-designed, created process (Wood and Cavanaugh 2001; Wood 2003a). Although this theory could provide new insight on the origin of species, it has not been extensively tested.

Along with creation biology, creation geology and climatology has significantly advanced over the past decade. As a result, we have an excellent – though incomplete – picture of the geological devastation wrought by the Flood. Ongoing field studies at Grand Canyon (Austin 1994; Austin 2003) and Mt. St. Helens (Coffin 1983a; Austin 1984; Austin 1986) have provided evidence that geological indicators of old age can be replicated in rapid, catastrophic events. The Catastrophic Plate Tectonics (CPT) model proposes that most tectonic events took place during or soon after the Flood. CPT explains evidence of plate tectonics plus data that cannot be explained by the conventional model (Austin *et al.* 1994). For example, CPT provides a mechanism for explaining the "Ice Age" (Vardiman 1994b) and successfully predicted rapid geomagnetic reversals (Austin *et al.* 1994).

Though creationists have made much progress in

understanding a general outline of the history of creation, little effort has yet been made to integrate the biological and geological theories and to test them in specific case studies. In large part, the biologists and geologists have been laboring in isolation and dealing with general trends and large-scale models. The Galápagos Islands provide an excellent opportunity to field-test creationist theories. The basaltic volcanoes of the islands give opportunity to test novel ideas about radioactive decay (Vardiman *et al.* 2000), paleomagnetic dating (Austin *et al.* 1994), and CPT (Austin *et al.* 1994). The organisms provide opportunity to apply baraminological methods (Robinson and Cavanaugh 1998a; Cavanaugh 2002; Wood 2004), theories of diversification (Wood and Cavanaugh 2001; Wood 2002a; Wood 2003b), and to understand mechanisms of post-Flood biogeography (Wise and Croxton 2003). Combining these theories could lead to the development of an integrated chronology of the islands, which would have important implications for broader questions about the Flood and post-Flood recovery.

In this monograph, I will discuss our present state of knowledge about the Galápagos Islands from a creationist perspective. I will attempt to apply the most recent creationist models of geology, climatology, and biology to the Galápagos, but it should be noted that my intention here is not to issue the final creationist interpretation of the islands. Instead, my goal is three-fold. First, I will show that the present creation model can explain the Galápagos at least as well as the various conventional models (plate tectonics, neodarwinism, etc.). Second, since biology is my expertise, I plan to test baraminology methods and highlight the areas of deficiency and strategies to address those deficiencies. Third and most importantly, I hope to inspire other creationists to join the research effort and work together to understand the history of the Galápagos and how the islands integrate with the Biblical record of earth history.

### 1.2. Overview

As a preliminary warning to the informed reader, I want to point out that the published literature on the geology, biology, and climate of the Galápagos is extensive. It is not possible for me to cover all of this information in a single review. The necessity to keep this work to a readable length has compelled me to center on certain issues while excluding others. The topics presented conform to one of three over-riding interests. Some topics are easily incorporated into the present creation model, with minor interpretive adjustment. Other topics are included because of their popularity. Many of these could be incorporated into the creation model but will require further research. Some organismal groups are chosen because of the availability of data on which baraminological techniques can be tested. In all cases, I recommend future creationist research projects that should lead to a better understanding of the Galápagos and creation in general.

I will open the body of this monograph by reviewing the relationship between Darwin's intellectual development and his experiences in the Galápagos. I will then survey the geological and climatological setting, with reference to creationist models that pertain to the recovery of the earth after the Flood. The bulk of the monograph will focus on the biology of the islands. I will begin with what are arguably the most famous island residents: the giant tortoises. Continuing with the reptiles, I will also discuss the curious marine iguana and lava lizards. Each of these reptile groups is well-known and must be discussed in a review of Galápagos. Next, I will present preliminary observations on the *Galapaganus* weevils, because like the Galápagos iguanids -the weevils seem to have evolved before the islands were in existence. Returning to the vertebrates, I will discuss various avian fauna of the islands, including the finches for their fame, and the pelecaniforms, the Galápagos penguin, and the Galápagos hawk. These bird groups make interesting subjects because of the availability of useful data and because of their previous analysis by creationists. The plants of the Galápagos constitute the next section. The Asteraceae and cacti are prominent flora on the islands, and the plant *Mollugo* relates to prior creationist work on mediated design in photosynthesis. My choice of biological subjects should not be taken as an exhaustive survey; many other groups from Galápagos (e.g. the snakes) could be the subject of fruitful creationist research. I will conclude the monograph with a proposed synthesis of the biogeography of the islands, a discussion of natural selection vs. mediated design and of baraminological methods, and specific recommendations for future research.

It should be noted, as most Galápagos authors do, that the present islands go by a variety of names (McEwen 1988; Woram 1989). Though the English named the islands first, the government of Ecuador has conferred upon the islands official Spanish names.

Thus, the Galápagos Islands are officially known as Archipelago de Colón, after Christopher Columbus. Even these names are not universally used, but I will consistently use the names illustrated in Plate 1.

# 2. Darwin and the Galápagos

The relationship between Darwin's intellectual development and his visit to the Galápagos has been much debated in recent history. The modern myth holds that: 1) Darwin discovered natural selection in a sort of Archimedean *eureka* while at the Galápagos and 2) the finches of the Galápagos were influential in that experience. For example, Julian Huxley (1953, p. 59) claimed that the finches "more than anything else convinced Darwin of the fact of evolution." Roger Tory Peterson (1967) stated that Darwin "noted that the finches differed from island to island, yet seemed to have had a common inheritance." Lester and Bohlin (1989, p. 17) more cautiously claim that the size variation in the finch beaks "added to his [Darwin's] curiosity." As we shall see, however, there is not much truth in this legend. First, the Galápagos had a significant influence on Darwin's thought only in the years following his visit, as he pondered the curious biogeography of the archipelago (Smith 1958, p. 32; Richardson 1981). Second, the fauna of the islands mostly contributed to his rejection of species stasis, not his development of natural selection theory. Third, of all the Galápagos biota, the finches played a relatively minor role in the development of Darwin's ideas (Sulloway 1982a, 1982b, 1983, 1984, 1985).

Despite the errors of the myth, the importance of the Galápagos on Darwin's developing evolutionary ideas is irrefutable. By his own admission, Darwin was greatly affected by his visit to the Galápagos. In his *Autobiography*, Darwin wrote, "During the voyage of the *Beagle* I had been deeply impressed ... by the South American character of most of the productions of the Galapagos [*sic*] archipelago" (Darwin 1958, pp. 41-42), an observation which appeared in *Origin* (Darwin 1859, p. 397-400). Darwin's son Frances (1909) and granddaughter Nora Barlow (1935) also emphasized the importace of Galápagos in Darwin's development of evolution.

What then is the actual relationship between Darwin's theory of evolution and his visit to and observations in the Galápagos? To answer this question, it is helpful to remember that the development of evolutionary theory in Darwin's mind came in two distinct stages. First, Darwin became convinced that species were not fixed entities but were capable of changing from one species to another. In other words, he became convinced of transmutation or to use his term, "common descent." Only later did Darwin arrive at the second step – a conviction that natural selection is the primary mechanism to explain transmutation. Seen in this light, we can recognize the important distinction between evidence of common descent and evidence of natural selection.

Darwin's writings on the subject make it very obvious that his visit to and consideration of the Galápagos contributed to his acceptance only of common descent. Almost without exception, Darwin's written comments on the Galápagos focus on the remarkable affinity of the Galápagos species to those on the South and Central American mainland. Indeed, as Desmond (1982, pp. 148-149) and others (Fichman 1977; Richardson 1981) have argued, biogeographical concerns figured prominently in the development and acceptance of transmutation by Darwin and his British contemporaries. Thus, though Darwin's finches may have had a very small influence on Darwin's theories, his general observations of the biogeography of the Galápagos contributed significantly to his thoughts on transmutation. We can see the interaction between Darwin's experiences in Galápagos and his development of evolution in a short review of Darwin's history and writings on the subject.

Darwin's voyage to the Galápagos actually began in 1828 when the *Beagle*'s captain Pringle Stokes committed suicide in South America. The new *Beagle* captain Robert Fitzroy requested a gentleman companion to accompany him on the ship's surveying mission to South America. When the British admiralty approved Fitzroy's request, Darwin's professors at Cambridge recommended that he fill the position. Darwin and his supporters persuaded his father Dr. Robert Darwin to pay passage for Charles and his servant. Darwin then successfully lobbied to turn the *Beagle*'s journey into a circumnavigation. Thus, at the age of only 22, Darwin embarked on a voyage around the world beginning in December, 1831 and lasting until October, 1836 (Larson 2001, pp. 62-64).

Though his name is so inextricably linked to Galápagos, Darwin actually spent very little time there. The *Beagle* visited and surveyed the Galápagos for only five weeks during the nearly five-year voyage, in September and October of 1835. During the visit, Darwin landed on San Cristóbal, Floreana, Isabela, and Santiago (Estes *et al.* 2000; see Figure 1), and he wrote 105 pages in his journal, 80 of which describe the geology of the archipelago and 25 of which discuss the zoology (Gruber and Gruber 1962). The emphasis of geology over zoology was typical of Darwin's *Beagle* notes. None of Darwin's notes known to be written during the visit to the Galápagos contain any clear statements on natural selection or even transmutation of species. Only one comment in any of the *Beagle* journals could be interpreted as early speculation on species mutability.

In his *Beagle* ornithology notebook, Darwin wrote, "the Zoology of Archipelagoes will be well worth examining; for such facts would undermine the stability of species" (quoted in Barlow 1935). Lady Barlow (1935) believed that this passage revealed

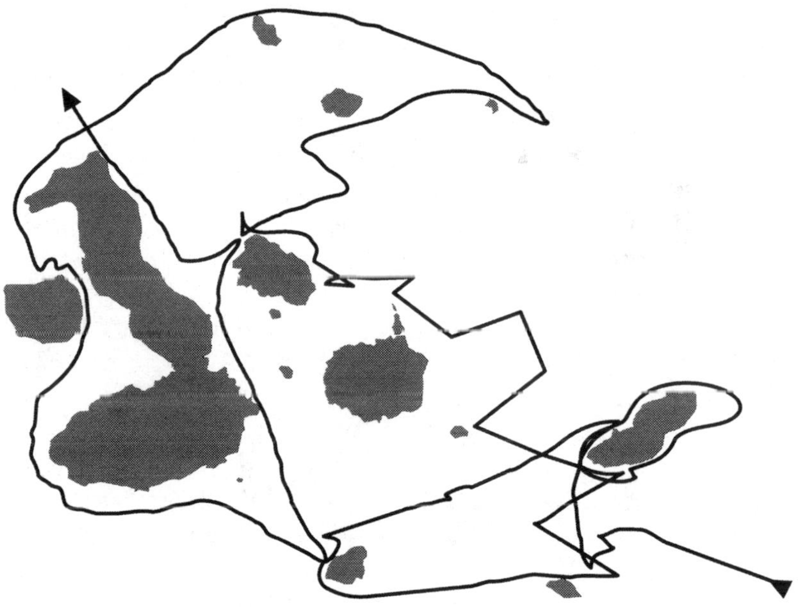

Figure 1. The path of the *Beagle* on its visit to the Galápagos Islands in September and October, 1835 (based on Estes *et al.* 2000).

an early speculation of Darwin's on species transmutation while he was still in the Galápagos, but others have suggested that the comment was actually written during the last few months of the voyage, nine months after his visit to the Galápagos (Gruber and Gruber 1962; Gruber 1974, p. 101; Sulloway 1984). During these months, Darwin began to organize and prepare his notes for publication upon his return to England. In so doing, he would naturally have been reflective on the meaning of the observations that he made. In that context then, it is not surprising to see a speculative statement on zoology and species stasis. Despite the uncertainty in dating the note, it was definitely made on the *Beagle*, within no more than a year of visiting the Galápagos. It also reveals a possible connection between his observations on Galápagos and other archipelagos ("Zoology of Archipelagos") and his thoughts on transmutation ("undermine the stability of species").

Ten months after the return of the *Beagle*, Darwin began his first journal on the "Transmutation of Species." In his diary, he noted "In July [of 1837] opened first notebook on 'Transmutation of Species' - Had been greatly struck from about month of previous March on character of S. American fossils - and species on Galapagos Archipelago. These facts origin (especially latter), of all my views [*sic*]" (quoted in Sulloway 1984). March of 1837 was only six months after the end of the *Beagle*'s voyage and seventeen months after leaving the Galápagos. Thus, Darwin's earliest recorded speculations on species transmutation occur very close to his visit to the Galápagos, which by his own admission significantly influenced his views on species transmutation. Darwin's son Francis (1909) considered this quote very significant in not only dating the emergence of evolutionary thinking in Darwin's mind but also in understanding the significance of the Galápagos archipelago to the development of transmutation and natural selection.

Sulloway (1984) persuasively argued that it was the identification of the Galápagos mockingbirds (genus *Nesosimus*) – and nothing to do with the finches – which precipitated Darwin's thoughts on transmutation and his comment on Galápagos in his diary. Darwin was intrigued by the variations he had observed in the Galápagos, particularly variations among the mockingbirds that came from separate islands. At the time of his visit to Galápagos, he conceded to the prevalent opinion that species were fixed and he hypothesized that the mockingbirds he had collected must have been varieties of a single species that had diversified into races or varieties, a phenomenon that was well-known and accepted at the time (Sulloway 1984).

When John Gould examined Darwin's collections from the *Beagle*, he recognized that the mockingbird specimens were actually three different species, each of which was limited to a specific island (Sulloway 1985). Darwin learned of Gould's diagnosis of the mockingbird species in March of 1837, probably between March 7 and 12, as Sulloway (1982b) argued. Note that this is exactly the time he noted in his diary passage: "Had been greatly struck from about month of previous March [of 1837] on character of S. American fossils - and species on Galapagos Archipelago." He is almost certainly referring to his meeting with Gould and probably also his February, 1837 meeting with Richard Owen to discuss the similarities of South American fossils with modern species (Sulloway 1984).

At his meeting with Gould, Darwin was impressed by the endemicity of the Galápagos mockingbirds (Sulloway 1984). To understand the significance of this, we must remember the prevalent scientific view of the day. Although modern scientists (and to some extent, Darwin himself) depict Darwin as wrestling against "creationism," the ideas of Darwin's day were actually quite diverse (G. Nelson 1978). In general, though, it was various forms of natural theology, and not creationism in any modern sense, that dominated British science at the time (Livingstone 1984). Most natural theologians advocated species stasis and believed species were optimally suited to their environment. Species originated either by creation in their present habitat or by creation and dispersal from various "centers of creation" (e.g. see Lyell 1832, Vol. 2, pp. 126-127). In this view, endemism would only be expected in unique environments, and similar species should only be found in similar environments. Darwin himself mentioned this concept in his discussion of the Galápagos land iguanas (Darwin 1839, p. 474).

In considering natural theology, we can see how the endemicity of mockingbirds would be so remarkable. Since Darwin recognized that the Galápagos were oceanic islands (never connected to the mainland), he expected that the species of the Galápagos could only have originated by immigration from other land masses (if they were not created *in situ*) (Sulloway

1982b). When Gould assured Darwin that the land bird species were in fact endemic and *not found on the mainland*, Darwin was left with the curious observation that the species of Galápagos were unique species yet very similar to American species (Darwin 1839, p. 474; Darwin 1845, p. 377). This fact would be difficult to explain by the natural theology concepts of perfect adaptation and species stasis, but it could easily be understood if the Galápagos species had arisen by transmutation from American ones.

The significance of the mockingbirds to Darwin's development is reinforced by Ospovat's (1981) analysis of the evolution of Darwin's views on transmutation. According to Ospovat, Darwin's earliest speculations on transmutation emphasized not interactions with other organisms (*i.e.* competition) but the interaction of organisms with their physical environment. Thus, the mockingbirds fitted neatly into Darwin's thinking since the birds occupied different islands and were different species. Darwin's early way of thinking would have caused him to see a causal connection between the isolated islands and the unique species that inhabited them. It would be much later (after his development of natural selection) that Darwin would come to view other organisms as the most important ingredient of environment, thereby paving the way for Lack's (1947) selectional interpretation of the finches that bear Darwin's name.

Fifteen months after opening his transmutation notebook, Darwin turned to an early form of natural selection as a mechanism to explain species transmutation (Stauffer 1959). As he read Malthus's *Essay on the Principle of Population*, Darwin's early ideas about the mechanism of evolution transformed into the natural selection that we know today. We can see from this chronology that by the time Darwin read Malthus in 1838, the organisms of Galápagos had already influenced Darwin's thinking and convinced him of common descent.

In 1842, Darwin drafted a 15,000-word sketch of his theory, and he produced a 52,000-word version in 1844 (Barrett and Freeman 1987; Darwin 1909; Stauffer 1959; Stauffer 1975b). Both of these manuscripts are organized along the same outline as *Origin*. He kept the manuscripts private but left a note for his wife Emma with instructions on publication of the 1844 manuscript should he suddenly die (reproduced in Darwin 1909). His comments on Galápagos in these two early sketches fill in some of the details about the role that the Galápagos played in Darwin's acceptance of common descent.

Darwin's 1842 sketch begins with variation and natural selection, then proceeds to the general evidences of common descent: classification, unity of type, and biogeography (Barrett and Freeman 1987). The Galápagos islands appear three times in this document, each time in the context of biogeography. The meaning of the first and third comments on Galápagos are obscured by Darwin's abbreviated writing style (Barrett and Freeman 1987, pp. 15, 27). Of the first comment, editor Francis Darwin noted "The discussion ... is not clear, and I find it impossible to suggest a paraphrase" (Barrett and Freeman 1987, p. 15, n. 66). In the second reference, Darwin cited the Galápagos and Tristan d'Acunha as volcanic islands that must have been populated recently by species from the nearby mainland, thus they possess a "similarity [to the mainland] of type, but not in species" (Barrett and Freeman 1987, p. 24, n. 24).

Darwin's 1844 essay is more polished, complete, and readable. The Galápagos appear eight times in this document (Barrett and Freeman 1987, pp. 65, 120, 121, 129, 130, 136, 140, 147). The first reference is a comment on the close affinity of land birds, such that naturalists have difficulty distinguishing species. The remaining seven references appear in chapter six, "On the geographical distrubution of organic beings in the past and present times." Here, Darwin commented both on the biogeographical affinity of Galápagos species with mainland South America and on the affinity of different species within the archipelago. In the latter context, he cited the Galápagos mockingbirds (Barrett and Freeman 1987, p. 121). According to Darwin, the "creationist" [*i.e.* the natural theologian who accepts perfect adaptation and species stasis] can only explain these facts by claiming that "it so pleased the Creator ... that the inhabitants of the Galápagos Archipelago should be related to those of Chile" (Barrett and Freeman 1987, p. 136).

In 1845, Darwin revised his 1839 *Journal of Researches* (Figure 2). Emboldened by the explanatory power of common descent, Darwin included new hints about his opinion on the mutability of species (Colp 1986). The chapter on Galápagos was considerably expanded, with much new information from studies that had been carried out since the first edition. As he revised the description of the Galápagos finches, Darwin wrote that it would be easy to imagine that they descended from an ancestral

JOURNAL OF RESEARCHES

INTO THE

GEOLOGY

AND

NATURAL HISTORY

OF THE

VARIOUS COUNTRIES

VISITED BY H. M. S. BEAGLE,

UNDER THE COMMAND OF CAPTAIN FITZROY, R.N.

FROM 1832 TO 1836.

BY

CHARLES DARWIN, Esq., M.A. F.R.S.

SECRETARY TO THE GEOLOGICAL SOCIETY.

LONDON:

HENRY COLBURN, GREAT MARLBOROUGH STREET.

1839.

Figure 2. The cover page of the first edition of Darwin's *Journal of Researches*, published in 1839. Courtesy Bryan College Library.

population "modified for different ends" (Darwin 1845, p. 380). In the first edition, when he commented on the similarity of the Galápagos species to mainland American forms, he speculated that "some authors" might explain this observation "by saying that the creative power had acted according to the same law over a wide area" (Darwin 1839, p. 474). He omitted that concession to natural theology from the revised version. Indeed, when discussing the very same biogeographical affinities in his 1844 essay, Darwin wrote, "it is absolutely opposed to every analogy, drawn from the laws imposed by the Creator on inorganic matter, that facts [*i.e.* the similarity of Galápagos and American species], when connected, should be considered as ultimate and not the direct consequences of more general laws [*i.e.* common descent]" (Barrett and Freeman 1987, p. 136).

Just a year earlier in 1844, Darwin shared his evolutionary views in a letter to Joseph Dalton Hooker, nervously likening his divulgence to "confessing a murder" (Colp 1986). Just four years later, in another letter to Hooker dated May 10, 1848, Darwin's confidence in evolution had matured as he boldly declared his theory "all gospel" (Colp 1986). In May of 1856, encouraged in part by Hooker, Darwin began to collect his notes into a third (and what he hoped was final) written version of his theory, the "big book" (Darwin 1958, p. 192) that he called *Natural Selection* (Stauffer 1975b). Because Wallace's manuscript describing natural selection arrived in 1858, Darwin began writing a smaller version of the theory, and the surviving big book manuscript is fragmentary (Stauffer 1975b). Of the ten and a half chapters originally written for *Natural Selection*, two were used in Darwin's 1868 *Variation of Animals and Plants under Domestication*, and the remaining eight and a half were recently published by Cambridge University Press (Stauffer 1975b). The shorter version of the theory was at last published in November of 1859 with the title *On the Origin of Species* (Stauffer 1959).

The final, unfinished chapter of *Natural Selection* ("Geographical Distribution") focuses on "the great amount of migration during the glacial epoch" (Stauffer 1975a, p. 564), but the biogeography sections of the 1844 manuscript (which prominently feature the Galápagos) are not paralleled by passages in *Natural Selection*. As a consequence, Darwin never finished the more detailed presentation of biogeography that he intended, which may explain the dearth of references to Galápagos (only six – two fewer than in the much shorter 1844 essay). The references to Galápagos in *Natural Selection* appear in four different chapters but not in the unfinished biogeography chapter. Only two of these references parallel passages in *Origin* where Darwin explicitly mentions Galápagos. The first (Stauffer 1975a, p. 115) pointed out the difficulty of distinguishing varieties from species and mentioned Galápagos birds. The second comment on the endemicity of the land birds of Galápagos (Stauffer 1975a, p. 257) actually appeared in *Origin*'s chapter twelve "Geographic Distribution continued."

The remaining four comments on Galápagos in *Natural Selection* that also do not appear in *Origin* are nevertheless biogeographical observations. In the first (Stauffer 1975a, p. 231), Darwin noted "the smaller the area, even though conditions be remarkably uniform, the more widely diversified will its inhabitants be" and cites Galápagos beetles as an example. The second appears only a few pages later, where Darwin discussed geographical isolation as an important factor for producing new species (Stauffer 1975a, p. 253). The third appears in a footnote to a discussion on the correlation between xeric environments and drab coloration in birds and insects (Stauffer 1975a, p. 282). The fourth and final appearance of Galápagos in *Natural Selection* occurs as an example of the paucity of migratory land birds on oceanic islands (Stauffer 1975a, p. 495). Of these four passages, the first three are paralleled in passages from *Origin* (Darwin 1859, pp. 114, 105, 133, respectively), but the explicit reference to Galápagos has been omitted.

In *Origin*, Darwin rarely mentioned the Galápagos. According to Sulloway (1984), the Galápagos appear in 1.1% of the text of *Origin*. In each instance, Darwin focused generally on the land birds of Galápagos. In chapter two, "Variation under Nature," he compared Galápagos and mainland birds and concluded, "I was much struck how entirely vague and arbitrary is the distinction between species and varieties" (Darwin 1859, p. 48). The Galápagos receive the most attention in Darwin's discussion of island biogeography in chapter twelve. To support his contention that the proportion of endemic species on islands was much higher than on continents, he cited the birds of Galápagos. He was particularly impressed that a higher proportion of endemics was found among land birds than among sea birds, which were able to migrate over the ocean more easily (Darwin 1859, pp.

390-392).

In the same chapter, he explained that species endemic to islands often closely resembled species on the nearest mainland. Again he cited the birds of the Galápagos as an example of this pattern (Darwin 1859, pp. 397-400). His final reference to Galápagos in this chapter dealt with the similarity of species within an archipelago, namely that endemic species of one island often resemble species of the nearby islands. To illustrate, he cited the mockingbirds of Galápagos (Darwin 1859, pp. 401-403). The Galápagos appear only once more, in the final chapter of *Origin*, again to illustrate the similarity of endemic to mainland species (Darwin 1859, p. 478). Though *Origin* underwent six revisions, Darwin never altered these references, nor did he add new ones.

Thus we see from the majority of Darwin's writings on the subject of evolution and natural selection that he mentioned the Galápagos Islands repeatedly and emphatically in the context of biogeography. The affinities of the Galápagos fauna to mainland America greatly impressed Darwin and contributed directly to his acceptance of species transmutation. Darwin was certainly not alone in his doubts about the fixity of species. In the early to mid-nineteenth century, belief in species transmutation was unpopular but not uncommon. Various forms of transmutation had been proposed by Lamarck and Schelling and had appeared in Robert Chambers's anonymous *Vestiges of Creation*. Even Richard Owen entertained a kind of progressivist view of the origin of species by secondary causes, though he remained a staunch opponent of Darwin's views on transmutation. And of course, let us not forget Darwin's own grandfather Erasmus, whose *Zoonomia* clearly articulated a theory of transmutation.

Despite the recurrence of transmutation in contemporary biological thought, many prominent naturalists of Darwin's day rejected it. Cuvier's anatomical doctrines did not permit alterations necessary for evolution (see Coleman 1964, Asma 1996). Even those who would eventually become supporters of Darwin, such as Hooker, accepted fixity prior to reading *Origin* (Colp 1986). The "father of uniformitarianism" himself, Lyell (1832, chap. 2), argued for the fixity of species in *Principles of Geology*. Today universal descent from a common ancestor is the rule in biology, rather than the exception, even though Darwin himself equivocated on the question (Darwin 1859, pp. 483-484; Barrett and Freeman 1987, p. 188, 190). During the twentieth century, it has become customary to refer to the theory of common descent as "fact" (e.g. Lack 1961, p. 29; Berry 1984; Lewis 1987-1988; Gould 1994).

Darwin's acceptance of common descent drove him to seek a mechanism to explain transmutation. As Colp (1986) pointed out, because transmutationists in Darwin's day (such as Chambers) were ridiculed and rejected by their scientific peers, Darwin would be motivated to keep his transmutationist beliefs to himself, revealing them only to select individuals. Darwin had to formulate a credible mechanism to explain transmutation before he could present his theory to the public. As explained above, after reading Malthus, he settled on natural selection as the primary mechanism of transmutation, only after toying with other evolutionary mechanisms (Ospovat 1981; Richardson 1981). Darwin's confidence in natural selection is illustrated by his reaction to *Vestiges of Creation*. In 1845, he wrote to Lyell that he had read Sedgwick's critique of *Vestiges* but that he was unshaken in his belief in transmutation because he had anticipated and answered all of Sedgwick's arguments (Colp 1986).

With these two stages of Darwin's thinking in mind, the relationship of the Galápagos to the formulation of the theory of evolution becomes clearer. The organisms of the Galápagos, primarily their biogeographical affinities with each other and with mainland species, helped to convince him of common descent, but Galápagos itself did not provide him with the mechanism of transmutation. Thus Darwin's references to Galápagos in *Origin* and its predecessors all deal with species relationships and biogeography and their explanation under common descent. Furthermore, Darwin's comment about archipelagos in the *Beagle* ornithology notebook questions the "stability of species." The close proximity of Darwin's transmutation notebooks to the end of the *Beagle* voyage and Darwin's own claim that Galápagos was a particular influence on his speculations both support the view that Darwin's acceptance of transmutation came about in part by observations made at Galápagos. Despite popular modern opinion, Darwin's visit to Galápagos did not play a significant role in his formulation of natural selection as the cause of transmutation.

Modern creationism rejects the species stasis accepted by natural theologians and instead embraces a limited common descent of species within baramins. Ironically, this portends the ultimate conclusion of this monograph – that none of the Galápagos observations, Darwin's or otherwise, are incompatible with modern creationist theory. They played an important role in the rejection of the natural theology of Darwin's day but should not be understood to be contrary to all creation theory.

# 3. Geology and Climate of the Galápagos

## 3.1. Geology

**3.1.1. Introduction.** While biological research flourished in the Galápagos, geological and climatological research lagged far behind. Darwin's observations and descriptions, although more than 160 years old, remain valuable contributions to Galápagos geology. More recent Galápagos studies in classical geology include Chubb (1933) and McBirney and Williams (1969), and in plate tectonic theory include Hey (1977), Hergt *et al.* (1994), and Hoernle *et al.* (2002).

The archipelago consists of 121 islands and islets (Snell *et al.* 1995), all of which are composed primarily of alkali and tholeiitic basalts (McBirney and Aoki 1966; McBirney and Williams 1969). The largest islands, Fernandina and Isabela, consist of seven recently active volcanoes (e.g. Simkin 1977) covering an area of 5300 km$^2$ (Snell *et al.* 1995), almost exactly the size of the state of Delaware. The next twelve largest islands consist of much older volcanoes and cover a collective area of 2500 km$^2$. Whereas Fernandina and Isabela contain large subaerial calderas, the remaining islands do not (Plate 1). Baltra and Santa Cruz are reported to contain layers of marine limestone, indicating that at least part of their present landmass formed below the water's surface (Hickman and Lipps 1985).

The archipelago lies just south of the conjunction of two aseismic, submarine ridges (Shumway 1954) (see Plate 2). The Cocos Ridge extends nearly 1000 km towards the coast of Costa Rica, from which it is separated by the Middle America Trench. The ridge is approximately 1 km below sea level and 3 km above the surrounding ocean floor (Meschede and Barckhausen 2000). The Carnegie Ridge extends towards the South American mainland nearly parallel to the equator, forming approximately a 45° angle with the Cocos Ridge. The Carnegie Ridge is 1350 km long and is also approximately 1 km below sea level. The eastern end of the Carnegie Ridge is separated from South America by the Peru-Chile Trench (Hey *et al.* 1977). The volcanoes that form the Galápagos Islands are found on the western end of the Carnegie Ridge.

**3.1.2. The Galápagos Archipelago in a Plate Tectonics Context.** The Galápagos Islands are found on or near six crustal plates (Cocos, Nazca, Pacific, North American, Caribbean, South American). The islands themselves and the Carnegie Ridge sit on the Nazca Plate near its northern edge, and the Cocos Ridge lies on the Cocos Plate near its southern margin. Shallow extensional earthquakes and transform faults between these two plates make up what is known as the Cocos-Nazca Spreading Center (CNSC) (Herron and Heirtzler 1967). Increasing radiometric ages from the CNSC both north and south confirm a spreading center interpretation. Some 1000 miles to the west, the Nazca and Cocos Plates share their western border with the Pacific Plate. Since that border is marked by shallow extensional earthquakes, transform faults, and the Mid-Pacific Rise, and the radiometric age of the ocean crust on either side of the border increases with distance from that border, the Mid-Pacific Rise is also interpreted as a spreading center. Compressional earthquakes along the eastern edge of the Cocos and Nazca Plates which deepen from ocean trenches eastward indicate that the Cocos Plate is subducting under the Caribbean Plate, and the Nazca Plate is subducting under both the South American Plate and the southern part of the Caribbean Plate.

Although they lie very close to a spreading center, the Galápagos Islands have usually been interpreted as hotspot rather than mid-ocean ridge volcanoes. First of all, although some Galápagos basalts have a Mid-Ocean Ridge Basalt (MORB) composition, others have an Ocean Island Basalt (OIB) composition (Graham *et al.* 1993; White *et al.* 1993). A horseshoe pattern is found, with OI basalts in the western, northern, and southern edges of the islands and MOR basalts in the center and eastern edge of the islands (Geist *et al.* 1998; Hoernle *et al.* 2000). This pattern can be explained by most of the Galápagos basalts being OI basalts sourced deep in the mantle, subsequently being intruded and divided north and south by spreading center (MOR) basalts (White *et al.* 1993; Geist *et al.* 1998; Hoernle *et al.* 2000). Secondly, whereas most mid-ocean volcanoes do not rise within 2 km of the ocean surface, the Galápagos Islands are not only subaerially-exposed, but they are also sitting atop the Galápagos Rise – a regional topographic high sitting several kilometers above the ocean floor (Detrick *et al.* 2002; Harpp *et al.* 2003). The elevation of the Galápagos Rise is thought to be due to the warmth of a hotspot.

The Cocos and Nazca Ridges are typically interpreted as the track a stationary Galápagos hotspot made as the plates moved over it. First of all, the heat of the hotspot would explain the elevated nature of the aseismic ridges and the Cocos-Nazca Spreading Center separating them would explain why the ridges create a v-shaped pattern which opens to the east. Secondly, whereas conventional radiometric ages of Galápagos Island basalts are 4 million radiometric years old or less (Cox, 1983), the radiometric age of samples dredged from the western end of the Carnegie Ridge are about 9 million radiometric years (Christie *et al.* 1992) and samples from the eastern end of the Cocos Ridge are about 14 million radiometric years (Werner *et al.* 1999). Thirdly, seismic, tomographic, and geomorphological data in Ecuador (Gutscher *et al.* 1999) and Costa Rica (Husen *et al.* 2002) are consistent with the subduction of eastward extensions of the Carnegie and Cocos Ridges respectively. Fourthly, Hoernle *et al.* (2000) show that similar geographical segregation of MOR and OI basalts can be found on the Cocos Ridge near the subduction zone off the coast of Costa Rica as are found in the Galápagos Islands themselves. Fifthly, enrichment of Sr, Nd, and Pb isotopes in Cocos Ridge dredge samples are more consistent with an OIB than an MORB source (Hoernle *et al.* 2000). Taken together, these data support the Cocos and Carnegie Ridges as hotspot tracks of the Galápagos hotspot for the past 14 million years of radiometric time.

Further support of an eastward-aging hotspot track comes from drowned islands east of the present archipelago. Christie *et al.* (1992) argued that the geomorphology of a seamount at 2° 01′ S 85° 40′ W is consistent with subaerial exposure in the past. Basalt in the form of rounded cobbles or pebbles has been dredged from the north slope of the island. Because such rocks are formed by wave erosion, Christie *et al.* (1992) interpreted their presence as indicative of a submerged island. Presently, the seamount is 10 km across and lies at 2000 m below sea level, approximately 675 km from the present hotspot below Isla Fernandina (Christie *et al.* 1992). The fact that a much older island is submerged and located to the east of currently emergent islands is consistent with eastward movement of the Cocos and Nazca Plates over a stationary hotspot.

Also consistent with this theory, several lines of evidence suggest that the ages of the current Galápagos Islands tend to increase from the west to the east. Lava flows throughout the islands have been subjected to potassium-argon and argon-argon ($^{40}Ar/^{39}Ar$) dating, as summarized by Cox (1983), Christie *et al.* (1992), and White *et al.* (1993). A tuff from Plazas dates to 4.21 million radiometric years, by far the oldest radiometric date in the islands. Candidates for the oldest lava flows occur on Santa Cruz (Cox 1983), Santa Fé (Cox 1983; White *et al.* 1993), Española (Cox 1983; White *et al.* 1993), and San Cristóbal (White *et al.* 1993). The oldest flows from Española date to 3.31 and 3.04 million radiometric years, and the oldest flows from Santa Fé date to 2.85 and 2.56 million radiometric years. In contrast, lava flows on the western island of Isabela date to less than a million radiometric years (Cox 1983; White *et al.* 1993).

Besides radiometric dating, paleomagnetic (Cox and Dalrymple 1966; Cox 1983), biostratigraphic (Hickman and Lipps 1985), and geomorphologic (Cox 1983; Hall 1983) dating methods have been applied to the islands. Paleomagnetically, for example, most of the lavas of the archipelago display a normal magnetic orientation. Young potassium-argon ages indicate that most of them cooled during the Brunhes Normal Polarity Epoch (0.72-0 million radiometric years ago) (Cox 1983). Lava flows with reversed magnetic orientation are found on Wolf, Rábida, Pinzón, Santa Cruz, Floreana, Baltra, and Española (Cox and Dalrymple 1966) (Figure 3). Based on the potassium-argon dates of these flows, they cooled during the Matuyama Reversed Polarity Epoch (2.47-0.72 million radiometric years ago). Several highly weathered flows with larger potassium-argon ages and a normal paleomagnetic orientation are found on Santa Fé, Española, San Cristóbal, and Santa Cruz (Cox 1983). Cox (1983) interpreted them as having been formed pre-Matuyama, probably during the Gauss Normal Polarity Epoch (>2.47 million radiometric years ago) (Figure 3).

Fossiliferous deposits occur throughout the islands and may be classified into six types: (a) submarine tuffs, (b) limestones and sandstones, (c) terrace deposits, (d) beachrock, (e) supratidal talus, and (f) recently uplifted tidal or subtidal rock (Hickman and Lipps 1985). Hickman and Lipps (1985) examined all six types on eight

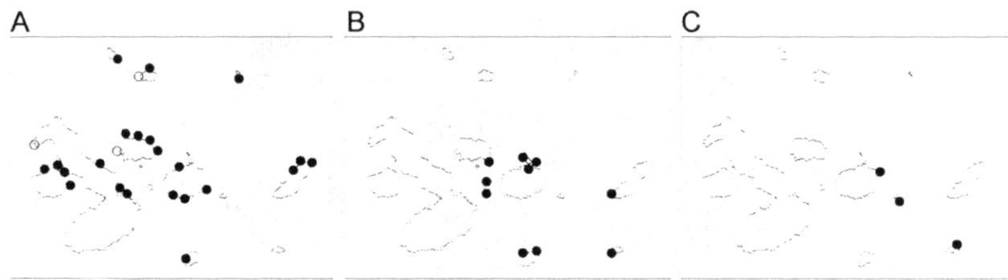


Figure 3. Summary of radiometric dating of Galápagos lava flows from the Brunhes normal polarity epoch (A), the Matuyama reversed polarity epoch (B), and pre-Matuyama normal polarity (C). Data from Cox (1983).

different islands and concluded that none could be substantially older than 3-4 million radiometric years. The limestones of Baltra and Santa Cruz are interbedded with basalt flows, implying the present landmass was generated by submarine eruptions followed by uplift. Even to these deposits, which apparently date to the origin of the islands of Baltra and Santa Cruz themselves, Hickman and Lipps (1985) assigned an age of approximately 2 million radiometric years.

Although paleomagnetism and radiometry can determine the age of a lava flow, other geological considerations (e.g. geomorphology) are necessary to determine if the lava was extruded subaerially. Isla Española, for example, has a peculiar half-circle shape with a gentle slope to several 600 m summits from the north and 300 m cliffs along its southern shore (Figure 4). Hall (1983) interpreted this shape as a heavily eroded shield volcano, with half of the island lost to faulting along its current southern shore. Within the 300 m cliffs, cinder cone deposits are seen, evidence that by that point in time the vulcanism on Española was subaerial. Radiometric dating of lava flows on Española indicate subaerial vulcanism dates back before 3 million radiometric years ago (Hall 1983).

Taken together, these dating evidences depict an archipelago that generally ages to the east. The youngest islands of Fernandina and Isabela with active volcanoes are found to the west, and progressively older islands occur eastward. The exception is Isla Wolf, which contains a lava flow deposited during the Matuyama Reversed Polarity Epoch (Cox 1983). But, because Wolf lies much closer to the CNSC and is not part of the Galápagos Rise

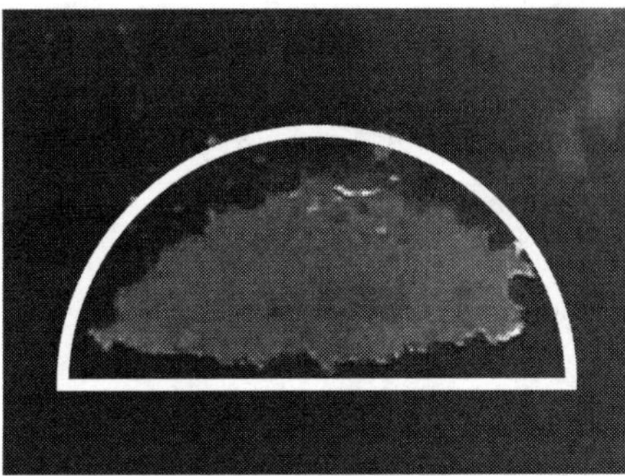

Figure 4. Satellite photo of Isla Española, highlighting its semicircular shape. Photo courtesy NASA.

of the Carnegie Ridge, Cox (1983) proposed that Wolf (and nearby Isla Darwin) has a different volcanic history than the rest of the archipelago. His proposal is supported by the chemical distinctiveness of Wolf and Darwin basalts (Christie *et al.* 1990; Harpp and White 1990). In general, however, the age trend of currently emergent islands is consistent with the evidence of the eastern-aging hotspot track already discussed.

There is also a fair amount of evidence which links the Galápagos basalts with the Caribbean Large Igneous Province (CLIP), which makes up most of the Caribbean Plate (Hauff *et al.* 2000; Hoernle *et al.* 2002). First of all, there are similar trace element ratios in Galápagos and CLIP basalts (Hauff *et al.* 2000). Secondly, high $^{3}He/^{4}He$ ratios usually thought characteristic of deep (Courtillot *et al.* 2003) or upper (Meiborn *et al.* 2003) mantle convection and found in Galápagos basalts (Graham *et al.* 1993) are also found in Quepas picrites from Costa Rica (Hauff *et al.* 2000). Thirdly, radiometric ages from Malpelo Island and coastal Panama and Costa Rica fall between the oldest radiometric dates of the Cocos Ridge and the youngest radiometric dates for the CLIP basalts, which have been dated to 70-100 million radiometric years ago (Hoernle *et al.* 2002). Fourthly, the Cocos and Carnegie Ridges increase in age to the east – precisely in the direction of the older CLIP basalts. Finally, the CLIP rocks are flood basalts, which are generally thought to be surface expressions of large mantle plume heads (Richards *et al.* 1989), predecessors of hotspot-generating mantle plumes. All this suggests that the basalts of the CLIP are part of the Galápagos hotspot track, and could be the surface expression of a large plume head early in the history of the hotspot.

Finally, seismic tomography studies point to a low shear velocity zone below the Galápagos Islands penetrating to a depth of over 500 km (Courtillot *et al.* 2003). This suggests a mantle plume currently exists beneath the Galápagos hotspot. Taken together, the long basalt track connected with a possible flood basalt province, high $^3He/^4He$ ratios, and a low shear velocity zone make up four of the characteristics Courtillot *et al.* (2003) considered diagnostic for a hotspot being due to a persistent mantle plume. Montelli *et al.* (2004) reported that the seismic tomography trace of the Galápagos plume at 1000 km depth is near Cocos Island, 600 miles to the northeast of its present location over the Galápagos Islands. Their results also show no evidence of the plume below 1000 km. This suggests that the Galápagos plume may neither be stationary in position nor deep in origin as originally suggested by Morgan (1971) for mantle plumes in general. This places the Galápagos into the middle of a current debate about the true nature of mantle plumes (e.g. DePaolo and Manga 2003; Foulger and Natland 2003; Smith 2003; Montelli *et al.* 2004). Different hotspots may be sourced at different depths in the mantle and some hotspots may actually move. For example, the Yellowstone hotspot seems to lack any plume trace at all beneath it (Christiansen *et al.* 2002), and the Hawaiian hotspot has evidence of having moved many degrees of latitude to the south (Tarduno *et al.* 2003).

**3.1.3. Conventional Plate Tectonic Model for the Galápagos Archipelago.** Because of the evidence laid out above, the Galápagos Islands can be considered the most recent volcanic expression of a hotspot over a long-term upper-mantle plume, which I will refer to as the Galápagos plume. The hotspot track which increases in age to the east from the current Galápagos Islands would suggest that the Cocos and Nazca Plates have been moving eastward over the top of the Galápagos plume. During this entire time the Galápagos plume produced over it a thick and warm basalt ridge and basaltic volcanoes – many of which probably erupted subaerially. As this ridge and islands were transported eastward with the motion of the plate, cooling caused the islands to sink beneath the ocean surface and the ridge to sink into deeper and deeper water. Also, since the Galápagos plume happens to lie on the Cocos-Nazca Spreading Center, as the ridge was generated by the Galápagos plume, it was split by the CNSC into the Cocos and Carnegie Ridges, creating a v-shaped pattern open to the east. In the present, the easternmost limits of the Cocos and Carnegie Ridges are subducting beneath Central and South America. Whereas early researchers (e.g. Baur 1891a, 1891b, 1897; Hemsley 1895) advocated a land connection between the Galápagos and the mainland, the more or less stationary relative position of the Galápagos plume with the Central and South American Plates would suggest that there has never been a continuous land bridge from the Galápagos to the mainland (Williams 1966).

In this model, continuous evidence of the history of the Galápagos plume can be found in the rocks of the Cocos and Carnegie Ridges back to about 14 million radiometric years ago. In simple plate tectonics theory, any older rocks would have been subducted and destroyed. Similarity between Galápagos and CLIP basalts on opposite sides of the subduction zone suggests an unusual scenario. According to such a scenario, at about 100 million radiometric years ago a single large oceanic plate known as the Farallon Plate was located over the Galápagos plume (Richards *et al.* 1989, 1991; Hoernle *et al.* 2002). A large plume head erupted onto the earth's surface between 100 and 70 million radiometric years ago to generate a large province of flood basalts on the ocean floor (Hergt *et al.* 1994; Hauff *et al.* 2000; Hoernle *et al.* 2002). As the Farallon Plate moved eastward, the flood basalts eventually encountered the Greater Antilles Subduction Zone. According to Hoernle *et al.* (2002) the flood basalts were too warm (and thus too buoyant) to be subducted, so they were pushed over the top of the subduction zone. After the flood basalts passed completely over the subduction zone, the MOR basalt on the west side of it broke off the flood basalts and resumed the subduction. This left the flood basalts on the east of the subduction zone as the CLIP of the Caribbean Plate and the Panama Isthmus as the trailing edge of the CLIP.

Sometime after subduction resumed, the Farallon Plate is thought to have split into the Cocos and Nazca Plates (Hey 1977), possibly because of global tectonic adjustments (Meschede and Barckhausen 2000). The split happened to occur through the Galápagos hotspot, perhaps because the warm ridge formed a zone of weakness. This generated the tectonic scenario we see occurring today. According to conventional plate tectonics theory this scenario has persisted for at least the last 14 million years, with the current Galápagos Islands forming within the last 3-4 million years.

**3.1.4. Creation Model for the Geology of the Galápagos Archipelago.** Though creationists have not commented specifically on the geology of the Galápagos, the Catastrophic Plate Tectonics (CPT) model of Austin *et al.* (1994) provides a global framework for understanding the geological history of the islands. According to the CPT model, the driving force of the Flood was runaway subduction (Baumgardner 1994) that completely altered the pre-Flood continental configuration. As the pre-Flood ocean floor was subducted, new ocean floor was formed by the partial melting of upper mantle rock. After the Flood, tectonic activity decreased exponentially, as the continental and new oceanic plates settled into their modern configuration. Unique among creationist Flood models, the CPT model also provides an explanation for magnetic field reversals (Humphreys 1986), post-Flood ice accumulation and advance (Vardiman 1996a), and the general decrease of volcanic activity after the Flood (Austin *et al.* 1994).

Even though the CPT model has a great deal of explanatory power, it has not been without its critics (e.g. Reed 2001; Oard 2002). Outstanding problems include the cooling of the newly-generated ocean floor (Baumgardner 1986; Austin *et al.* 1994) and evidence of pre-Pangaea continental motion (Austin *et al.* 1994). Despite these drawbacks, CPT can explain a vast amount of observational data, including virtually all the evidence explained by conventional plate tectonics theory. In the Galápagos region, for example, CPT is the only creationist model which explains such things as the geometry, topography. and chemistry of mid-ocean ridges, the geometry and topography of ocean trenches, the geographic and vertical distribution of compressional and extensional earthquakes, trends in relative ages of basalts, and hotspot traces. CPT is also the only creationist model which explains mantle plumes (e.g. Austin *et al.* 1994; Baumgardner 2003). This makes it the only creation geology model which might be able to explain the seismic tomography trace of a mantle plume beneath the Galápagos, the flood basalts of the CLIP, Galápagos basalts with OIB vs. MORB chemistry, and raised hotspot topography. Finally, as Baumgardner (2002) continues to insist, CPT explains some observational data which conventional plate tectonics cannot explain. Consequently, even though questions persist, I will adopt the CPT model for the general framework used to interpret Galápagos geology.

In order to interpret Galápagos geological history, it is important to review the geological data with respect to interpretation of such data in a creationist context. Taken as a whole, the evidence of a hotspot trace, mantle plume, and association of Galápagos with the CLIP might seem very strong, but creationists have offered various interpretations of such evidence, and these interpretations could alter the geological model adopted for the Galápagos Islands. As a result, these interpretations warrant discussion and commentary.

The relationship of mantle plumes and hotspots to conventional plate tectonics has been a subject of ongoing debate. This debate has been used by Froede (2001) as an argument against plate tectonics and CPT. Froede (2002) claimed that stationary deep-mantle-sourced plumes are a "*very* important uniformitarian concept" [his emphasis] and that evidence of moving hotspots "might not support" plate tectonics. Contrary to Froede's claims, the plume debate in conventional literature demonstrates that plate tectonics and stationary deep-mantle-sourced plumes are independent models. Foulger and Natland (2003), for example, claim that mantle plumes were not predicted by plate tectonics. Alternatively, some researchers, such as Anderson (2000), have attempted to integrate hotspot and plate tectonics models, leading to the ongoing controversy. Anderson's (2000) model explains hotspots as plate tectonics-generated temperature variations without recourse to deep mantle plumes. Furthermore recent evidence and modeling of a moving Hawaiian hotspot helps to explain the bend in the Emperor seamount chain, which is not explained by stationary hotspot and plate tectonics (Tarduno *et al.* 2003; Steinberger *et al.* 2004). In the creation model, much of this debate is moot since mantle plumes are predicted by Baumgardner's mantle modeling. Thus, catastrophic plate tectonics is a geophysical model that integrates mantle hotspots with plate tectonics.

As noted above, flood basalts have been interpreted as the explosive volcanism associated with the rise of plume heads. Various creationists have tried to interpret flood basalts within a creationist context, with widely differing results (Nevins 1974;

Garner 1996; Woodmorappe and Oard 2002). Garner (1996) argued for a Flood/post-Flood boundary below the Triassic because of the occurrence of continental flood basalts in the Mesozoic. Nevins (1974) interpreted the Columbia River (Tertiary) basalt as a post-Flood feature, while Woodmorappe and Oard (2002) placed the origin of the same formation in the Flood. Despite their frequent appearance in the creationist literature, there has been little attempt to explain the source of flood basalts in a creationist context. By attributing them to explosive plumes from mantle-wide convection, the CPT model of Austin *et al.* (1994) seems to be the only creationist model with the potential for explaining the origin of flood basalts.

At present, creationists have not proposed an adequate explanation of the observational data associated with radiometric dating. As a result, the direct interpretation of the dating of the emergence of the extant islands becomes difficult. A general concept of accelerated decay currently enjoys popularity (Humphreys *et al.* 2003; Vardiman *et al.* 2003), but geochemical models also provide powerful and competing explanations (Snelling 2003). Despite the shortcoming in radiometric models, creationists have frequently classified some formations as late- or post-Flood formations, primarily on grounds of geomorphology or other factors (e.g. see Froede *et al.* 1998; Walker 2001). For example, since the basalts formed by volcanoes on the Uinkaret Plateau flow into the Grand Canyon, they necessarily post-date the cutting of the canyon, which necessarily post-dates the formation of the strata through which the canyon cuts (Austin 1994, p. 123). Since many young-earth creationists agree that the strata cut by the canyon formed during the Flood, the Uinkaret Plateau volcanoes would seem to date from after the Flood.

Consequently, although direct interpretation of the radiometric dating of basalts of the Galápagos Islands and adjacent seamounts is not possible, it may be possible to compare the radiometric dating of the Galápagos basalts to the radiometric dating of other formations judged by creationists to be post-Flood. A cursory sample of such formations is given in Table 1. Naturally, since disagreement over the placement of the Flood/post-Flood boundary persists, formations with older radiometric dates (>25 million radiometric years) have been interpreted as either late Flood or post-Flood (Snelling 2000; Walker 2002), but those with radiometric dates less than 10 million radiometric years have

Table 1. Geological formations assigned by creationists to the post- or late Flood.

| Formation | Date (in million radiometric years) | Method | Inferred Creationist Timeframe | Reference |
|---|---|---|---|---|
| Banks Peninsula | 2 Ma | | Post-Flood | Walker 2001 |
| Uinkaret Plateau basalt | 1.2-3.67 Ma | K-Ar | Post-Flood | Austin 1994, p. 123 |
| Hickey Basalt | 10.1-14.6 Ma | K-Ar | "Withdrawal of the Floodwater during the Ice Age Timeframe" | Froede *et al.* 1998 |
| John Day Formation | 31.1-31.5 Ma | K-Ar | Post-Flood | Nevins 1974 |
| coastal submarine tin placer | 40 Ma | | "Recessive stage" of Flood | Lalomov and Tabolitch 2000 |
| Devils Tower | 40 Ma | | late Flood, recession of water | Walker 2002 |
| Tertiary basalt flow | 47.5 Ma | K-Ar | Post-Flood | Snelling 2000 |

been referred to the post-Flood by Austin (1994, p. 123), Froede *et al.* (1998) and Walker (2001). Radiometric ages of lavas in the extant Galápagos Islands date within the last 3-4 million years (Cox 1983). A comparison with entries in Table 1 would suggest that the Galápagos Islands date from the post-Flood period. The effectiveness of this argument is, of course, mitigated by my imperfect sample of formations referred to the post-Flood, but it could be tested by surveying basalt flows which are less than 10 million radiometric years to determine how many exhibit signs of subaerial formation after the Flood.

A similar conclusion can be derived from conventional stratigraphy. Although utilization of the stratigraphic column to identify the beginning and end of the Flood has been an issue of strong debate among creationists (e.g. Woodmorappe 1981; Snelling 1996), I will assume with Snelling *et al.* (1996) that the stratigraphic record is a valid description of the earth's geology and with Austin *et al.* (1994) that the Flood/post-Flood boundary may be approximated by the Cretaceous/Tertiary (K/T) boundary.

Placing the Flood/post-Flood boundary at the K/T is consistent with Vardiman's (1996b) sea floor sediment model and Reed's (2002) interpretation of the Palo Duro basin. A K/T Flood/post-Flood boundary also explains the fossil record of the Equidae (Cavanaugh *et al.* 2003) and other mammalian baramins (e.g. Wise 1994a; Wood *et al.* 1999) as post-Flood diversification.

As seen above, according to conventional radiometric, paleomagnetic, biostratigraphic, and geomorphological dating, the extant Galápagos Islands are entirely uppermost Tertiary and Quaternary (Cox 1983). If the K/T is assumed to mark the end of the Flood, then the extant Galápagos Islands are entirely post-Flood. The tectonics models which include the CLIP in the history of the Galápagos hotspot extend the tectonic history of the region to a radiometric age of approximately 100 million radiometric years (Hergt *et al.* 1994). If the K/T is assumed to mark the end of the Flood and radiometric ages produce reliable relative dates, then the history of the Galápagos plume almost certainly extends to the late stages of the Flood. A CPT interpretation might attribute the CLIP to an explosive plume event near the end of the Flood, sourcing either in the shallow or deep mantle. The explosive plume events of CPT (Austin *et al.* 1994) may better explain the explosive vulcanism associated with plume events in general and the CLIP in particular. Indeed the association of flood basalts with the rifting of plates (Storey 1995) tends to support the catastrophic nature of these massive volcanic events and their association with plumes.

Subsequent plate movement at the end of the Flood or immediately thereafter may have thrust the CLIP across a subduction zone between the North and South American Plates, as Hoernle *et al.* (2002) proposed. In fact, it may turn out that the rapid plate motion of the CPT model may better explain how the CLIP would still be buoyant enough to override the subduction zone. The higher energy of the CPT model may also be more likely to provide the energy needed to break the MOR basalts from the western edge of the CLIP to reinitiate subduction. Following reinitiation of subduction, the remnants of the plume maintained the Galápagos hotspot and continued to create volcanic islands during the centuries following the Flood. The reduction of geologic energy from the production of the flood basalts of the CLIP to the production of basaltic volcanoes is also consistent with the decreasing geologic energy postulated in the CPT model. The CPT model may also better explain the source of the energy necessary to split the Farallon Plate into the Cocos and Nazca Plates (which may have occurred in early post-Flood times). Based on carbon-14 dating to be discussed in the following section on the climate of the Galápagos Islands, the development of both the Cocos and Carnegie Ridges as well as the extant Galápagos Islands probably occurred within 200 years of the end of the Flood.

Although the splitting of the Farallon Plate, accretion of new ocean floor, and the formation of the Carnegie and Cocos Ridges are significant geological events, they are orders of magnitude less intense than the tectonic events taking place during the Flood itself, such as the origin of the CLIP flood basalts and insertion of the CLIP between the North and South American Plates. Thus, though some might object that such high energy events that I have attributed to the post-Flood would be more appropriate to the Flood event itself, I nevertheless attribute them to the residual catastrophism that immediately followed the Flood. High-resolution modeling of Flood tectonics should help resolve the chronology of the origin of the Cocos and Carnegie Ridges and the Galápagos Islands. Such modeling would also have important implications for the general Flood/post-Flood boundary debate.

## 3.2. Climate

**3.2.1. Introduction.** The common stereotype of oceanic islands as tropical paradises certainly does not apply to the Galápagos Islands. The Galápagos actually sit in a region of low rainfall in the Pacific (the Central Pacific Dry Zone), resulting in a generally arid climate (Plates 3 and 4). The average annual rainfall in the Galápagos is typically less than 500 mm, while the average annual rainfall just a few hundred miles to the north can exceed 3000 mm (Palmer and Pyle 1966). The poor rainfall and volcanic landscape combine to produce very little standing water in the islands. Over the centuries, travelers to the islands repeatedly note the lack of freshwater lakes or streams (Slevin 1959). Ambrose Cowley wrote on his first visit in May, 1684, possibly about Isla San Cristóbal, "wee went a shoare and found the Largest Land Turtle that ever I saw but the Iland rocky and barren without wood or water" (transcribed in Slevin 1959). The strange landscape and lack of water quickly led to the colloquial name *Las Encantadas*, the "enchanted islands" (Larson 2001, pp.

3), which English buccaneer Edward Davies mentions in his 1694 journal (Slevin 1959).

Long-term study of the atmosphere and ocean in the Pacific has explained many of the peculiarities of the Galápagos climate, primarily the arid environment and the cool coastal waters, but at least one regular occurrence, El Niño, remains a subject of ongoing research and debate (McPhaden 2004). El Niño, a persistent increase in sea surface temperature in the Pacific, recurs every 3-7 years and lasts 12-18 months. In the western Pacific, droughts occur in Australia, Indonesia and the Philippines during El Niño. In the eastern Pacific, the increased sea surface temperature contributes to torrential rainfall along the west coasts of the Americas. In Galápagos, the warmer ocean water and higher rainfall produce widespread mortality of the animals that depend on cool ocean waters to provide needed food. The heavy rainfall in the Galápagos described by Captain James Colnett during the 1794 visit of the H.M.S. *Rattler* (transcribed in Slevin 1959) was probably caused by an El Niño.

In this section, I include two somewhat disparate but related subjects. First, I will describe the modern climate of the islands, with some emphasis on the devastating affects of El Niño. Related to this topic, I will also discuss evidence of past climate and how that evidence relates to creationist hypotheses of post-Flood climate recovery. My second major topic will be a brief discussion of carbon dating of organic sediments from two lakes of the Galápagos (Colinvaux and Schofield 1976; Riedinger *et al.* 2002). My purpose here is two-fold: to provide a climatological context for the biological topics that follow and to suggest possible ways that existing creationist research can interact with Galápagos science. The research and concepts explored here should provide a basis for future climatological research in the Galápagos from a creationist perspective.

**3.2.2. Modern Climate.** The climate of the Galápagos is dominated by an interannual cycle called the El Niño Southern Oscilation (ENSO). ENSO consists of wet periods called El Niños and dry periods called La Niñas, with a total cycle time of approximately 3-7 years. Although technical definitions of El Niño (and La Niña) vary (Trenberth 1997), the general attributes are well known. During a normal year, the region of the ocean called the thermocline that separates the warm, surface waters from the cold, deep waters is tilted down to the west in the

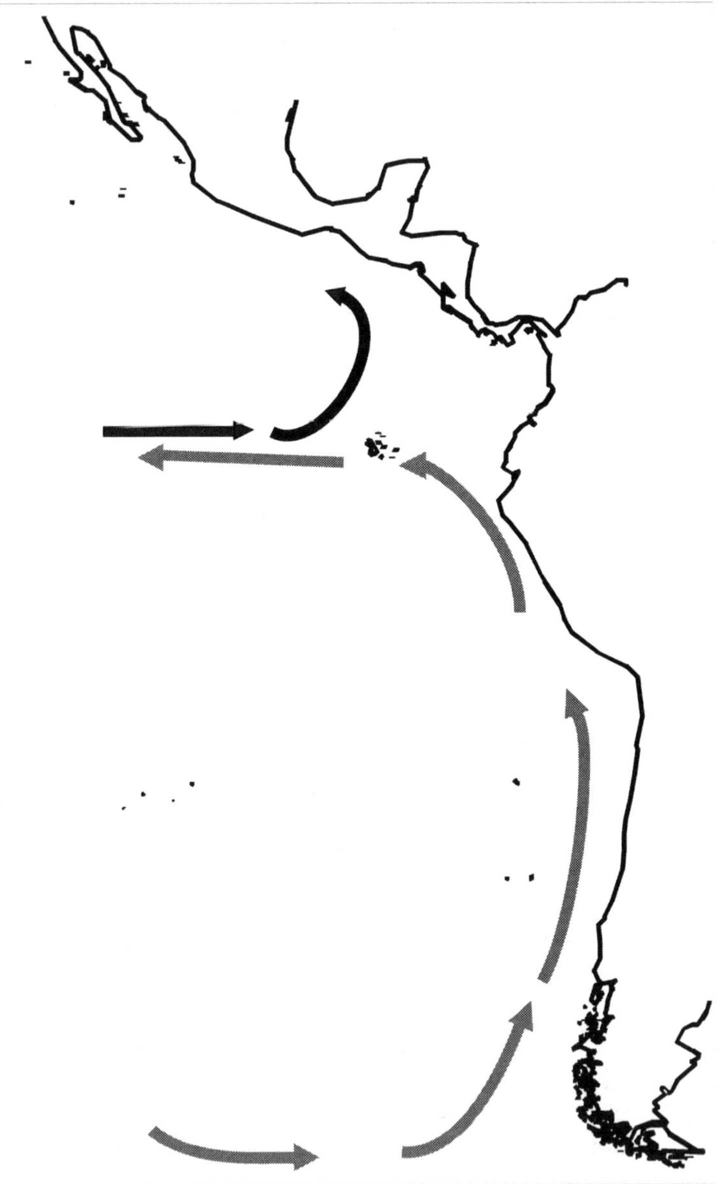

Figure 5. Currents that influence the Galápagos Islands, the Humboldt and South Equatorial Currents (grey arrows) and the Cromwell Current (black arrows).

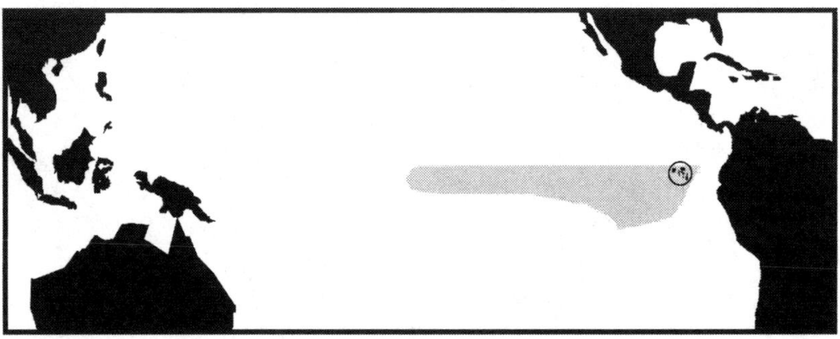

Figure 6. The Central Pacific Dry Zone wth the Galápagos circled. Adapted from Palmer and Pyle (1966).

Pacific basin. In the east, the shallow thermocline brings colder waters to the surface, inducing trade winds that drive the South Equatorial Current (SEC) (Figure 5). As they move cold, upwelled water to the west, the trade winds and SEC create a "cold tongue" of surface water extending to approximately 160°W longitude (McPhaden 1999, 2004) (Figure 6).

As the trade winds move west, they absorb heat and moisture from the ocean, causing them to rise over the Pacific warm basin in the west. As they rise, deep convection gives rise to large cumulonimbus clouds, dumping rain in the western Pacific, particularly over Australia, Indonesia, and the Philippines. In the upper atmosphere, the air currents cool and move east again, in a cycle called the Walker cycle. Because of these coupled atmospheric and oceanic affects, air over the Galápagos is typically dry and the water from the upwelling is cool. During El Niño, the Pacific warm basin shifts to the east, flattening the thermocline, and reducing the trade winds. The sea surface temperature (SST) in the east increases, and as a result, the Walker cycle shifts to the east and induces dry weather in the western Pacific and torrential rain in the east. These changes can effect changes in global weather patterns, for example by reducing hurricane damage in the eastern United States (Pielke and Landsea 1999). During La Niña, the thermocline tilt is increased, the eastern SST is reduced, and the trade winds are stronger than normal, resulting in even drier conditions in the east Pacific and wetter conditions in the west (McPhaden 1999, 2004).

Despite the importance and regular occurrence of El Niño, the causes of ENSO are still a subject of debate (McPhaden 2004). Numerous ENSO models have been devised, none of which have been completely successful in predicting the onset, duration, and severity of any particular El Niño (Barnston *et al.* 1999; McPhaden 2004). Even though the onset of the 2002/2003 El Niño was the first to be predicted six months in advance (Kerr 2002), Fedorov *et al.* (2003) concluded that the interaction of ENSO with local weather patterns make it inherently unpredictable, while Chen *et al.* (2004) claimed that El Niño can be predicted accurately with a simple SST model. Since a comprehensive review of the causes and predictability of El Niño is unnecessary for this review, I refer the interested reader to the relevant literature cited above. An understanding of the difficulty of predicting El Niño is sufficient for appreciating the impact of the ENSO on Galápagos weather.

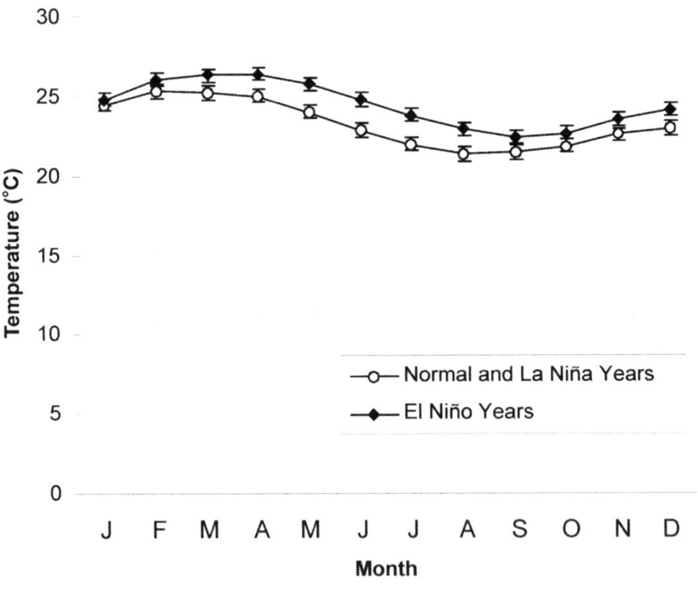


Figure 7. Monthly mean sea surface temperature for the period 1965-1998 measured at the Charles Darwin Research Station, Academy Bay, Santa Cruz. Data from Snell and Rea (1999, table A5).

In non-El Niño years in the Galápagos, SST is generally cool, and the annual variation in SST is very slight. Based on 34 years of weather records kept by the Charles Darwin Research Station (CDRS) from 1965 to 1998, Snell and Rea (1999) found that August and September were the coolest months, with average sea surface temperatures of 21.8°C and 21.7°C respectively. The warmest month was March with an average sea surface temperature of 25.5°C (see Figure 7). The average annual sea surface temperature for the same period ranged from a low of 21.7°C in 1988 to a high of 26.2°C in 1998.

In typical, non-El Niño years, precipitation is sparse and varies by elevation. The coastal areas are drier, the highlands wetter. On Santa Cruz, the rainy season is January to May at both elevations, but during June to December, the highlands receive moisture from a regular mist called *garúa*. As a result, June through December in the highlands is known as the "wet" season and January through May is called the "dry" or "rainy" season. In the coastal regions, where the garúa does not bring much moisture, the period June through December is known as the "dry" season, and January through May is the "wet" or "rainy" season (Bowman 1961). For coastal regions and highlands, the warmest air temperatures occur in February, March, and April, and the coolest air temperatures occur in August, September, and October (Bowman 1961; Snell and Rea 1999). The highlands are approximately 1°C cooler than the coast during the coolest months of the year.

As Houvenaghel (1974) has shown, mean annual rainfall on Santa Cruz correlates well with mean annual SST ($r > 0.875$). Thus, during El Niño the total annual rainfall increases dramatically as the SST rises (Figure 8), with most rain falling in the regular wet season of December through July (Figure 9). El Niños in Galápagos typically devastate populations of indigenous animals. As the sea surface temperature increases, the upwelling of cold water decreases (McPhaden 2004; Houvenaghel 1974), reducing the food available for marine animals such as the sea birds and marine iguanas. On land, plants growth increases, providing a temporary increase in food availability for land animals such as the finches (Laurie 1983a). After El Niño, however, plant growth and food availability return to normal, causing a crash in the population numbers of land animals dependent on plant food.

Since the CDRS has kept records, strong El Niño events took place in the rainy seasons of 1975-1976, 1982-1983, 1986-1987,

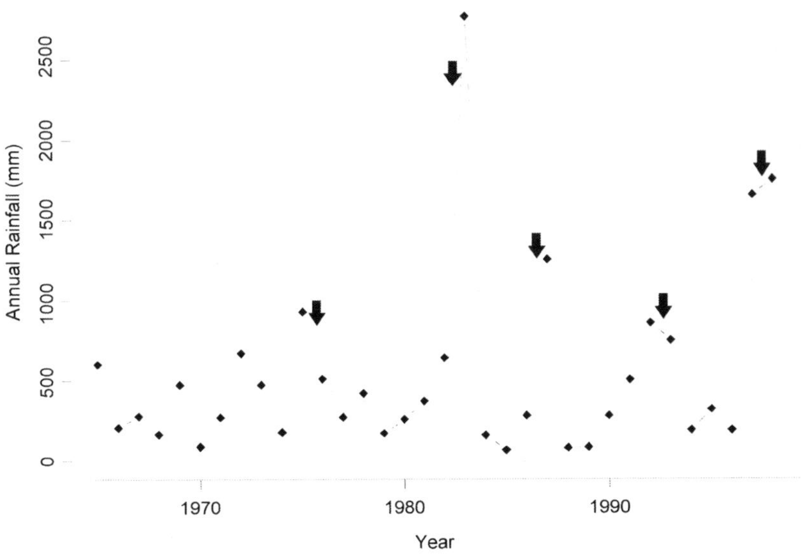


Figure 8. Annual rainfall at the Charles Darwin Research Station, Academy Bay, Santa Cruz. Data from Snell and Rea (1999, table A1). Occurrences of El Niños are indicated by arrows.

1993-1994, and 1997-1998 (Snell and Rea 1999). The El Niño event of 1982-1983 is remembered as particularly severe (Cane 1983; Halpern *et al.* 1983; P.R. Grant 1984, see Figure 8). Based on the records kept by the CDRS at Academy Bay, Santa Cruz, the total rainfall for 1983 was more than five times greater than the total rainfall for 1981 (Snell and Rea 1999). On Genovesa, the total rainfall during the El Niño (measured from November 1982 to July 1983) was more than ten times the rainfall for the same period of the previous three years (P.R. Grant 1984; P.R. Grant and B.R. Grant 1987). Weather records had just begun to be kept at five stations on Floreana, and all stations showed dramatic increases in monthly rainfall (as much as 1468%) from the months preceding the El Niño (Cruz and Beach 1983). During a single storm on Santa Fé on December 16-17, 1982, 254 mm of rain fell in only 20 hours (Laurie 1983a).

During the 1982-83 El Niño, animals dependent on the ocean for food suffered the immediate effects of the abnormally high

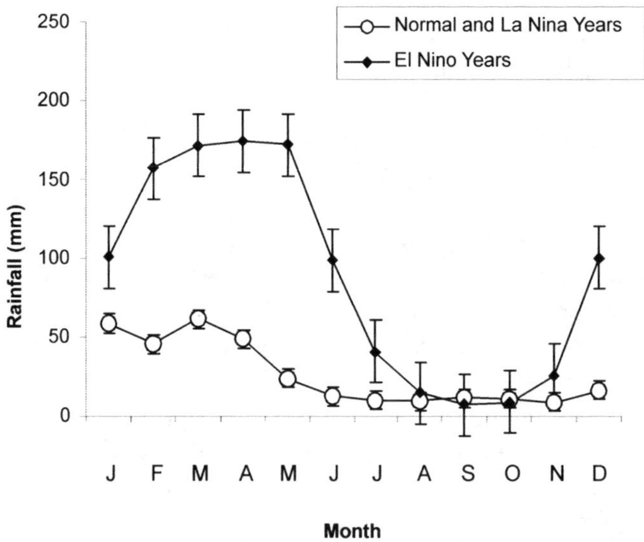


Figure 9. Monthly mean coastal rainfall for the period 1965-1998 measured at the Charles Darwin Research Station, Academy Bay, Santa Cruz. Data from Snell and Rea (1999, table A1).

sea surface temperature. Mortality among the marine iguanas was as high as 50% in some Isabela populations (Laurie 1983b). Censuses of penguin and cormorant populations revealed a size reduction of 77% and 49% respectively (Valle *et al.* 1987). Of the fifteen species of sea birds reviewed by Valle *et al.* (1987), ten did not breed during El Niño and the remaining five bred with greatly reduced success. Land organisms fared somewhat differently, with some groups thriving and others suffering. The growth of Convolvulaceae species increased tremendously, while the prickly pears suffered physical damage due to torrential floods, high winds, and excessive water uptake (Merlen 1985; P.R. Grant and B.R. Grant 1987). Alarmed by the massive rainfall, the giant tortoises made a mass exodus from the interior highlands to the coastal plains, causing one researcher to abandon her study of tortoise/plant interactions (Merlen 1985). The sudden appearance of standing water in the islands saw an explosion of insect populations, including a large increase of mosquitos on

Española (Merlen 1985).

The cactus finches (*Geospiza conirostris*) on Genovesa responded dramatically to the 1982-1983 El Niño (P.R. Grant and B.R. Grant 1987). Darwin's finches normally breed for approximately three months during the wet season (Lack 1947, p. 33), but during the El Niño, *G. conirostris* bred continuously for approximately seven months. The fraction of unmated males fell from 16.7-24.0% to 3.3%, and the mean number of clutches per pair increased from 1-4 to 7. Although the total reproduction was unusually prolific for *G. conirostris*, the survival of fledglings (12.1%) was not significantly different from prior years. Furthermore, as food resources became increasingly scarce in later years, the number of surviving *G. conirostris* individuals that first fledged in 1983 dropped to only 4% in 1985 and 2% in 1986 (P.R. Grant and B.R. Grant 1987). A similar extension of the breeding season was seen among *Geospiza* species on Daphne Major during the 1982-1983 El Niño (Gibbs and Grant 1987) but not during the 1997-1998 El Niño (P.R. Grant and B.R. Grant 1999), highlighting the unpredictability of the biological affects of El Niños.

Evidence of past El Niños comes from the research of Riedinger *et al.* (2002) at Bainbridge Crater Lake. This lake is a hypersaline shallow lake on Bainbridge Rocks off the southeastern coast of Santiago. Riedinger *et al.* (2002) obtained a 4.2 m sediment core from the lake and carbon dated 49 different depths from the core, with a maximum age of 6100 $^{14}C$ years bp. Intermingled with the organic sediments, Riedinger *et al.* (2002) found siliciclastic lamination, which they interpreted as evidence of erosion due to the heavy rains of El Niño. If their interpretation is correct, their results show a low frequency and intensity of strong El Niño events in the first 3000 $^{14}C$ years and an increase in frequency and intensity of strong El Niños during the last 3000 $^{14}C$ years. Put another way, the frequency of siliciclastic lamina is higher in the upper ~2.8 m of the core than in the bottom ~1.4 m of the core. If the many creationist attempts to understand radiocarbon dating are correct (see below), radiocarbon dates are artificially inflated as the sample becomes older. This would require a reinterpretation of Riedinger *et al.*'s (2002) data and may imply a much higher frequency of El Niño events in the period of 6000 to 3000 $^{14}C$ years bp.

Even in the recent past, however, other variables than El Niño have impacted the climate of the Galápagos Islands. According to work by Dunbar *et al.* (1994), the period of A.D. 1607-1953 experienced decadal periods of warming and cooling of SST in the Galápagos. They obtained this record from specimens of *Pavona clavus* coral from a region of Urvina Bay, Isabela that was uplifted in 1954 as the result of a magmatic intrusion beneath Volcán Alcedo. The annual mean $\delta^{18}O$ from a calibration sample of *P. gigantea* taken from the present Urvina Bay strongly correlates with the average mean temperature recorded at Academy Bay by the CDRS ($r = -0.81$). By measuring the $\delta^{18}O$ record from *P. clavus*, Dunbar *et al.* (1994) estimated that extended periods of SST cooling took place in 1600-1660 and 1800-1825. The periods 1660-1680, 1710-1800, and 1870-1895 experienced unusually warm SSTs in the Galápagos. They note that the variability of annual $\delta^{18}O$ has a periodicity of 11 and 22 years, consistent with other measures of past climate. The periodicity is coincident with periods of low and high sunspot activity.

**3.2.3. Post-Flood Climate at the Galápagos.** The Flood model of Austin *et al.* (1994) postulates a warmer ocean (due to the replacement of the ocean floor by new basalt) and cooler continents (due to lower specific heat of dry land and volcanic ash in the atmosphere) immediately after the Flood. Vardiman (1994a; 1994b) has simulated the affects of a warmer ocean and cooler land masses but mostly to understand the formation of the ice sheets after the Flood (Vardiman 1996a). In general, his models imply much greater precipitation (Vardiman 1998) and more intense storms (Vardiman 2003) after the Flood, diminishing in intensity in a roughly exponential fashion as the oceans cooled. A superficial understanding of these models might imply that rainfall was generally much greater in the Galápagos during the first few centuries after the Flood.

The oldest climatological record in the Galápagos comes from El Junco Lake, San Cristóbal, one of the only standing freshwater lakes in the islands. Colinvaux (1972) obtained three cores from the lake, which revealed three distinct layers. The lowest layer common to all three cores was 12 m of a red sediment dominated by clay. The upper 3-m layer was a laminated layer of organic-rich mud (gyttja). In a single core, EJ5, the lower layer was interrupted by a short segment of gyttja. The lowest portion of the upper layer of gyttja carbon dates to $10,170 \pm 140$ $^{14}C$ years bp. The lower layer of gyttja in EJ5 dates to between 34,300 and

48,000 $^{14}C$ years bp. Colinvaux (1972) hypothesizes that the red clay arises from weathering of the surrounding basalt when there is no standing water in the lake – *i.e.* during an extended drought. The gyttja is formed during moister periods when the lake is filled with standing water. Thus, according to Colinvaux (1972), the oldest sediments of the lake (which probably formed very shortly after the islands themselves) record a very dry climate. How then can we reconcile this with Vardiman's prediction of much higher rainfall after the Flood?

Before attempting to reinterpret Colinvaux's results within Vardiman's atmospheric models, it is important to remember that Vardiman's modeling has been global rather than local in scope. As a result, the simulations are good global overviews of post-Flood climate, but they may not be suitable for prediction of conditions at a specific locality. With that in mind, it is easy to imagine that some locations on the earth did not receive extreme amounts of precipitation after the Flood, and in fact, Vardiman's (1998) simulations of precipitation induced by a hot mid-ocean ridge showed extremes over the north Atlantic and Antarctica but not over the Galápagos. In these simulations, the Galápagos appeared to receive less than 5 mm of precipitation per day. If rain fell at 5 mm/day every day for a year, the total precipitation of 1825 mm could hardly be called a xeric environment, even though it does not exceed the total rainfall of the 1983 El Niño (2768.7 mm) (Snell and Rea 1999). An average daily rainfall of less than 5 mm/day still leaves the possibility that there was *no* rainfall at the Galápagos, thus it is still possible that Colinvaux (1972) is correct in his interpretation of the red clay as an extended drought.

In light of the coarse scale of Vardiman's simulations, it is important to reconsider the erosional deposits from which Colinvaux infers a dry climate. The inorganic, erosional deposits at the bottom of El Junco Lake constitute 104,000 $m^3$ by Colinvaux's (1972) estimate. The volume would be roughly equal to the erosion of 3 m of the crater rim surrounding the lake. While that could be feasible in 15,000 years at less than the modern rates of precipitation, it seems unlikely that such a massive amount of erosion could take place in only a few centuries without rain. Colinvaux and Schofield's (1976) radiocarbon dates indicate that the upper gyttja layer began approximately 10,000 $^{14}C$ years bp. Brown's (1990), and Humphreys's (1986) creationist $^{14}C$ models differ by a millennium in their dating of the Flood, but both models place a $^{14}C$ age of 10,000 years within two centuries after the Flood. By making a very crude assumption that San Cristóbal formed within one year after the Flood, I can calculate an average erosional rate of 520 $m^3$ per year (104,000 $m^3$ in 200 years) or a vertical erosion of the crater wall of 1.5 cm/yr. Such an enormous rate of erosion and weathering would have required a similarly high rate of rainfall. Consequently, I might also conclude that the red clay was deposited during a period of very high precipitation, such that the water level in El Junco Lake was so high that it constantly topped the crater rim and flowed down to the sea. The result would be the extreme weathering necessary to account for the 15 m layer of inorganic material, but a constant flow of water to prevent the accumulation of organic debris at the bottom of the lake.

Were the Galápagos Islands very dry or very wet after the Flood? Based on the present data, it is impossible to answer with certainty. The erosion needed to produce the sediment deposits at the bottom of El Junco Lake on San Cristóbal seems to require very high precipitation, enough to create a constant water flow out of the present lake basin. At the same time, Vardiman's (1998) global climate simulations may not support such extremes of precipitation in the Galápagos Islands. Since Vardiman's simulations are limited in resolution, I would provisionally accept the occurrence of extreme precipitation in the Galápagos immediately following the Flood, and I would recommend further, fine-scale climate simulations be conducted to examine possible precipitation rates at Galápagos after the Flood.

**3.2.4. Radiocarbon Interpretations.** The lake sediment cores from Bainbridge Crater Lake (Riedinger *et al.* 2002) and El Junco Lake (Colinvaux 1972) were both interpreted using radiocarbon dating. As described above, the Bainbridge core is 415.8 cm deep and is composed of two types of laminae: carbonate and siliciclastic. Radiocarbon dating of the Bainbridge core puts the oldest carbonate laminae at 6100 $^{14}C$ years bp. Colinvaux (1972) described three cores taken from El Junco Lake on San Cristóbal. As noted previously, the cores revealed two very distinct layers: an upper layer of gyttja and a deeper layer of red clay. The base of the gyttja layer dates to 10,000 $^{14}C$ years bp. In one core (EJ5), the red clay is interrupted by a small layer of gyttja, which dates to 48,000 $^{14}C$ years bp. Superficially, these radiocarbon dates contradict a straightforward biblical chronology that places the

Flood at 4500 years bp, but since much creationist research has been done on the radiocarbon problem, we may re-interpret these results in a creationist context.

A complete review of radiocarbon dating is beyond the scope of this monograph, but at least two previous studies relate to the radiocarbon results from Galápagos. First, Brown's (1975, 1986, 1988) studies of depth vs. $^{14}C$ age profiles for peat and sediment cores can be expanded using the Colinvaux and Schofield (1976) data, which were not included in his studies. Second, recent research suggests that detectable $^{14}C$ can survive in materials that should have no longer have any measurable $^{14}C$ content (Giem 2001; Baumgardner *et al.* 2003). Because these materials date to approximately 40,000 $^{14}C$ years bp, their interpretation bears directly on the interpretation of the lower gyttja layer from El Junco Lake core EJ5, which dates to 34,000-48,000 $^{14}C$ years bp (Colinvaux and Schofield 1976).

Brown (1986) surveyed 309 published $^{14}C$ age vs. depth profiles for deep cores of sea sediment, continental sediment, soil, and peat. His results showed that very few of these profiles are linear and thus do not indicate a constant deposition of sediment with $^{14}C$ time. Instead, the majority reveal an increase in $^{14}C$ year per centimeter with increasing sediment depth. In his earlier terminology (Brown 1975), the majority of $^{14}C$ age vs. depth profiles were C-type curves. Brown (1988) considered four factors that could produce such a global bias in $^{14}C$ age profiles: compaction of deeper sediments, contamination, decomposition (of peats), and an increasing $^{14}C/^{12}C$ ratio over time. Although he did not consider an earlier hypothesis of decreasing sediment accumulation over time (Brown 1975) in his later study (Brown 1986), he nevertheless tentatively concluded that the cause of the global bias was an increasing $^{14}C/^{12}C$ ratio.

As I have already mentioned, Vardiman's (1994a; 1996a; 1998; 2003) extensive climate simulations revealed an extremely high rate of precipitation after the Flood, due to the warm oceans (Austin *et al.* 1994; Vardiman 1998). As a direct result of this high precipitation rate, the sediment deposition would also be increased, and as the oceans cooled to their present temperatures, the sedimentation rate should have decreased. Based on this reasoning, Vardiman (1996b) assumed a sedimentation accumulation rate that exponentially decays with increasing time after the Flood. Because of a potential increase of nutrients available in the oceans, Roth (1985) argued for a transient, post-Flood increase of biogenic sedimentation as a result of microbial blooms after the Flood. Thus, we might expect both a exponentially-decreasing lithogenic and biogenic sedimentation rate after the Flood. A decreasing rate of biogenic sedimentation would produce a global tendency towards C-type $^{14}C$ age vs. depth profiles, as indicated by Brown (1975).

Still, we have yet another reason to believe that the $^{14}C/^{12}C$ ratio has increased over time. Since cosmic rays acting on nitrogen produce $^{14}C$, a reduction in cosmic ray influx on the earth would result in a lower $^{14}C/^{12}C$ ratio. Humphreys's (1986) geomagnetic models predict such a lower cosmic ray influx as a result of a stronger geomagnetic field – especially after the Flood. At the Flood, the strength of the magnetic field was drastically reduced in Humphreys's model (see Humphreys 1986, figure 6). If Humphreys is right, there may have been a *very* high production rate of $^{14}C$ immediately after the Flood – much higher than the present. Combined with the loss of pre-Flood $^{12}C$ in Flood-generated carbonates, a steep rise in $^{14}C/^{12}C$ ratios would be expected in the centuries immediately following the Flood. As noted above, an increasing $^{14}C/^{12}C$ ratio over time would produce a preponderance of C-type $^{14}C$ age vs. depth profiles (Brown 1988).

Taken together then, the increased biogenic sedimentation rates and geomagnetic field strength immediately after the Flood would predict a bias towards C-type $^{14}C$ age vs. depth profiles, exactly as Brown (1975; 1986) observed. In his 1988 review, Brown did not consider the contribution of an increased sedimentation rate in the past and instead interpreted the bias towards C-type profiles solely as an indication of an increasing $^{14}C/^{12}C$ ratio. By representing all three types of $^{14}C$ age vs. depth profiles, the three cores from El Junco Lake (Figure 10) remind us to consider the influence of sedimentation rate on $^{14}C$ age vs. depth profiles. If the bias towards C-type profiles resulted only from an increasing $^{14}C/^{12}C$ ratio, we would expect a sample of sediment cores from a single lake to show the same bias towards C-type profiles. If an increased sedimentation rate also contributed to the increased frequency of C-type profiles, we might expect that local variations in sedimentation rates could produce any type of profile in a single lake of sufficiently large area to experience variations in sedimentation rate. Such local perturbations would not disturb

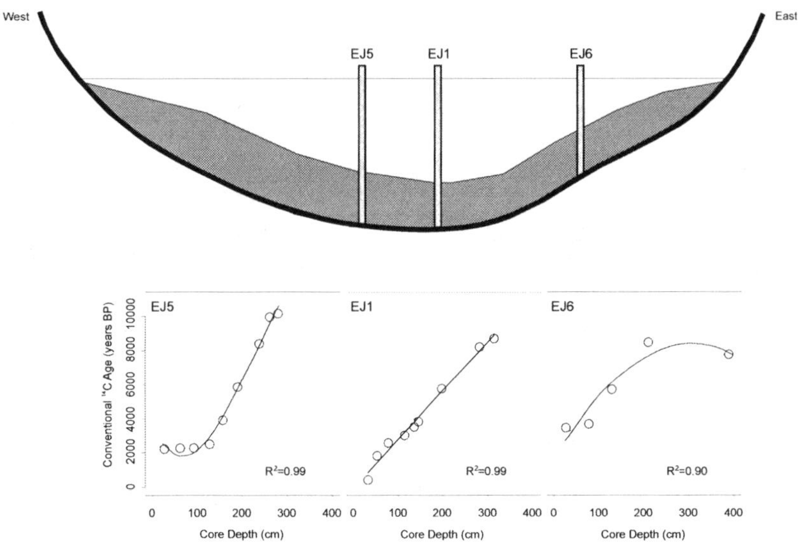


Figure 10. A diagrammatic cross section of El Junco Lake (top), adapted from Colinvaux and Schofield (1976). Dark solid line represents bedrock; thin solid line represents lake surface, and shaded region represents the sediment layer. Colinvaux and Schofield's cores are located along a linear transect as indicated. Radiocarbon age vs. sediment depth profiles for each core are also shown (bottom) with curves of highest correlation.

the global pattern, however, as the decreasing precipitation and geomagnetic field strength after the Flood would assure a predominance of C-type curves. I conclude therefore that the three types of $^{14}C$ age vs. depth profiles observed at El Junco Lake probably arise from local variations in sedimentation. That the global pattern is not disturbed is evidenced by the occurrence of a C-type curve in an independent sample from a different Galápagos lake (Riedinger *et al.* 2002, their figure 2).

The deeper layer of gyttja from El Junco Lake, dated between 34,000 and 48,000 years bp (Colinvaux and Schofield 1976), provides additional evidence pertinent to creationist interpretation of $^{14}C$ dating. Many creationsts (e.g. Wysong 1976, p. 151) have pointed to discrepancies in $^{14}C$ dating as evidence that the radiocarbon dating method is unreliable. Hall (1990, p. 65), for example, cited carbon dating done on materials old enough by conventional dating that they should have no measurable $^{14}C$

left (samples of "infinite" $^{14}C$ age). Nevertheless, such materials often have measurable $^{14}C$, and thus a $^{14}C$ age can be calculated. Other creationists have attempted to determine the causes of such discrepancies (Brown 1988; Giem 2001; Baumgardner *et al.* 2003).

Brown (1988) surveyed a very small sample of materials of infinite $^{14}C$ age for which $^{14}C$ content could be measured in order to calculate the concentration of $^{14}C$ in the atmosphere before the Flood. In doing so, he assumed that any carbon samples of infinite age would have formed during the Flood and thus their $^{14}C$ content would be dependent on the pre-Flood $^{14}C/^{12}C$ ratio. Because his sample was so small, Brown (1988) refrained from drawing definite conclusions, but he suggested that the pre-Flood $^{14}C$ atmospheric content might have between 0.014 and 0.002 of the modern $^{14}C$ content.

Giem (2001) reviewed the published $^{14}C$ content of 77 samples of infinite $^{14}C$ age. He found that the biogenic samples had a consistently higher $^{14}C$ content than samples of graphite. Although he conceded that some of these samples showed $^{14}C$ content due to contamination *in situ* or during sample preparation, he concluded that the majority of the $^{14}C$ content appears to be residual content. Giem interpreted these results in terms of the age of the earth, as an argument against the conventional dating of the Phanerozoic samples containing residual $^{14}C$. Baumgardner *et al.* (2003) updated Giem's review to 90 published samples and added ten coal samples for which they commissioned $^{14}C$ dating. Like Giem, they concluded that the $^{14}C$ represented residual carbon and challenged the conventional dating of the coal.

In light of these results, the lower gyttja layer of El Junco Lake probably represents deposition very soon after the Flood. The published samples surveyed by Giem (2001) and Baumgardner *et al.* (2003) range from 0.71 to 0.014 $\pm$ 0.010 pmc, and Baumgardner *et al.*'s (2003) coal samples range from 0.46 $\pm$ 0.03 to 0.10 $\pm$ 0.03 pmc. This $^{14}C$ data would correspond to conventional $^{14}C$ dates of 40,900-73,400 years bp and 44,500-57,100 years bp respectively. The lower gyttja layer at El Junco Lake dates to 34,000-48,000 $^{14}C$ years bp, which is younger than but overlaps the range of samples reviewed by Giem (2001) and Baumgardner *et al.* (2003). This suggests a date from the early post-Flood period. Although Colinvaux (1972) gave the thickness of the lower gyttja layer as 0.5 m, he did not specify the depth at which the gyttja layer is found. Colinvaux (1972) only indicates that it "interrupted" the red clay. Thus, although it was formed soon after the Flood, without precise depth information, I cannot speculate further on the date of the formation of the lower gyttja layer.

Furthermore, the radiocarbon recalibrations developed by Brown (1990) and Humphreys (1986) both place the lower deposits of the upper gyttja layer to within two centuries of the Flood. If, as I previously argued, the Galápagos Islands are entirely post-Flood, the lower red, inorganic layer and the included lower gyttja layer must also have been deposited within two hundred years of the Flood. Thus the lower gyttja layer of El Junco Lake helps to pinpoint the formations of one of the oldest islands in the archipelago, San Cristóbal, to soon afer the Flood – certainly within the first two centuries after the Flood.

**3.2.5. Conclusion.** The Galápagos Islands present several opportunities for creationist research into climate models. As we will see in the biology section of this monograph, the extreme climate variations of the islands, produced by ENSO, cause measurable biological reactions, in terms of both population growth and organismal characteristics. Organismal changes are attributed to natural selection, which can lead to an uncritical belief that natural selection accounts for all organismal differences in the islands. Whether this belief withstands scrutiny is a significant theme in the rest of this document. In addition to research opportunities afforded by present climate, creationist attempts to model the climate after the Flood and re-interpret radiocarbon dating also find opportunities to interact with Galápagos science. As I have shown, the sediment cores of El Junco Lake, San Cristóbal could be interpreted as showing a significant increase or decrease in annual rainfall during the two centuries following the Flood, with the rate of erosional deposits supporting an increase within a biblical chronology. The radiocarbon dating of the El Junco Lake cores supports a model of sedimentation rate variation affecting the attributes of $^{14}C$ age vs. depth curves, in addition to changes in the $^{14}C/^{12}C$ ratio.

# 4. Biology of the Galápagos

## 4.1. Introduction

Before reviewing selected organisms of Galápagos, it is helpful to review the development of modern methods in baraminology, a creationist biosystematic method. Against the wishes of George McCready Price (see Numbers 1992, pp. 126-130), Frank Lewis Marsh (1941) and Harold Clark (1940) suggested in the 1940s that speciation and natural selection could be accommodated within the creation model. Price initially wanted to retain species stasis, but he eventually relented and approved Marsh's ideas (Price 1945). Marsh devoted most of his writings (e.g. Marsh 1947, 1950, 1976) to advocating the "created kind" or *baramin*. According to Marsh, members of a baramin were identified by their God-given ability to hybridize, an extremely practical criterion, even if the philosophical underpinnings were somewhat muddled (Wood *et al.* 2003).

Scherer and colleagues (Scherer 1993a) adapted the Marshian hybridization criterion to produce basic type biology, which identifies basic types on the following three criteria: Two organisms (species) belong to the same basic type if (1) they are able to hybridize, (2) they are able to hybridize with the same third organism (species) or (3) a hybrid embryo progresses beyond the expression of genes from both parents before dying. As Scherer (1993b; 1998) noted, however, the hybridization criterion has limitations, not the least of which is the inapplicability to fossils and organisms that do not reproduce sexually.

Citing the shortcomings of hybridization, ReMine (1990), Wise (1990), and Wood *et al.* (2003) have advocated a system of multiple criteria and statistical methodology for identifying baramins. ReMine calls his system "discontinuity systematics," while Wise and Wood *et al.* call theirs baraminology. Both systems rely on successive approximation for identifying baramins. Rather than posit a single, defining characteristic, Wood *et al.* (2003)

proposed that baramins merely occupy a continuous region of biological character space. Consequently, baramins are identified by two methods: identification of continuity between species and discontinuity between larger groups. Evidence used to identify continuity is termed "additive evidence" and the resulting groups of continuous species are called *monobaramins*. Evidence of discontinuity is called "subtractive evidence" and groups of species bounded by discontinuity are called *apobaramins*. A group of species simultaneously continuous with each other (a monobaramin) and discontinuous with species outside the group (an apobaramin) is properly termed a *holobaramin*. The holobaramin approximates the membership of a continuous region of biological character space surrounded by discontinuity, a *baramin*.

The most obvious advantage of such a system is its widespread utility. Baraminological research can be performed even in groups that either cannot hybridize or from which hybrids are unknown. Furthermore, failure to identify the holobaramin in a single analysis is not actually a failure. Because the holobaramin is simultaneously a monobaramin and apobaramin, any monobaramin or apobaramin can be considered an approximation of a holobaramin. Presumably, further baraminological research of the same questionable group should resolve ambiguities of holobaraminic membership.

Within this framework, numerous techniques and criteria for identifying baraminic units have been proposed (for a recent review, see Wood and Murray 2003). Wood and Murray (2003, chap. 6) revised Wise's (1992) original forensic baraminology technique for identifying apobaramins. The method involves answering a series of questions about a group of organisms for which discontinuity is hypothesized (*i.e.* the group may be an apobaramin). The questions are designed to detect discontinuity and are organized in the form of a matrix. Each question is phrased such that answering "yes" implies the presence of discontinuity and answering "no" indicates a lack of evidence for discontinuity. After completing the discontinuity matrix, the strength of an apobaraminic hypothesis can be assessed by the number of "yes" and "no" answers. Thus far, the technique has been applied only to turtles (Wise 1992).

Robinson and Cavanaugh (1998a) introduced the baraminic distance as a technique for evaluating hypotheses of continuity and discontinuity. Given a character state matrix, the baraminic distance between taxa *i* and *j* can be calculated as the fraction of characters in which the states are both known and different between *i* and *j* over the total characters for which the states of *i* and *j* are known. According to Robinson and Cavanaugh (1998a), baraminic distances can be evaluated by a test of correlation. Given organisms *i* and *j* in some larger sample of organisms *X*, a linear correlation coefficient is calculated for the distances between *i* and all other organisms in *X* and the corresponding distances between *j* and all other organisms in *X*. If *i* and *j* are adjacent in biological character space, they will be similarly distant to all other organisms in *X*, hence the correlation coefficient will be positive and statistically significant. Conversely if *i* and *j* are far apart in biological character space, corresponding distances to other organisms in *X* can result in negative correlation. Robinson and Cavanaugh interpreted positive correlation as evidence of continuity (membership in the same monobaramin) and negative correlation as evidence of discontinuity (membership in different apobaramins).

Possibly owing to the publication of datasets used in cladistic analyses that can also be used in baraminic distance analysis, the baraminic distance correlation method has been widely applied. In only two cases, the Felidae (Robinson and Cavanaugh 1998b) and the Poaceae (Wood 2002b), has the technique revealed a holobaramin, *i.e.* a group united by significant positive correlation (continuity) and separated from a sample of outgroup species by significant negative correlation (discontinuity). In both cases, the authors justifiably concluded that a holobaramin had been identified. Application of the technique to fossil Equids (Cavanaugh *et al.* 2003) and composites of the tribes Heliantheae *sensu stricto*, Helenieae, and Eupatorieae (Cavanaugh and Wood 2002) revealed ambiguous results. In both of these cases, the technique revealed a contradictory mixture of positive and negative correlation with no clear demarcation of a holobaramin. In both cases, the authors concluded that the taxa in question belonged to a single monobaramin, arguing that negative correlation does not by itself constitute evidence of discontinuity.

Although it may seem arbitrary to interpret negative baraminic distance correlation as evidence of discontinuity in some cases but not in others, such special pleading is partly justified by the Analysis of Patterns (ANOPA) technique (Cavanaugh

2002). ANOPA is a pattern projection technique that reduces multidimensional data to three dimensions, much in the same way that a two-dimensional shadow is a projection of a three-dimensional object. The technique treats each character as a different dimension in biological character space. The character states are recoded numerically, and the dimensions are reduced by reference to a polar coordinate system around a hyperline between the organismal centroid and an outlying taxon or set of taxa chosen by the researcher. ANOPA offers significant advantages to baraminology by allowing taxa clusters to be observed apart from calculation of baraminic distances. Also, ANOPA can reveal clusters of unusually regular geometry, such as trajectories (Wood and Cavanaugh 2003), which are otherwise difficult to detect in the more simplistic baraminic distance correlation test. Indeed, the presence of complex geometries revealed by ANOPA justified the rejection of negative baraminic distance correlation as evidence of discontinuity in studies of fossil equids (Cavanaugh *et al.* 2003) and Heliantheae *sensu lato* (Cavanaugh and Wood 2002).

Another technique useful in identifying complex geometry is the application of classical multidimensional scaling (MDS) to baraminic distance matrices, as proposed by Wood (2004). In re-analyses of two previous ANOPA studies, the aforementioned Equidae (Cavanaugh *et al.* 2003) and Heliantheae *s. l.* (Cavanaugh and Wood 2002), Wood found that MDS of baraminic distances strongly confirmed the exact geometry of the equid 3D ANOPA and corroborated the general results of the Heliantheae 3D ANOPA. One major advantage of MDS is the introduction of *stress*, a measurement of how the observed baraminic distances are distorted by the reduction in dimensionality. In particular, Wood's (2004) analysis of stress for these previously-published studies revealed that the Heliantheae dataset is highly complex, with its minimum stress in a 20-dimensional structure. In contrast, the Equidae dataset reaches its minimum stress in a five-dimensional structure, for which a 3D pattern captured most of the relevant geometry. Because the 20D Heliantheae dataset is poorly described in three dimensions, the geometrical taxic pattern in 3D ANOPA and 3D MDS were quite different. Further details on MDS can be found in the Appendix.

Other creationists have suggested biosystematic techniques outside of mainstream baraminology. García-Pozuelo-Ramos

(1998; 1999; 2002) applied morphometric techniques to canids, but in doing so, he assumes their common ancestry. He attempted to relate the results of canid variability to variability in other mammalian groups (e.g. hominids), but the analogy suffers from a lack of justification for why canid variability should relate to variability in non-canid mammals. Woodmorappe (2001; 2002; 2003) recently introduced and utilized a method to detect "discontinuity" (*sensu* ReMine 1990). His technique actually tests a model of orthogenetic phylogeny, but since modern researchers reject orthogenesis, the utility of the method is unclear.

Despite the blossoming of statistical techniques for baraminology and my own personal enthusiasm for the system (e.g. Wood and Murray 2003), the baraminology perspective has been largely untested. Indeed, it is difficult to imagine how such a test might be conducted. Instead of evaluating baraminology itself, I will attempt to evaluate two of the basic assumptions behind the system. First is the ubiquitous and – according to Marsh (1947, p. 101) – self-evident discontinuity between groups of organisms. Repeated failure to detect discontinuity using the variety of methods here described could be taken as evidence against the assumption of ubiquitous or self-evident discontinuity. Furthermore, Wood and Murray (2003, p. 71-72) argue that discontinuity should be detectable at the taxonomic rank of family. If baraminology methods repeatedly fail to detect discontinuity at or near the family rank, Wood and Murray's prediction would be falsified.

A second assumption peripherally related to baraminology but used in the justification of the ANOPA technique (Wood and Murray 2003, p. 125) is that the tree structure (*i.e.* the unique nested hierarchy) is too limiting for adequate description of complex taxic clustering. From this we might suppose that groups traditionally viewed as difficult to classify might only be difficult to classify into a unique nested hierarchy. Presumably, techniques such as ANOPA or MDS, which are not bound by the tree structure, could reveal a reason for the difficulty and/or an alternative non-nested or non-hierarchical classification structure. If, however, the tree represents the best method of displaying taxic clustering, I would expect 3D ANOPA or MDS patterns to resemble the phylogenetic trees derived from the same dataset.

As I now turn to discussing the Galápagos organisms from a creationist perspective, I intend to test these claims in addition to proposing possible creationist explanations for the species diversity and biogeography. Specifically, I will use two methods wherever possible: the baraminic distance correlation method of Robinson and Cavanaugh (1998a), and the classical MDS technique proposed by Wood (2004). Given adequate datasets and the presence of actual discontinuity, these studies should reveal a consistent and consilient picture of discontinuity and continuity, as Marsh predicted. In addition, the pelecaniforms and iguanid lizards have been groups that are difficult to classify. If this difficulty arises from the imposition of an artificial and unnatural unique nested hierarchy, baraminological techniques should reveal the problem. If baraminological techniques also have difficulty in classifying these organisms, the problem cannot be attributed simply to the assumptions inherent in the classification methods. Even with the present examples, however, the paucity of baraminological studies cannot be judged a comprehensive test of the assumptions. At best, I can only contribute to the future evaluation of the methods and their assumptions.

In addition to concerns of systematics, the creation biology model encompasses other unconventional ideas that need to be explored in much more detail. For example, creation biologists have argued that the period immediately following the Flood saw rapid and dramatic speciation within baramins (e.g. Wieland 1992; Wise 2002, p. 217-218; Wood 2002a). Because this kind of biological change is unlike any biological change happening today (*i.e.* the changes stopped after some unknown duration), Wood and Murray (2003, p. 170) recommended the term diversification (initially suggested by Wise 1994a) be used to refer to rapid, post-Flood, intrabaraminic speciation. I follow that recommendation here, and I refer to the period of rapid, post-Flood diversification as the "diversification period." Because of a lack of mechanism, diversification has become the subject of some ridicule of the young-earth creation position (Ross 2004, chap. 11). Wood and Murray (2003, chap. 11) actually reviewed several mechanisms that have been proposed to account for diversification and concluded that none of them completely account for the phenomena involved. Wood's (2002a; 2003b) model of altruistic genetic elements (AGEs) and genomic modularity would seem to hold the most promise in explaining diversification. Additional systematic studies of Galápagos organisms will indirectly aid study of diversification by providing additional case studies of organismal change.

More immediately relevant to the organisms of the Galápagos is the diversification-related concept of mediated design (Wood 2003a). Mediated design is a marriage of theological and biological concepts of biological change. An organism that changes by mediated design exhibits a "new" trait that was already present in their genome or developmental capabilities. The trait was designed, in that it was created and intended by God, but the design was not immediately implemented but instead was mediated via some mechanism of biological change. Thus it *appears* to be both designed and evolved. The concept behind mediated design was initially devised in a study of the origin of the complex $C_4$ photosynthetic pathway (Wood and Cavanaugh 2001), and Wood (2003a) introduced the term "mediated design" to describe changes in photosynthetic pathways and other complex biological phenomena that appear suddenly, after the Creation.

Another general model of biological change is the popular notion of degenerative changes (e.g. Wieland 1991; Scherer 1993b). According to this model, biological change is in the direction of lost information or reduced fitness or degraded quality of life. This model appears to be consistent with the theological notion of a fall from grace, as in God's Curse on creation as a result of Adam's sin and Adam's subsequent expulsion from the Garden of Eden (Gen. 3). Degeneration is frequently invoked to explain pathological attributes of the post-Fall creation (Stambaugh 1991; McCoy 1992; Wood 2001, 2002c; Mace *et al.* 2003). Since degeneration and mediated design are not mutually exclusive, the question arises as to the dominance of one type of change or the other. The insistence of Wieland (1991) that *all* biological change is degenerative would seem to rule out the possibility of mediated design, although there seems to be no theological necessity for exclusively degenerative biological change. The organisms of Galápagos will offer several opportunities to explore potential mechanisms and models of biological change within the creation biology model.

## 4.2. Galápagos Tortoise (*Geochelone elephantopus*)

**4.2.1. Introduction.** One of the most recognizable denizens of the islands is the Galápagos tortoise (*Geochelone elephantopus*; for recent discussion of Galápagos tortoise nomenclature see

Pritchard 1996 and Zug 1997). Older individuals can weigh as much as 300 pounds, making *G. elephantopus* the largest tortoise in the world. The tortoises appear in the earliest descriptions of the islands. Fr. Thomás de Berlanga described them as "such big tortoises, that each could carry a man on top of itself" (quoted in Larson 2001, p. 22). Darwin himself confirmed this by riding on several different tortoises during his visit to the islands (Darwin 1839, p. 465). Because the tortoises are slow (they are one of the few animals on which lichens grow; see Hendrickson and Weber 1964) and remarkably hardy, they are easily caught and soon became a valuable food source for passing ships. They could be stowed aboard ships and kept for months with no food or water. Not only could their meat be eaten upon slaughter, but also an oil could be made from their fat and drinkable water could be obtained from their bladders (Darwin 1839, p. 464-465). Excessive hunting (and competition with feral donkeys and goats) greatly reduced the numbers of tortoises during the nineteenth century (MacFarland *et al.* 1974; Pritchard 1996). Today, through the captive breeding program at the Charles Darwin Research Station and protective laws, tortoise populations are slowly recovering (e.g. see Márquez *et al.* 1987, 1991).

The Galápagos tortoises were initially classified as *Testudo indicus*, since all giant tortoises of the time were believed to be the same species (Darwin 1839, p. 465; Pritchard 1996; Sulloway 1982b). Today, the extant giant tortoise species from Galápagos and Aldabra are classified as separate species in the genus *Geochelone*. Half of all extant tortoise species are also classified in *Geochelone*. In total, 24 extant species (Ernst *et al.* 2000) and 95 species known only from fossils (Auffenberg 1974) are referred to the genus. Eleven subgenera are recognized (Ernst *et al.* 2000), with the giant Galápagos and Aldabran tortoises referred to *Chelonoidis* and *Aldabrachelys* respectively (Hendrickson 1966; Auffenberg 1974; Pritchard 1996).

The South American mainland is currently home to three *Geochelone* species, the Chaco tortoise (*G. chilensis*), the red-footed tortoise (*G. carbonaria*), and the yellow-footed tortoise (*G. denticulata*). Whereas *G. elephantopus* subfossils are known from Isla Floreana (Steadman 1986), true fossil remains are not known from any Galápagos locality. The fossil record of South and Central America and the Caribbean contains nine *Geochelone* species, seven of which belong to the subgenus

*Chelonoidis* (Auffenberg 1974). Thus, the geographically closest fossil species are also phylogenetically close to the Galápagos tortoise. A mitochondrial DNA phylogeny implies that the closest mainland relative to the Galápagos species is the smallest of the South American *Geochelone* species, the Chaco tortoise (Caccone *et al.* 1999). That the giant tortoise of Galápagos could be closely related to a small tortoise should come as no surprise since tortoise gigantism is somewhat common. In *Geochelone*, three subgenera, *Chelonoidis*, *Megalochelys*, and *Aldabrachelys*, all contain giant species. The largest of the giant tortoises was the Pleistocene *G.* (*Megalochelys*) *sivalensis*, which grew to approximately twice the shell diameter as the modern Galápagos species (Wood 1976).

The classification of the Galápagos tortoises varieties has not been as straightforward as the classification of the species itself. That morphologically distinct populations exist is indisputable, but the taxonomic interpretation of these populations is an area of some contention. Aside from the obvious differences in the shape of the carapace (Figure 11), attempts at breeding Galápagos tortoises have revealed that an individual tortoise experiences a lower reproductive success with tortoises from different islands and a higher reproductive success with tortoises from the same island (MacFarland *et al.* 1974). Various descriptions of the tortoise populations recognized between ten and fifteen subspecies (Hendrickson 1966; Pritchard 1996), but Ernst *et al.* (2000) argue that the subspecies should be recognized as full species. Ongoing mtDNA research aimed at identifying genetically different populations have confirmed the monophyletic status of many of these populations (Caccone *et al.* 2002), but corresponding studies of nuclear DNA have revealed very low sequence diversity (Caccone *et al.* 2004). Tortoise subspecies from Española, San Cristóbal, Pinzón, Santiago, Pinta, and Volcan Darwin on Isabela all correspond to separate, monophyletic mitochondrial lineages. Although Ernst *et al.* (2000) argue for specific recognition for these populations, I will refer to the different populations as subspecies to maintain consistency with the majority of current references.

As noted above, the most recognizable characteristic that distinguishes various subspecies is the shape of the carapace. For example, tortoises from San Cristóbal have a dome-shaped carapace, while tortoises from Española have a distinctive "saddleback" shape (Fritts 1983) (Figure 11). Although Nicholas

Figure 11. Domed (top) and saddleback (bottom) Galápagos giant tortoises *Geochelone (Chelonoidis) elephantopus*. Photos courtesy Corel Corporation.

O. Lawson, vice-governor of the Galápagos during the *Beagle*'s visit, boasted to Darwin that he could identify the island origin of any tortoise based on the carapace shape (Darwin 1839, p. 465), this is an unlikely boast. Careful morphological analyses can distinguish different morphological forms (Fritts 1983, 1984), but attempts to visually identify the island origin of tortoises have not been successful (Pritchard 1996; Sulloway 1982b).

The saddleback form has been correlated with a greater vertical reach than the dome form (Fritts 1984). This observation has led to the suggestion that the saddleback form is adaptive, in that it allows tortoises to exploit additional food resources in xeric environments (e.g. Fritts 1984). The correlation of saddleback forms with xeric environments (Fritts 1983), the correlation of genetic lineages with geography (Caccone *et al.* 2002), and the recent origin of the genetic lineages (Caccone *et al.* 2002) would be consistent with formation of subspecies within the present islands and the origin of the saddleback form by adaptation. Among creationists, adaptation of carapace form has been accepted by Harris (1976, pp. 88-89), but questioned by another creationist (Anonymous 2001).

**4.2.2. Turtle baraminology** has a longer history of creationist research than any other group, with turtles (order Testudines) having been examined in four different studies (Frair 1984; Frair 1991; Wise 1992; Robinson 1997). Nevertheless, widespread agreement on the baraminic relationships of turtles has not been forthcoming. One conclusion on which creationists seem to agree is that the peculiar anatomy of the turtles constitutes evidence against the evolution of turtles from a non-turtle ancestor (Gish 1995, pp. 112-114; Roth 1998, p. 182; Weston 1999). This claim was criticized by Petto (1983), who reviewed evidence of turtle phylogeny. He constructed a four-part argument to support the contention that turtles and other reptiles evolved from a common ancestor. His critique might have some bearing on past claims that evolution cannot account for the origin of turtles. Using the refined baramin concept (Wood *et al.* 2003), however, Wood and Murray (2003, p. 94) made a different claim that turtle anatomy constitutes evidence of significant, holistic difference (*i.e.* of discontinuity). Because discontinuity is a positive, testable claim, it is not properly refuted by hypothetical evolutionary scenarios for the origin of turtles.

Several other baraminic hypotheses have been proposed for

the Testudines. Frair published two different hypotheses. In 1984, he suggested that all turtle species might constitute a "polytypic created 'kind'" with four "diversification lines": the side-necked turtles (suborder Pleurodira), the sea turtles (superfamily Chelonioidea), the softshells (family Trionychidae) and the rest of the hidden-necked turtles (suborder Cryptodira except for trionychids and chelonioids) (Frair 1984). The Marshian concept of the polytypic created kind or baramin (Marsh 1947) has no modern corollary, but a diversification line of a polytypic baramin would be approximately equivalent to a holobaramin *sensu* ReMine (1990). Frair (1991) later revised his hypothesis and proposed that all turtles (pleurodires and cryptodires) descended from a created ancestor, possibly the Triassic fossil *Proganochelys*. He did not, however, discard his original hypothesis of four diversification lines, considering it a "reasonable hypothesis worthy of further consideration" (Frair 1991).

After introducing baraminology in 1990, Wise (1992) produced a study of turtle baraminology in order to illustrate the practical application of the technique. Wise concluded that turtles are apobaraminic and that some evidence supported Frair's (1984) original interpretation of four holobaramins. Robinson's (1997) analysis of mitochondrial DNA further supported Wise's contention that the turtles are apobaraminic. Robinson's analysis of turtle monobaramins was limited to sea turtles (family Cheloniidae) and the genus *Gopherus*. In both cases, he concluded that the evidence supported their monobaraminic status.

Since Robinson's mtDNA study, no new turtle baraminology research has been published, even though significant advances in baraminology methods (Robinson and Cavanaugh 1998a; Cavanaugh 2002) and turtle phylogenetics (e.g. Rieppel and Reisz 1999; Lee 2001; Rieppel 2001) have been made. Creationists have commented on the developments in turtle phylogeny only rarely. Martin (1996) criticized Lee's (1993) research, and Junker (2003) argued for a form of discontinuity between turtles and other reptiles. Neither of these authors offered a baraminological interpretation of the evidence. Here, I will first discuss recent findings relating to the phylogeny of turtles and then present an analysis of three recently published datasets to evaluate the hypothesis of the turtle apobaramin. I will then comment on the possibility of all turtles belonging to a single monobaramin.

**4.2.3. The Need for a New Analysis.** In 1988, Gaffney

and Meylan proposed that turtles were related to the Paleozoic Captorhinidae, based on four synapomorphies. Reisz and Laurin (1991) proposed that a group of Permian and Triassic reptiles called procolophonids are the sister taxa to turtles based on ten synapomorphies. Their work was discussed in the *NCSE Reports* by Padian (1991), but his comments were not specifically anti-creationist. Lee (1993) followed their report with a cladistic analysis that supported a sister relationship between turtles and the Upper Permian pareiasaurs based on sixteen synapomorphies. Lee also proposed a scenario for the evolution of the turtle shell by fusion of osteoderms and posterior migration of a reduced pectoral girdle. Lee's work was attacked in the *CRSQ* by Martin (1996), who argued that turtles remained a "model of the creationist view of origins."

Laurin and Reisz (1995) responded to Lee's (1993) paper with an extensive analysis of amniote phylogeny. They combined data from their original study (Reisz and Laurin 1991) and from Lee's (1993) work, and they found a single most parsimonious tree that supported a sister relationship between turtles and procolophonids, supported by seventeen synapomorphies. Lee (1996) quickly responded with yet another cladistic analysis of turtles, which included data from all previous studies plus new data identified for that study. In addition, Lee (1996) included ten separate pareisaur species rather than a composite pareisaur taxon. He found a single most parsimonious tree that again confirmed not only that turtles and pareiasaurs were sister taxa but also that pareiasaurs were paraphyletic with turtles. In his interpretation of the cladogram, Lee (1996) noted that pareiasaurs become progressively smaller and more heavily armored with osteoderms the closer to turtles they appear in the cladogram.

As if this story is not complicated enough, deBraga and Rieppel (Rieppel and deBraga 1996; deBraga and Rieppel 1997) argued that turtles were not even anapsids but instead clustered with the diapsids, as the sister taxon of the Sauropterygia. Their dataset consisted largely of newly coded characters, and they were the first to include a variety of diapsids in their cladistic analysis of turtle phylogeny. Their clade of Testudines + Sauropterygia was supported by ten synapomorphies, but the bootstrap support for the same clade was only 43%. Not surprisingly, this new proposal of turtles as diapsids met with immediate skepticism from several groups. Wilkinson *et al.* (1997) reexamined the same data as deBraga and Rieppel (1997) and concluded that trees with turtles as diapsids or anapsids were not significantly different. Lee (1997) criticized some of deBraga and Rieppel's (1997) character coding and found that a recoded dataset supported turtles as anapsids. Although not precisely a criticism, Motani *et al.* (1998) added ichthyosaurs to Lee's (1997) recoding of deBraga and Rieppel's (1997) dataset and found that turtles clustered with the anapsids. At this point, molecular phylogenies of the turtles began to appear, all of which seemed to support an alternative clustering of turtles within the diapsid-bird clade (Platz and Conlon 1997; Mannen *et al.* 1997; Zardoya and Meyer 1998; Hedges and Poling 1999; Kumuzawa and Nishida 1999; Cao *et al.* 2000; Rest *et al.* 2003).

In 1999, Rieppel and Reisz produced a new morphological study of turtles, accepting "the majority" of Lee's (1997) criticism of deBraga and Rieppel's (1997) dataset. They recoded and rescored other characters and once again found that the most parsimonious tree supported placing the turtles with the diapsids, but their bootstrap support for their most parsimonious tree topology was still weak. Furthermore, a developmental study of the turtle shell seemed to contradict Lee's theory of turtle shell evolution (Gilbert *et al.* 2001). Instead of showing a deflection of the pectoral girdle posteriorly as Lee (1993) suggested, Gilbert *et al.* (2001) found that the ribs are deflected dorsally to the scapula during development. They also found that ossification centers in the carapace homologous to osteoderms (e.g. of the pareiasaurs) are secondary to more important ossification centers that resemble perichondral ossification. Thus, instead of being primitive as Lee (1993) predicted, Gilbert *et al.* (2001) found that osteoderm-like ossification occurs late in turtle development, after the ossification of the carapace has already begun.

Lee's (2001) response to these developments was a combined morphological and molecular analysis that showed turtles grouping with anapsids, with pareiasaurs as their sister taxa. His analysis of just the molecular dataset, however, confirmed previous findings that turtles group with diapsids and birds. His conclusions were more conservative than they had been in previous papers: he acknowledged that turtles might group with diapsids even though his analysis of the complete dataset showed turtles clustering with anapsids. If turtles are anapsids, their closest relatives would be the pareiasaurs, with their dermal armor. If turtles are diapsids, their closest relatives would be rhynchosaurs, which have beaks.

Where do turtles come from? In a recent commentary on turtle evolution, Rieppel (2001) made no firm claim as to what the turtles' progenitors really were. Instead, he claimed that the turtle shell is unique and can only be explained by alterations in the early development of the turtles' ancestor. In the abstract of that paper, he claims that this kind of change is "not compatible with scenarios of gradualistic, stepwise transformation."

**4.2.4. Evaluating the Discontinuity of Testudines.** In order to evaluate the baraminological status of turtles with modern methods and data, I performed classical MDS (see Appendix) on three published, morphological datasets. The first dataset is the Laurin and Reisz (1995) dataset of thirteen taxa and 124 characters, which showed a close relationship between turtles and procolophonids. The second is Rieppel and Reisz's (1999) dataset of 38 taxa and 138 characters, which showed some evidence that turtles are diapsids. The last dataset is Lee's (2001) morphological dataset of 29 taxa and 216 characters, which showed evidence of a sister relationship between turtles and pareiasaurs.

For the Laurin and Reisz (1995) dataset, 101 characters were retained for baraminic distance calculation at a 0.9 relevance cutoff. I performed MDS on the baraminic distance matrix, which resulted in a minimal stress of 0.026 at eight dimensions. Stress at three dimensions was 0.119. Next I scaled the baraminic distance matrix by adding the greatest distance in the matrix (0.753 between Limnoscelidae and Testudines) to each baraminic distance value. MDS of the scaled matrix yielded a minimum stress of 0.270 at nine dimensions. The three-dimensional stress for the scaled matrix was 0.434. As in previous results, MDS of calculated baraminic distances more closely matched the original distances than MDS of the scaled distances. The 3D MDS pattern of the unscaled baraminic distances from the Laurin and Reisz (1995) dataset reveals two distinct clusters of taxa: Testudines + Procolophonidae + Pareiasauria in one cluster and everything else in another cluster (Figure 12). As was expected from the cladistic results for the same dataset, Procolophonidae was the closest taxon to Testudines, at a calculated baraminic distance of 0.296. Pareiasaurs were more distant from Testudines, at a calculated baraminic distance of 0.418.

For the Rieppel and Reisz (1999) dataset, 113 characters were used to calculate baraminic distances after filtering the dataset at a 0.9 relevance cutoff. MDS was calculated for the unscaled

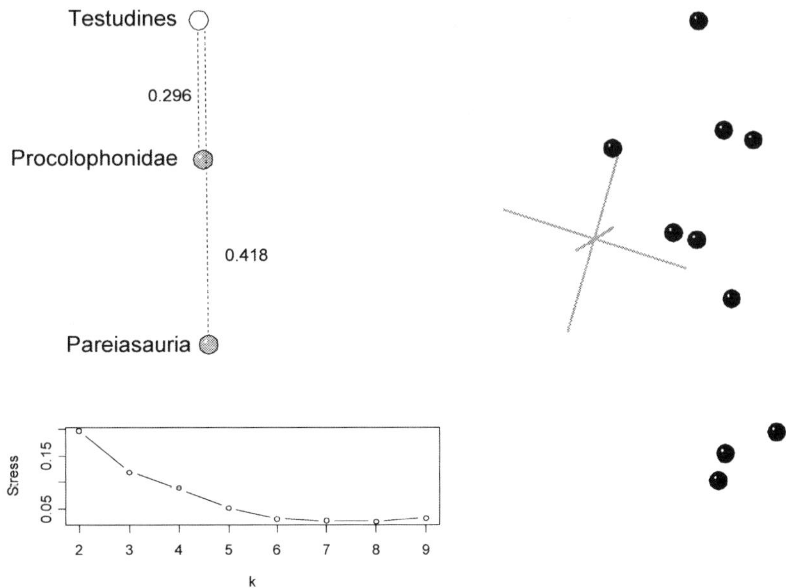


Figure 12. Three-dimensional classical MDS applied to uncorrected turtle baraminic distances calculated from the Laurin and Reisz (1995) dataset. Also shown is the stress of *k*-dimensional MDS on the same baraminic distance matrix plotted as a function of the number of dimensions (*k*). Distances indicated are baraminic distances and not inferred from the 3D MDS.

baraminic distance matrix, yielding a minimal stress of 0.049 at eight dimensions. Three-dimensional stress for the unscaled distance matrix was 0.202. Scaling of the dataset by addition of the maximum distance (0.589 between Ophiacodontidae and *Placodus*) resulted in a minimal MDS stress of 0.231 at nineteen dimensions. Stress for the 3D MDS on the scaled distance matrix was 0.468. The 3D MDS (Figure 13) revealed a much more complex taxic clustering than seen in the Laurin and Reisz (1995) dataset. At one end of the cluster is Testudines, with proposed sister taxa arrayed in an arc around the turtles. The closest were the diapsids *Cyamodus* and Eosauropterygia, as suggested by the cladistic results of the same dataset. The next closest taxa were the procolophonids *Owenetta* and *Procolophon*. The most distant of these proposed sister taxa were the pareiasaurs *Bradysaurus* and *Scutosaurus*.

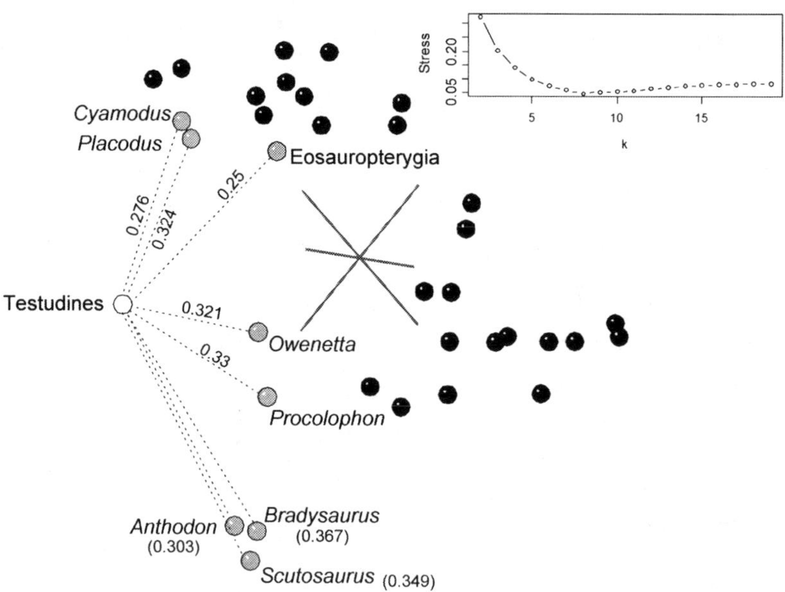


Figure 13. Three-dimensional classical MDS applied to uncorrected turtle baraminic distances calculated from the Rieppel and Reisz (1999) dataset. Also shown is the stress of *k*-dimensional MDS on the same baraminic distance matrix plotted as a function of the number of dimensions (*k*). Distances indicated are baraminic distances and not inferred from the 3D MDS.

For the Lee (2001) morphological dataset, 111 characters were used for baraminic distance calculation after filtering the dataset at a 0.9 relevance cutoff. Using the unscaled baraminic distance matrix, MDS was calculated for all possible dimensions, revealing a minimal stress of 0.057 at eight dimensions and a stress of 0.175 at three dimensions. The largest distance in this baraminic distance matrix was 0.585 between Lanthanosuchidae and Trilophosauridae. Addition of this value to each element of the distance matrix yielded a minimal MDS stress of 0.254 at fifteen dimensions and a 3D MDS stress of 0.462. The three dimensional MDS calculated for the unscaled baraminic distances (Figure 14) reveals a taxic clustering pattern somewhat similar to that of the Laurin and Reisz (1995) dataset. Testudines, Pareiasauridae, and Procolophonoidea form a loose cluster, but the cluster is only set off slightly from the other taxa. Consistent with Lee's cladistic

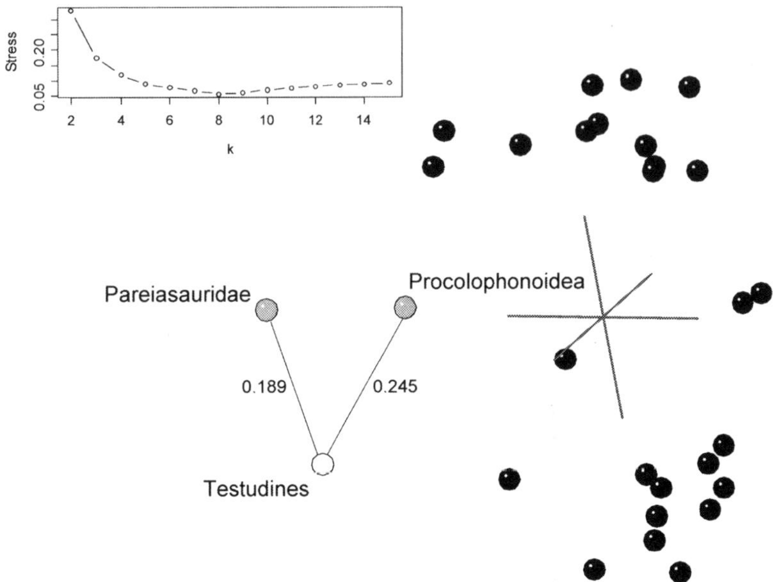


Figure 14. Three-dimensional classical MDS applied to uncorrected turtle baraminic distances calculated from the Lee (2001) dataset. Also shown is the stress of *k*-dimensional MDS on the same baraminic distance matrix plotted as a function of the number of dimensions (*k*). Distances indicated are baraminic distances and not inferred from the 3D MDS.

analysis, the Pareiasauridae is the closest taxon to the Testudines at a baraminic distance of 0.189. Procolophonoidea is more distant at 0.245.

What then is the sister taxon to the Testudines? The answer to this question depends entirely on which dataset is used, and the datasets depend on the judgments of the researchers as to which structures are homologous and systematically relevant. If the turtles are actually discontinuous with other organisms, then we should expect ambiguity and confusion when a non-existent sister taxon is sought. The fact that the turtles are visibly offset from other taxa in each of the three MDS analyses here presented suggests that their distinctiveness is robust to the dataset used. The consistent distinction of turtles from other vertebrates in turn would further support the conclusion of discontinuity around turtles. I conclude therefore that the assertion of Wise (1992) that the turtles are apobaraminic is supported despite advances in turtle phylogenetic research.

**4.2.5. Turtle Holobaramins.** Because the definition of the holobaramin requires a demonstration of both discontinuity and continuity, it is important to establish monobaramins within the turtle apobaramin to determine the number of turtle holobaramins. As noted above, Frair has suggested that the turtles could constitute a single holobaramin or four different holobaramins (*sensu* ReMine). As noted above, Frair's four proposed holobaramins consist of the side-neck turtles (suborder Pleurodira), the sea turtles (superfamily Chelonioidea), the softshells (family Trionychidae), and the rest of the turtles (Cryptodira except for trionychids and chelonioids). Wise's (1992) analysis of turtle discontinuity weakly confirmed discontinuity within the turtles.

To evaluate Frair's suggestions, I obtained a published morphological consisting of 115 characters and 30 turtle taxa (Shaffer *et al.* 1997). The 30 taxa consist of seven extant pleurodires, sixteen extant cryptodires, six fossil cryptodires, and *Proganochelys*. I performed a baraminic distance correlation analysis on this dataset as described previously (Robinson and Cavanaugh 1998a; Wood 2002b). At the default relevance cutoff of 0.95, only 60 characters were included in the analysis. Lowering the relevance cutoff to 0.9 resulted in the inclusion of an additional 33 characters, bringing the total number of analyzed characters to 93 (80.8% of the initial dataset). Because of the greater number of characters included, the baraminic distances described here were calculated at a relevance cutoff of 0.9.

The baraminic distance correlation results for the complete dataset are shown in Figure 15. Immediately apparent from these results are two different groups of turtles. The first consists of the pleurodires and the Triassic fossil form *Proganochelys*. Each pleurodire species is positively correlated with all other pleurodires, and *Proganochelys* positively correlates with four of the pleurodire species (from two different families). The turtles of the traditional suborder Cryptodira form the second major group. Almost every cryptodire species pair shows significant positive correlation, with the exception of *Meiolania* and *Carettochelys*, *Meiolania* and *Lissemys*, and *Meiolania* and *Apolone*.

To confirm these results, I performed MDS (see Appendix) on the baraminic distance matrix. For the uncorrected distance matrix, the minimal stress was 0.073 at five dimensions. The stress

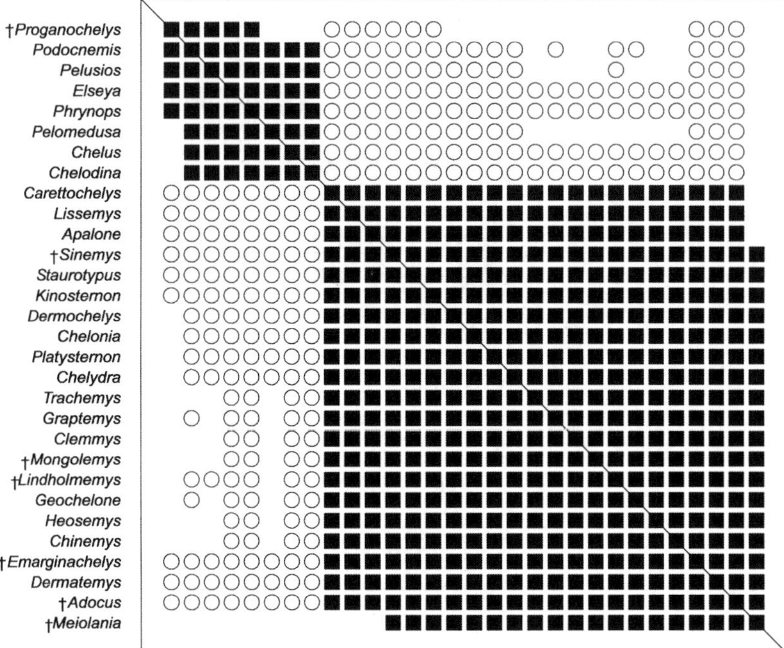


Figure 15. Baraminic distance correlation for the Shaffer *et al.* (1997) turtle dataset, using a relevance cutoff value of 0.9. Taxa with significant ($p<0.05$) positive correlation are indicated as filled squares. Taxa with significant ($p<0.05$) negative correlation are indicated as open circles. Fossil taxa (†) are also indicated.

at three dimensions was 0.101. I also corrected the matrix to be a metric matrix by adding the maximum distance in the distance matrix, which was 0.598 between *Proganochelys* and *Apalone*. MDS on the corrected distance matrix yielded a minimal stress of 0.316 at 16 dimensions and a 3D MDS stress of 0.504. Because of the substantially lower stress, I will describe the 3D MDS only of the uncorrected distance matrix.

The taxic clustering revealed by the 3D MDS of the baraminic distance matrix reveals a number of clusters that do not correspond to the groups implied by the distance correlation results (Figure 16). *Proganochelys*, instead of clustering closely

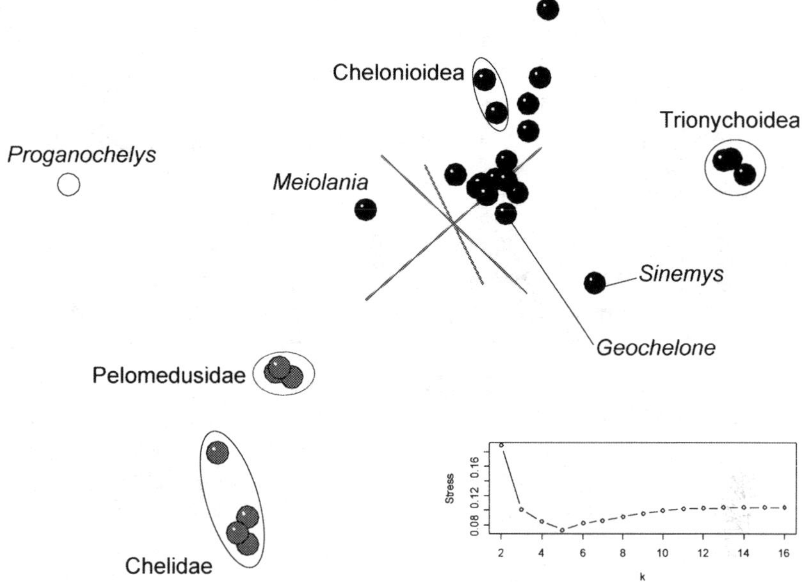


Figure 16. Three-dimensional classical MDS applied to uncorrected turtle baraminic distances calculated from the Shaffer *et al.* (1997) dataset. Also shown is the stress of *k*-dimensional MDS on the same baraminic distance matrix plotted as a function of the number of dimensions (*k*). Cryptodires (black circles), pleurodires (grey circles), and *Proganochelys* (white circle) are distinguished.

with the pleurodires, is visibly distant from them. The pleurodires, instead of clustering closely together, actually form two distinct clusters that correspond to the two pleurodire families, Chelidae and Pelomedusidae. The cryptodires form a diffuse taxic cluster, with *Sinemys*, *Meiolania*, and the Trionychoidea (Trionychidae + Carettochelyidae) as notable outliers.

The baraminic distance correlation results alone would suggest that the turtles form two holobaramins, but the 3D MDS seems to show between four and seven different clusters that could potentially be separated by discontinuity. To test this possibility, I calculated baraminic distance correlations for subsets of the taxa in the complete distance matrix. Correlation calculations on subsets of the full distance matrix can be justified because the geometry of taxic patterns can adversely influence baraminic distance correlation results (e.g. by revealing significant negative distance correlation without discontinuity, see Cavanaugh *et al.* 2003). Removal of taxa that dominate correlation calculations might reveal significant negative or positive correlation patterns undetectable in the full dataset.

The first subset I examined consisted of just *Proganochelys* and the pleurodires, and the correlation results revealed significant negative correlation between *Proganochelys* and Chelidae species and no significant correlation between *Proganochelys* and the Pelomedusidae species (Figure 17). I further reduced this set to include just the pleurodires, and I found significant negative correlation between the Chelidae and Pelomedusidae species (Figure 18). Baraminic distance correlations calculated for a subset of just the cryptodire species revealed negative correlation between the Trionychoidea species and the rest of the Cryptodires (Figure 19). A subset of non-trionychoid cryptodires showed very little significant negative correlation (Figure 20), but did show three groups of turtle species with no significant positive correlation between them. The three groups are *Sinemys*, the Chelonioidea, and the Testudinoidea + Chelydridae.

Frair's original proposal of a single turtle "polytypic kind" is not supported by the present results. Baraminic distance correlation

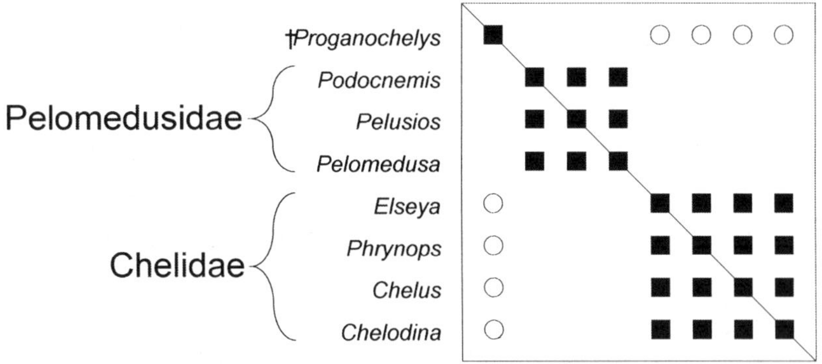


Figure 17. Baraminic distance correlation for the Shaffer *et al.* (1997) turtle dataset, using a relevance cutoff value of 0.9. Correlations are calculated for the pleurodires and *Proganochelys* only. Taxa with significant ($p<0.05$) positive correlation are indicated as filled squares. Taxa with significant ($p<0.05$) negative correlation are indicated as open circles. Fossil taxa (†) are also indicated.

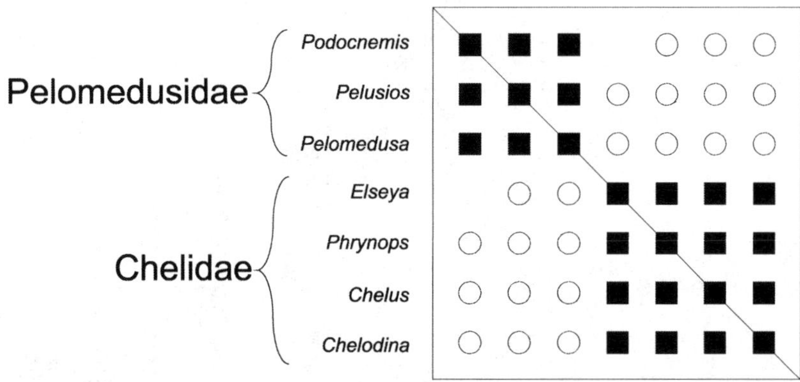


Figure 18. Baraminic distance correlation for the Shaffer *et al.* (1997) turtle dataset, using a relevance cutoff value of 0.9. Correlations are calculated for the pleurodires only. Taxa with significant ($p<0.05$) positive correlation are indicated as filled squares. Taxa with significant ($p<0.05$) negative correlation are indicated as open circles. Fossil taxa (†) are also indicated.

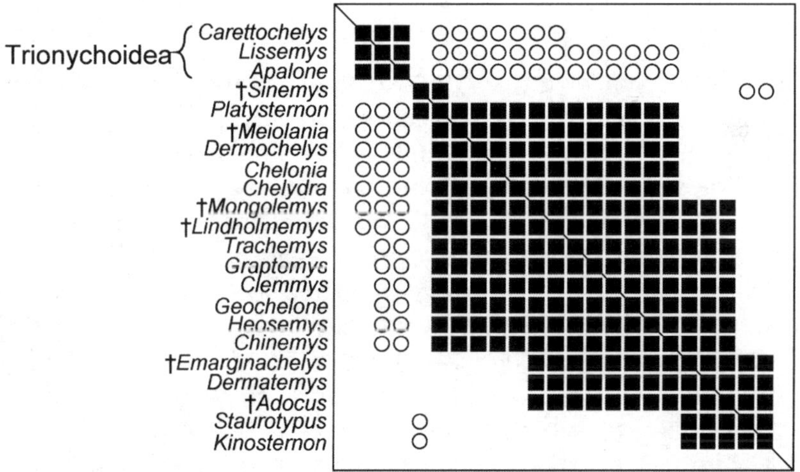


Figure 19. Baraminic distance correlation for the Shaffer *et al.* (1997) turtle dataset, using a relevance cutoff value of 0.9. Correlations are calculated for the cryptodires only. Taxa with significant ($p<0.05$) positive correlation are indicated as filled squares. Taxa with significant ($p<0.05$) negative correlation are indicated as open circles. Fossil taxa (†) are also indicated.

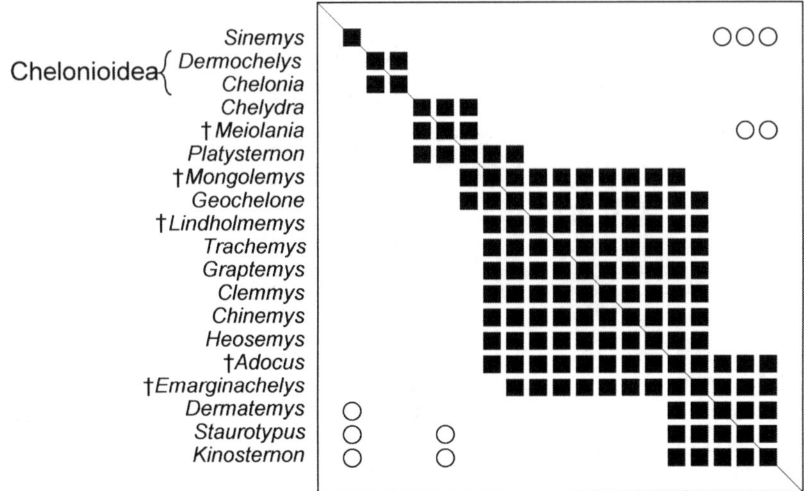


Figure 20. Baraminic distance correlation for the Shaffer *et al.* (1997) turtle dataset, using a relevance cutoff value of 0.9. Correlations are calculated for all cryptodires except Trionychoidea. Taxa with significant ($p<0.05$) positive correlation are indicated as filled squares. Taxa with significant ($p<0.05$) negative correlation are indicated as open circles. Fossil taxa (†) are also indicated.

of the full Shaffer *et al.* (1997) dataset implies the presence of a discontinuity between *Proganochelys* + pleurodires and the cryptodires. This discontinuity is confirmed in the 3D MDS pattern, which shows a gap between these two groups of turtles. Frair's hypothesis of four turtle holobaramins, corresponding to the Pleurodira, Chelonioidea, Trionychidae, and Testudinoidea + Chelidridae, fairs better when compared to the present analysis (Table 2). The noticeable gaps in the taxic pattern revealed by 3D MDS suggest further discontinuities in both the Pleurodira and Cryptodira, which are confirmed by baraminic distance correlation analysis of taxic subsets of the Shaffer *et al.* (1997) dataset.

The first holobaramin proposed by Frair was the side-neck turtles, or pleurodires. My results confirm a discontinuity between pleurodires and cryptodires, but I also find evidence of discontinuity within the pleurodires. The 3D MDS pattern reveals an obvious gap between the two families of pleurodires, Chelidae and Pelomedusidae. That this gap may be a discontinuity is

Table 2. Comparison of baraminological conclusions of this study and Frair (1984).

| Turtle Taxon | Baraminic Status from This Study | Frair's Hypothesis |
|---|---|---|
| Pleurodira | Apobaramin | Holobaramin |
| Chelidae | Holobaramin | |
| Pelomedusidae | Holobaramin | |
| Trionychoidea | Holobaramin | Holobaramin (without *Carettochelys*) |
| Other Cryptodira | Holobaramin? | Two holobaramins: Chelonioidea and others |
| *Proganochelys* | Holobaramin | |

implied by baraminic distance correlation of just the pleurodires, which reveals significant positive correlation within each family but significant negative correlation between the families. Thus, Frair's first holobaramin hypothesis is partially confirmed: the side-neck turtles are indeed an apobaramin, but further analysis suggests that the pleurodire apobaramin contains two holobaramins, the Chelidae and Pelomedusidae.

Frair's second holobaramin proposal was the sea turtles, superfamily Chelonioidea. The baraminic status of this group is not entirely clear. In all baraminic distance correlation analyses, I find significant, positive correlation between the green sea turtle (*Chelonia*) and the leatherback turtle (*Dermochelys*). Thus, I would conclude that the sea turtles are a monobaramin; however, my analysis here does not support discontinuity around the sea turtles. There is no obvious gap between sea turtles and other cryptodires in the 3D MDS pattern. Furthermore, in baraminic distance correlation calculations on a subset of just Cryptodira, I find significant positive correlation between the sea turtles and *Platysternon*, *Meiolania*, *Chelydra*, *Mongolemys*, *Lindholmemys*, *Trachemys*, *Graptemys*, *Clemmys*, *Geochelone*, *Heosemys*, and *Chinemys*. In a subset of cryptodires without the Trionychoidea, I do not find significant positive correlation between the sea turtles and any other turtles in the dataset, but I also do not find any significant negative correlation between sea turtles and other turtles. I conclude therefore that Frair was again partially right that the sea turtles form a monobaramin, but I find no evidence that they are also an apobaramin.

The softshell turtles were Frair's third proposal for a turtle holobaramin. In the Shaffer *et al.* (1997) dataset, the softshell turtles are represented by two genera, *Apalone* and *Lissemys*. As with the sea turtles, these two taxa exhibit significant positive baraminic distance correlation in the full Shaffer *et al.* (1997) dataset and in a subset that excludes the pleurodires and *Proganochelys*. In the same analyses, the softshells also correlate positively with the Fly River turtle, *Carettochelys*. The 3D MDS pattern confirms the close association between the softshells and *Carettochelys* and shows that all three of these taxa are distinct from other cryptodires. The baraminic distance correlation analysis of just the cryptodires reveals significant negative correlation between these three taxa and other cryptodires. I conclude again that Frair was partially right, there is evidence that the softshells are a holobaramin (continuous with each other but discontinuous with other turtles), but I would include *Carettochelys* in the same holobaramin. Interestingly, in a separate serological study, Frair (1985) found that *Carettochelys* is most similar to softshells.

The final holobaramin proposal of Frair was something of a wastebasket, consisting of all the rest of the turtles. The continuity of these taxa would be confirmed by the significant positive baraminic distance correlation observed in all subsets of the Shaffer *et al.* (1997) dataset and by the diffuse but closely-clustered taxic pattern revealed in the 3D MDS. Discontinuity between these turtles and pleurodires is evidenced by the significant negative baraminic distance correlation observed in the full dataset, and by the significant negative correlation between the Trionychoidea (softshells and *Carettochelys*) and the remaining cryptodires. I would again partially agree with Frair's assessment, in that I would conclude that the cryptodires including the sea turtles but not the softshells or *Carettochelys* form a turtle holobaramin.

In summary, based on my analysis of the Shaffer *et al.* (1997) dataset, I propose that the turtles are composed of five different holobaramins (Table 2): Pelomedusidae, Chelidae, Trionychoidea, cryptodires except for trionychids, and *Proganochelys*. The holobaraminic status of Proganochelys is evidenced by the significant negative baraminic distance correlation observed between *Proganochelys* and the chelid taxa in the pleurodire + *Proganochelys* subset of Shaffer *et al.*'s (1997) dataset and by the gap observed between *Proganochelys* and the cryptodires and pleurodires in the 3D MDS. Due to a lack of correlation within cryptodires when Trionychoidea are excluded, it is possible that *Sinemys* and the sea turtles could be additional holobaramins. Further research will be necessary to clarify these relationships.

**4.2.6. Biogeography.** My interpretation of turtle baraminology implies that the Galápagos Tortoises share a true genetic relationship with tortoises of the mainland. As noted above, mtDNA evidence suggests that the Chaco tortoise (*G. chilensis*) is the closest living relative of the extant Galápagos tortoise (Caccone *et al.* 1999). This relationship raises several important questions about the origin of the giant tortoises. First, how did the tortoises get to the islands? Many authors have commented on the hardiness of the modern Galápagos tortoise, proposing that the tortoises are pre-adapted to long-distance dispersal (e.g. see Thornton 1971, pp. 125-128; Caccone *et al.* 2002). If we accept species transmutation, however, it is possible that the ancestors of the modern giant tortoises were neither hardy nor even giant. Furthermore, modern tortoises do not seem to disperse even between islands or even between volcanic peaks on Isabela (Caccone *et al.* 2002, 2004).

The second important question derives directly from the first: Were the original tortoise colonizers of the Galápagos small or large? Genetically, the Galápagos tortoises resemble each other much more than they resemble their nearest mainland relative, the Chaco tortoise (Caccone *et al.* 1999, 2002). If we assume that the Galápagos tortoise lineage began diverging upon arrival in the islands, their high degree of genetic similarity might imply that the tortoise ancestor was already large when it arrived.

Of significance to these questions is the occurrence of other giant tortoises on isolated islands of the Indian Ocean (Arnold 1979), of which the surviving species is the Aldabran tortoise, *Geochelone gigantea* (Figure 21). Though classified in the same genus as the Galápagos Tortoise, they are in separate subgenera and are not considered to be closely related (Arnold 1979; Austin and Arnold 2001). Although the apparent correlation of large size with oceanic islands might suggest convergence in response to a common insular environment, Arnold (1979) and Hayes *et al.* (1988) rejected this hypothesis. Fossil forms of *Geochelone* that

Figure 21. Aldabran giant tortoise *Geochelone* (*Aldabrachelys*) *gigantea* in the Knoxville Zoo. Photo courtesy Stephanie Mace.

exhibit varying degrees of gigantism are known from continental localities, demonstrating that the origin of gigantism is not necessarily related to insular habitats (Auffenberg 1974). Instead, Arnold (1979) proposed that the large size of tortoises provided stability for rafting to remote islands. Studies of body size in island vertebrates reveal that insular gigantism is not limited to tortoises, suggesting that the cause is a general phenomenon that can act on other animals (Foster 1964; Case 1978).

**4.2.7. Shell Morphology**. What are we to make of the adaptationist interpretation of the difference in shell morphology between the saddleback (SB) and the domed tortoises? According to Fritts (1983), SB morphology is associated with islands of low elevation. His tabulation of "islands" (treating the volcanoes of Isabela as separate 'islands' of tortoise habitation) revealed that of the six islands below 800 m in maximum elevation, all are or were inhabited by SB tortoises. Similarly of the eight islands of maximum elevation >800 m, only two are occupied by SB tortoises. Although this difference is statistically significant (Fisher test $p = 0.007$), Fritts gives no justification for dividing the islands into two classes at 800 m elevation, other than the obvious association with SB tortoises. Division of the islands at a different elevational cutoff results in an insignificant correlation between SB tortoises and islands of low elevation. For example, if the islands were divided into those higher and lower than 950 m elevation, six of eight islands <950 m are occupied by SB and five of six >950 m are occupied by domed tortoises (Table 3). This division is not statistically significant (Fisher test $p$ = 0.13). Thus, the association between SB tortoises and islands of low elevation seems marginally significant at best. Fritts's (1983) more rigorous demonstration of a significant, positive correlation between maximum elevation and mean carapace length provides much stronger support for his contention that the smaller SB tortoises occur preferentially on islands of low elevation.

Fritts (1983) offered two hypotheses to account for the SB morphology by adaptation: the increase vertical reach afforded by the SB morphology provides (1) additional grazing resources or (2) advantages during aggressive encounters with other tortoises. Although both hypotheses are untested, the former is generally favored (e.g. McMullen 1999, p. 325). Tortoise grazing has often been linked to the evolution of arborescent forms of prickly pears

Table 3. Contingency tables comparing correlation of tortoise carapace shape to elevation of islands.[1]

| | Islands <800 m | Islands >800 m |
|---|---|---|
| SB tortoise populations | 6 | 2 |
| Domed tortoise populations | 0 | 7 |

Fisher exact probability test $p$ = 0.007

| | Islands <950 m | Islands >950 m |
|---|---|---|
| SB tortoise populations | 6 | 2 |
| Domed tortoise populations | 2 | 5 |

Fisher exact probability test $p$ = 0.132

[1]Data taken from Fritts (1983, table 2). Numbers do not add up to total number of islands because Volcan Wolf is occupied by SB and domed tortoises.

of genus *Opuntia* (Dawson 1966), but if this were the case, we would expect to find that the prickly pears grow just out of the tortoise's reach and no higher. Further, we would expect that the taller prickly pears would be found preferentially on islands of low elevation, where the SB morphology is more prevalent. Both of these expectations are falsified. Galápagos prickly pear species grow as tall as 12 m, and the islands of low elevation support the short and sprawling prickly pear species (Wiggins and Porter 1971). Thus, at an intuitive level, the SB tortoise's increased vertical reach does not seem to be adaptive to a food source that is increasing in vertical height. Fritts's alternative hypothesis of advantages in aggression with other tortoises has not been evaluated in detail.

Regardless of its adaptational advantage, where does the SB morphology come from in the first place? In considering this interesting question, I note that the SB and domed tortoises do not correspond to monophyletic mtDNA lineages in Caccone *et al.*'s (2002) analysis. Instead, domed and SB tortoises can be found mixed in closely-related groups. Based on conjectural considerations of the extinct San Cristóbal population, Caccone *et al.* (2002) concluded that the ancestral tortoise was domed. Considering, however, that three of the four most basal tortoises in their mtDNA phylogeny are SB, the opposite conclusion would seem better supported by their data, namely that the SB is the most primitive form in the Galápagos. Perhaps the increased reach afforded by the SB morphology provided a selective advantage during rafting, since SB tortoises could hold their heads higher above the waves. Any "adaptation" to environmental conditions in Galápagos would then be a secondary benefit. Such possibilities are speculative, however, especially considering that the three extant tortoises of South America are not SB. Further analysis of the phylogeny of the extant Galápagos tortoises and possibly extraction of DNA from preserved specimens from extinct populations should aid in the testing of selectional hypotheses. Further baraminological research also needs to be done on possible continuity or discontinuity within the cryptodires, to determine the actual ancestry of the Galápagos species.

### 4.3. Iguanid Lizards

**4.3.1. Introduction.** The Galápagos islands are home to 10 species of iguanid lizards: seven species of lava lizards (genus

*Tropidurus*), two species of land iguana (genus *Conolophus*), and the world's only species of marine iguana (*Amblyrhynchus cristatus*) (Plate 5) (Thornton 1971 pp. 88ff). The iguanas specifically are prominently featured in historical records related to the islands, probably due to their size and prominence. Fr. de Berlanga mentioned them in his account of the islands (Larson 2001, p. 22), and Darwin recounted experimenting on the marine iguanas by throwing them into the water to see if they would swim (they invariably scrambled straight back to shore) (Darwin 1839, p. 468; Stauffer 1975a, p. 496).

The taxonomy of iguanid lizards has been somewhat contentious. While most agree on the identity of eight different monophyletic lineages within the group, there has been disagreement on their relationship to each other and how the groups should be classified. According to Frost and Etheridge (1989), the eight lineages consist of the morunasaurs (3 genera, South America), the anoloids (11 genera, North and South America), the basiliscines (3 genera, Central America), the iguanines (8 genera, Central and South America, Fiji, Tonga, and Galápagos), the crotaphytines (2 genera, North America), the sceloporines (10 genera, North and Central America), the oplurines (2 genera, Madagascar and Comoro Islands), and the tropidurines (14 genera, South America, Caribbean, and Galápagos). These eight groups constitute the traditionally-recognized family Iguanidae. Within this family, Galápagos iguanas belong to the iguanine group, and the lava lizards belong to the tropidurine group.

Based on a cladistic analysis of 67 morphological characters from 37 taxa (31 traditional iguanids and 6 acrodonts), Frost and Etheridge (1989) elevated these eight lineages to family status, in part because they were unable to derive statistical support for a monophyletic "Iguanidae." Recent molecular work by Macey *et al.* (1997) supported the monophyly of Iguanidae, and they reduced Frost and Etheridge's families back down to subfamily rank. Further analysis of the tropidurine group (which contains the Galápagos lava lizards) suggested that it may be paraphyletic (Schulte *et al.* 1998). Despite morphological and molecular approaches, there still exists no accepted phylogeny relating the eight subfamilies of Iguanidae. In keeping with tradition, I will refer to the iguanids as family Iguanidae and to Frost and Etheridge's eight lineages as subfamilies.

**4.3.2. Baraminology Analyses.** In order to clarify the

baraminic position of the Galápagos iguanas and lava lizards, I analyzed two morphological datasets (skeletal and soft tissue characters) using the baraminic distance correlation method of Robinson and Cavanaugh (1998a; 1998b) and the MDS technique recommended by Wood (2004; see Appendix). The first dataset came from Frost and Etheridge's (1989) afore-mentioned study of iguanids and consists of 67 characters. To supplement this analysis and to focus specifically on the lava lizards, I also analyzed the dataset from Frost's (1992) study of the *Tropidurus* group, consisting of 77 characters and 27 taxa. For the Frost and Etheridge data, I used a relevance cut-off of 0.9 and retained 57 characters for the analysis. I used the recommended relevance cut-off of 0.95 for Frost's *Tropidurus* data, which resulted in 66 characters used in the analysis.

The results of the baraminic distance correlation analysis on the Frost and Etheridge data are shown in Figure 22. Frost and Etheridge (1989) originally derived 225 equally-parsimonious trees of 208 steps from their dataset. Their strict consensus, shown here in reference to the baraminic distance correlation results (Figure 22), was an unresolved polytomy consisting of nine separate lineages (the iguanid subfamilies and the acrodonts) originating from a single node. In the baraminic distance results, the outgroup acrodont taxa *Priscagama*, chameleons, *Agamas*, *Physignathus*, *Uromastyx*, and *Leiolepis* exhibit only negative correlation with the ingroup iguanids. This negative correlation is most common with the oplurines, tropidurines and anolines, but completely absent with subfamily Corytophaninae. Between other subfamilies, the occurrence of negative correlation is sporadic. For example, the chameleons are negatively correlated with all sceloporines but not with the oplurines. The anoles are negatively correlated with all acrodont outgroup taxa except the chameleons. "*Enyaloides*" is not significantly correlated with any of the acrodont outgroups.

Considering the traditional iguanid subfamilies in light of the baraminic distance correlation results, we find that each possible pair of taxa within a subfamily shows significant, positive correlation. Between the subfamilies, we see positive correlation between the oplurines (Oplurinae) and tropidurines (Tropidurinae), between the iguanines (Iguaninae), basiliscines (Corytophaninae), and crotaphytines (Crotaphytinae), and between morunasaurs (Hoplocercinae) and anoloids (Polychrinae). Individual taxa

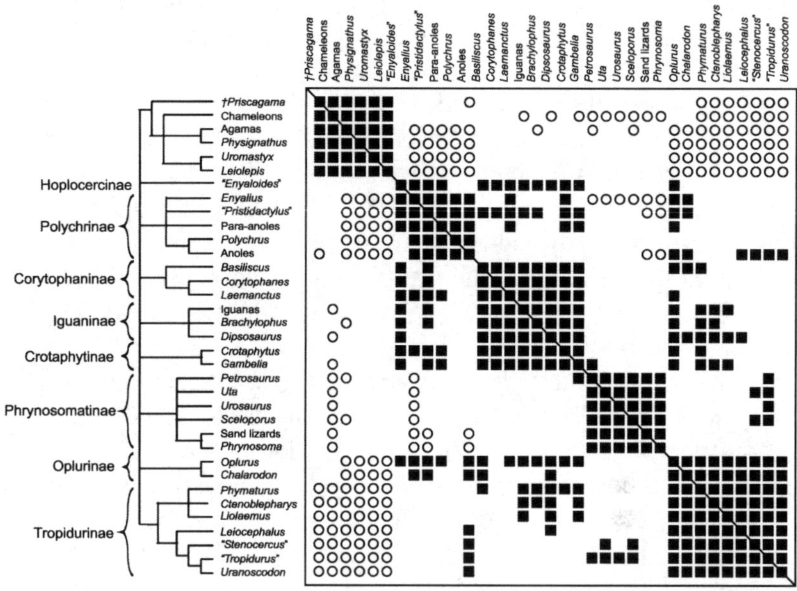


Figure 22. Baraminic distance correlation for the iguanid dataset of Frost and Etheridge (1989). Taxa with significant ($p<0.05$) positive correlation are indicated as filled squares. Taxa with significant ($p<0.05$) negative correlation are indicated as open circles. Taxa are ordered according to the strict consensus of 208 most parsimonious trees calculated by Frost and Etheridge (1989, Fig. 8), as shown on the left.

show positive correlation across multiple subfamilies. For example, *Crotaphytus* and *"Enyaloides"* correlate with members of each subfamily except Phrynosomatinae and Tropidurinae, and *Sceloporus* unites Phrynosomatinae with Tropidurinae. The only negative correlation seen within the family Iguanidae occurs between members of the subfamilies Phrynosomatinae (sceloporines) and Polychrinae (anoloids). Phrynosomatinae is not significantly correlated positively or negatively with most other iguanids; it shows significant negative correlation with anoles, *Enyalius*, and *"Pristidactylus"* and significant positive correlation mostly with *Tropidurus*. *Tropidurus* however is positively correlated with anoles, which therefore reveals a connection of positive correlation between the Phrynosomatinae and the Polychrinae.

Although it clusters with the outgroup taxa in at least one of Frost and Etheridge's (1989) trees, the paraphyletic "*Enyaloides*" (traditionally referred to Hoplocercinae) does not correlate positively with any outgroup taxa in the baraminic distance correlation analysis. Instead, it positively correlates with twelve of the 28 iguanid taxa, and it negatively correlates with no taxa. This result would imply that "*Enyaloides*" should be classified as an iguanid. Specifically, "*Enyaloides*" correlates positively with all members of the iguanines, crotaphytines, and basiliscines included in the study. This result is consistent with eight of Frost and Etheridge's (1989) 225 trees, which placed "*Enyaloides*" as the sister taxon to the iguanines.

The results of the classical MDS of the uncorrected baraminic distances are shown in Figure 23. Three-dimensional MDS of a baraminic distance matrix corrected by addition of the maximum distance (0.585 between anoles and *Uromastyx*) revealed a stress of 0.506, which is much higher than the 0.235 stress of the uncorrected distance matrix. The minimum stress for the uncorrected distance matrix is 0.080 at eight dimensions. The three dimensional geometry of the MDS of uncorrected distances reveals a clear and noticeable gap between the six acrodonts and the iguanids. The iguanids form a loose cluster, with "*Enyaloides*" very near the center of the cluster. The anoles, *Tropidurus*, and the phrynosomatines are furthest from the center of the cluster. The phrynosomatines in particular are separated by a noticeable gap from the main iguanid cluster.

The three-dimensional MDS geometry of the iguanid and acrodont taxa helps to explain some of the patterns of baraminic distance correlation. The gap between the six acrodonts and the iguanids presumably explains the presence of negative baraminic distance correlation between the outgroup taxa and the ingroup iguanids. The distance separating the anoles from the phrynosomatines would explain the observation of significant negative correlation between these taxa. The gap between the phrynosomatines and the remaining iguanids would explain the general lack of positive correlation between these taxa. Significant positive baraminic distance correlation is observed between the phrynosomatines and *Tropidurus*, which are adjacent in the three dimensional MDS results. In general, then, the MDS results confirm the observations made from the baraminic distance correlation results alone.

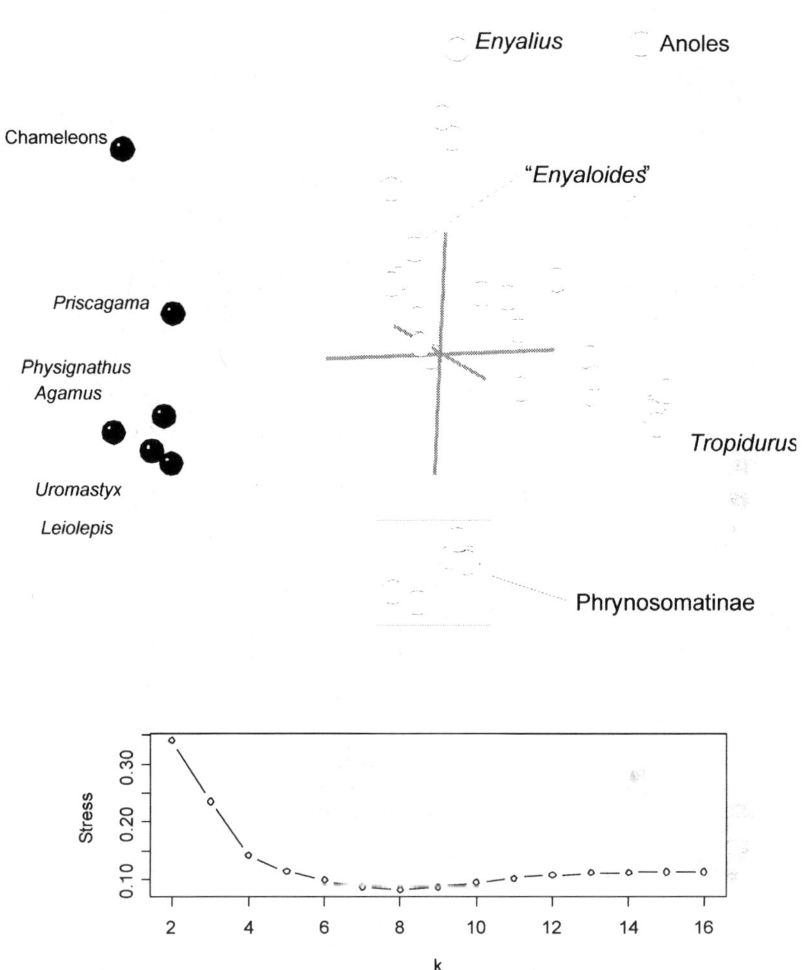


Figure 23. Three-dimensional classical MDS applied to uncorrected iguanid baraminic distances (top) and the stress of *k*-dimensional MDS on the same baraminic distance matrix plotted as a function of the number of dimensions (*k*). Iguanidae (white) and outgroup taxa (black) are distinguished.

Because the Galápagos is home to only ten iguanids, most of which are members of *Tropidurus*, I also analyzed a morphological dataset from Frost's (1992) analysis of the *Tropidurus* group. With a data matrix of 77 morphological characters and 27 taxa, Frost found 36 equally-parsimonious trees, which gave the consensus shown in Figure 24. Based on this tree, Frost recommended the reduction of genera in this group from six to four: *Uranoscodon*, *Plesiomicrolophus*, *Microlophus*, and *Tropidurus* (including *Tapinurus*, *Plica*, *Strobilurus*, and *Uracentron*) (see Figure 24). The Galápagos species were represented in his dataset by *T. bivittatus*, which is re-classified as *Microlophus* in Frost's proposal.

The results of the baraminic distance correlation analysis of Frost's *Tropidurus* dataset are shown in Figure 25. Instead of self-evident clusters of genera, two poorly-defined groups exhibit a high frequency of positive correlation among their respective members. The first group is composed of genera *Uranoscodon*, *Tapinurus*, and *Tropidurus*. The outgroup species *Uranoscodon*

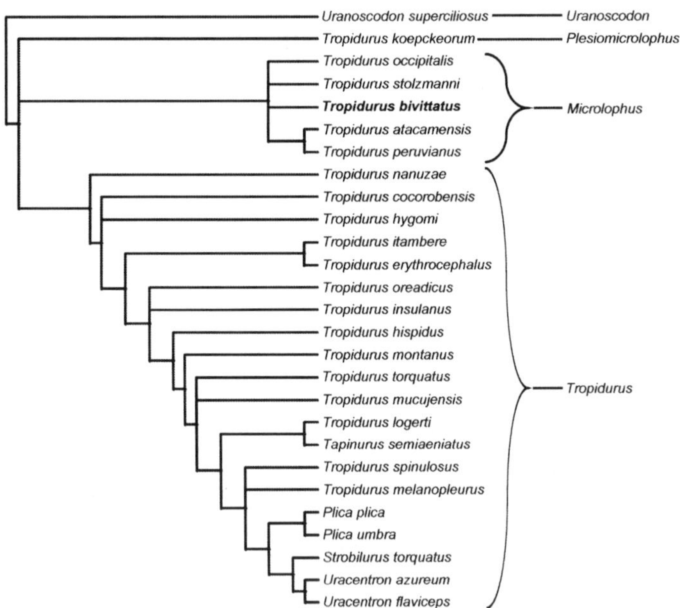


Figure 24. Strict consensus tree of 36 equally parsimonious trees of the *Tropidurus* lizard group, as calculated by Frost (1992, fig. 33). Frost's proposed genera are also indicated. The Galápagos native *Tropidurus bivitattus* is highlighted in bold font.

*superciliosus* correlates positively with members of *Tropidurus*, which correlate positively with most of the remaining species of *Tropidurus* and *Tapinurus semitaeniatus*. The second group consists of genera *Strobilurus*, *Plica*, and *Uracentron*. Exact delineation of these groups is impossible due to the overlapping positive correlation. For example, *Strobilurus torquatus* correlates positively with *Tropidurus* species *melanopleurus* and *spinulosus*. Significant negative correlation is common between *Uracentron* species and *Tropidurus* species, but since both *Uracentron* species correlate positively with *Strobilurus torquatus*, *Uracentron* and *Tropidurus* can be connected via positive correlation with *Strobilurus*.

The results of 3D classical MDS of uncorrected *Tropidurus* baraminic distances are shown in Figure 26. The stress at three dimensions is 0.104 for the uncorrected distance matrix and 0.461 for a distance matrix corrected by addition of the maximum distance. Again, I limit the following description to 3D MDS

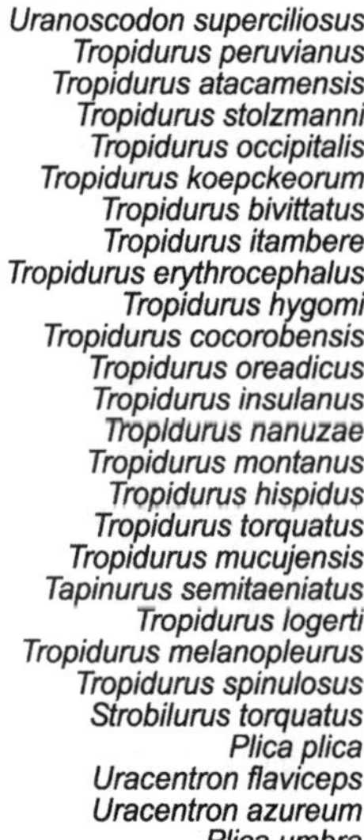


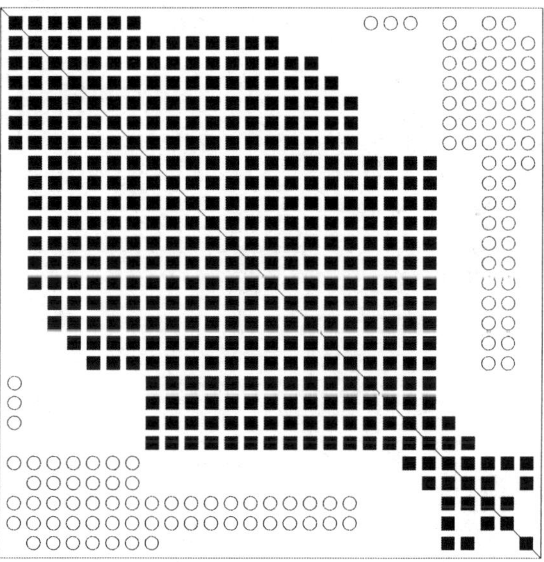

Figure 25. Baraminic distance correlation for the *Tropidurus* lizard group dataset of Frost (1992). Taxa with significant ($p<0.05$) positive correlation are indicated as filled squares. Taxa with significant ($p<0.05$) negative correlation are indicated as open circles.

of uncorrected baraminic distances, as in all previous cases. Minimal stress of 0.048 occurs at six dimensions. The 3D MDS pattern reveals a complex geometry of diffuse taxa. The genera *Uranoscodon, Uracentron, Plica,* and *Strobilurus* lie at a notable distances from the central *Tropidurus/Tapinurus* cluster, which is also quite diffuse.

**4.3.3. Interpretation and Discussion.** The results of the baraminic distance correlation and 3D MDS analyses show poor agreement with the conclusions of Frost and Etheridge (1989) regarding the relationships of the eight subfamilies. Based on their 225 equally-parsimonious trees, Frost and Etheridge (1989) summarized possible relationships in a set of twelve trees shown in their figure 7. Ten of these trees indicate a monophyletic relationship between the Oplurinae and Tropidurinae, which is very consistent with the pattern of baraminic distance correlation,

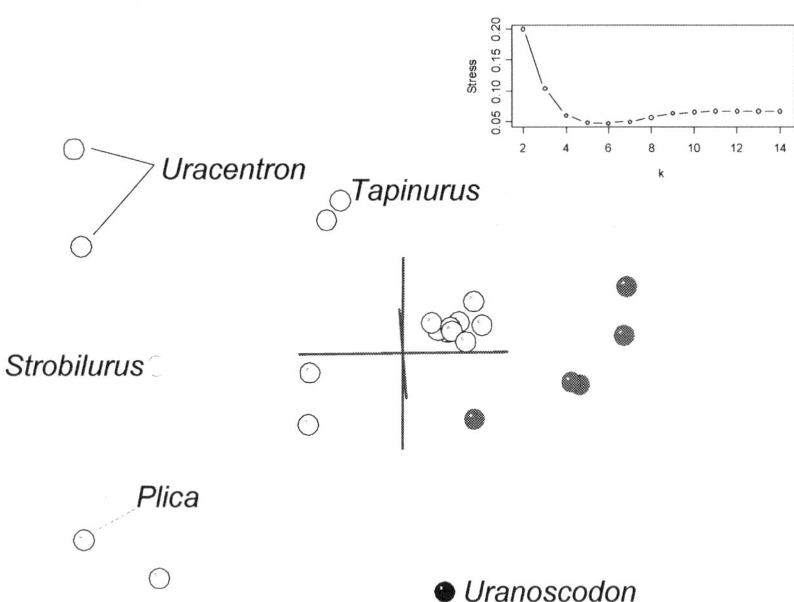


Figure 26. Three-dimensional classical MDS applied to uncorrected baraminic distances of the *Tropidurus* lizard group and the stress of *k*-dimensional classical scaling on the same baraminic distance matrix plotted as a function of the number of dimensions (*k*). Frost's (1992) proposed genera *Tropidurus* (white), *Microlophus* and *Plesiomicrolophus* (grey), and *Uranoscodon* (black) are indicated.

which reveals that all members of both subfamilies are positively correlated. None of their trees show a clade of Corytophaninae + Iguaninae + Crotaphytinae + Hoplocercinae, a grouping strongly supported by positive baraminic distance correlation. In all of Frost and Etheridge's (1989) twelve summary trees, these four subfamilies form a paraphyletic group.

As noted above, Robinson and Cavanaugh (1998a, 1998b) suggested that significant, positive baraminic distance correlation indicates continuity while significant, negative correlation indicates discontinuity. Based on my present baraminic distance results using the Frost and Etheridge (1989) data (Figure 22), I propose that the traditional family Iguanidae is a holobaramin. Significant, positive correlation within the Iguanidae connects all eight of the subfamilies, and the outgroup acrodonts show significant, negative correlation with members of five of the eight subfamilies. Thus, the iguanids exhibit continuity within the group and discontinuity with their most similar outgroup, fulfilling the definition of the holobaramin (Wood *et al.* 2003). The negative correlation between the Phrynosomatinae and Polychrinae should not be counted as evidence of discontinuity within the Iguanidae, since negative correlation within a monobaramin has been observed previously in the horses (Cavanaugh *et al.* 2003) and sunflowers (Cavanaugh and Wood 2002). In each of the previous cases, negative correlation within a baramin was caused by unusual geometric spacing of taxa in character space, which is consistent with the present spacing of the iguanid taxa. Further, continuity between the Phrynosomatinae and Tropidurinae and between the Polychrinae and Tropidurinae establishes a link of continuity between the Phrynosomatinae and Polychrinae.

When compared to Frost's (1992) conclusions and description of genera *Tropidurus* and *Microlophus*, the baraminic distance correlation (Figure 25) and MDS results (Figure 26) offer virtually no support. Frost's *Microlophus* and *Plesiomicrolophus* species form a curvilinear structure coming from the central *Tropidurus* cluster in the 3D MDS (Figure 26). Indeed, the recognition of a separate genus *Plesiomicrolophus* seems especially tenuous since this taxon has identical 3D MDS coordinates as the Galápagos lizard *T. bivittatus*. Frost's *Microlophus* and *Plesiomicrolophus* species also correlate positively with members of Frost's monophyletic *Tropidurus* and with the outgroup taxon *Uranoscodon*. These results imply that Frost's (1992) *Plesiomicrolophus* should be referred to *Microlophus*. The frequent negative correlation and infrequent positive correlation between *Tropidurus* species and *Uracentron, Plica*, and *Strobilurus* (Figure 25) would be inconsistent with Frost's (1992) referral of these three genera to *Tropidurus*. Indeed, the gap between these three genera and the *Tropidurus* species in the 3D MDS results would suggest that the genera should be retained. Frost's placement of *Tapinurus semitaeniatus* within *Tropidurus* is his only proposed taxonomic change that is consistent with my findings, which show that *Tapinurus* is positively correlated with fourteen other *Tropidurus* species.

Unlike the Frost and Etheridge (1989) dataset, the baraminic distance correlation results on Frost's (1992) dataset do not reveal a group clearly bounded by negative baraminic distance correlation. Instead, negative baraminic distance correlation occurs, but a connection of significant, positive can be drawn between all taxa in the dataset. These patterns are reminiscent of the baraminic distance correlation and 3D ANOPA patterns observed in fossil equids by Cavanaugh *et al.* (2003). In the case of the equids, Cavanaugh *et al.* (2003) concluded that all taxa belonged to the same baramin. In the absence of strong evidence for discontinuity and by analogy to the fossil equids, I would conclude here that all the taxa in Frost's (1992) dataset belong to a single monobaramin. This conclusion would be consistent with my proposal of a holobaramin Iguanidae. If Iguanidae is a holobaramin, I would expect to see a high degree of continuity among the members of the *Tropidurus* group, as a subset of the full holobaramin.

Based on these baraminic distance and classical MDS analyses, I conclude that the Galápagos iguanid species, including the seven lava lizards and the marine and land iguanas, belong to the same baramin and are descended from an ancestor that survived the Flood aboard the Ark. To account for the differences observed in the Galápagos iguanids, I now turn to specific discussions of both groups, the land and marine iguanas and the lava lizards.

**4.3.4. Iguanas.** There can be no doubt that the marine (*Amblyrhynchus cristatus*) and land iguanas (*Conolophus subcristatus*) belong to the same baramin, as evidenced by their successful hybridization on Plaza Sur off the east coast of Isla Santa Cruz (Rassmann *et al.* 1997). Since the discovery was limited to a single hybrid adult male, the fertility of the individual was not reported. Rassmann *et al.* (1997) conclude that hybridization probably does not contribute to the genetic variation of either species, implying that either the hybrids are sterile or that they simply do not occur with sufficient frequency to produce detectable introgression.

A close relationship between the marine and land iguanas is supported by morphological (Norell and de Queiroz 1991), immunological (Wyles and Sarich 1983), and mitochondrial DNA (Sites *et al.* 1996; Rassmann 1997) analyses. That this similarity indicates a sister-taxa relationship between *Amblyrhynchus* and *Conolophus* is generally agreed upon (Sites *et al.* 1996), but the statistical support for the relationship is weak (Rassmann 1997). Rassman (1997) concluded that the Iguaninae ancestor diverged rapidly, resulting in the inability to resolve relationships within the subfamily. Wyles and Sarich (1983) agreed with this assessment and suggested two possible interpretations: (1) Either the iguanas colonized the Galápagos in two separate events, or (2) their common ancestor colonized the Galápagos and subsequently diverged into the two genera and three species that presently inhabit the islands.

Separate colonization of the Galápagos by an *Amblyrhynchus* ancestor and a *Conolophus* ancestor is generally not favored by researchers acquainted with the evidence. Instead, a single colonization by the common ancestor of both genera is the preferred explanation. This raises the question of how such a great difference between the two genera could have arisen in the presumed short lifespan of the present islands. Both Wyles and Sarich (1983) and Rassman (1997) claimed that the divergence of the Galápagos iguanas pre-dates the existence of the present archipelago; however, the specific calibration of their clocks is invalid from a creationist perspective. Rassmann relies on the divergence of ungulates and reptiles, and Wyles and Sarich calibrate the immunological clock by analogy with divergence rates of other groups (mammals, etc.). Since reptiles and mammals did not share a common ancestor and different groups may evolve at different rates, neither calibration should be considered reliable. Regardless of calibration, however, the difference between the land and marine iguanas is at least as substantial as differences between other iguanine genera. Within the creation model, multiple colonizations of the Galápagos by iguana ancestors could be explained by post-Flood debris serving as rafts (Wise and Croxton 2003), and the great differences between the two genera could be accounted for by the rapidity of diversification (Wood 2002a).

The presence of a marine organism (*A. cristatus*) in an otherwise terrestrial baramin raises interesting questions regarding design and diversification. Since the marine iguana shares an ancestor (presumably terrestrial) with other land iguanas, its unique specializations to a marine way of life must have arisen in the course of intrabaraminic diversification. To some creationists, the claim that a marine and terrestrial vertebrate share a common ancestor might seem to strain credibility. In the case of whales at least, creationists have resisted the inclusion of terrestrial animals in a whale baramin (Woodmorappe 2002; Young 2003), but the differences between extant whales and their proposed terrestrial and semi-aquatic ancestors are much greater than between *Amblyrhynchus* and *Conolophus*.

The aquatic specializations commonly attributed to *Amblyrhynchus* are actually found in other iguanids (Dunson 1969; Dawson *et al.* 1977). The aerobic and anaerobic metabolic rates of *Amblyrhynchus* are similar to those of terrestrial iguanids. Of particular importance is the temperature-independence of anaerobic metabolism, in contrast to the temperature-dependence of aerobic metabolism. Thus, while *Amblyrhynchus* dives, a steady supply of energy can be derived from anaerobic respiration, despite the cool water. According to Dawson *et al.* (1977), the much celebrated diving habits of the marine iguana may have been exaggerated. While it is true that they feed preferentially on algae, they will graze on the algae growing on rocks exposed during low tide (Plate 6). Also, similar to Darwin's experience (1839, p. 468), Dawson *et al.* (1977) reported that marine iguanas forced into the water will immediately return to shore. Even the marine iguana's tolerance of anoxic conditions has been observed in terrestrial species.

Most surprising in our consideration of the marine lifestyle of *Amblyrhynchus* is the apparent origin of the iguana's salt glands. Salt glands excrete extremely saline fluids from a wide variety of reptiles and birds; the glands function in osmoregulation and ionic regulation. Despite their ubiquity, however, salt glands of different organisms are not homologous. For example, the marine iguana has special nasal salt glands, but the salt glands of sea turtles are modified lachrymal glands (Peaker and Linzell,

p. 232). Peaker and Linzell (1975, p. 264) proposed that salt glands evolved at least five different times: once each in birds, lizards, sea snakes, crocodiles, and turtles. Presumably extinct marine reptiles such as plesiosaurs and ichthyosaurs also had salt glands, requiring yet more convergent evolution of salt glands. In the case of the iguanids, salt glands are present not only in the marine iguana, but also in the Galápagos land iguana *Conolophus subcristatus* (Dunson 1969) and in seven other genera (Peaker and Linzell 1975, p. 259; Hazard *et al.* 1998). In a review of avian salt glands, O'Daniel (2002) proposed that only two theories could account for their origin: evolution or creation "by God as He spoke the feathered creatures into existence." The presence of convergent salt glands in marine birds, reptiles, and even in terrestrial reptiles (e.g. Lemire *et al.* 1980; Hazard 2001) would support O'Daniel's contention that evolution is an inadequate account of their origin. Further, the presence of salt glands in non-marine iguanas such as *Conolophus* would suggest a pre-adaptation to a marine existence in *Amblyrhynchus*.

**4.3.5. Lava Lizards.** The seven species of Galápagos lava lizards occupy different islands, with no two species on the same island (Wright 1983). Fernandina, Isabela, Santiago, Bartolomé, Daphne, Baltra, Santa Cruz and Santa Fé are occupied by a single species, *T. albemarlensis*, whereas Pinta, Marchena, San Cristóbal, Española, Floreana, and Pinzón are inhabited by separate species endemic to each island. Based on genetic and immunological differences, Wright (1983), Lopez *et al.* (1992), and Heise (1998) have all argued that *T. albemarlensis* should be divided into at least two different species, but Kizirian *et al.* (2004) argued that the *T. albemarlensis* populations are only weakly divergent and so should be recognized as a species complex rather than separate species. (Unlike Frost, I have chosen to retain the *Tropidurus* genus for the Galápagos species rather than using *Microlophus*, in keeping with my baraminic distance correlation results). In Heise's system, nine different species occupy ten major islands, with only one species (*T. albemarlensis*) occupying more than one major island.

The systematics of *Tropidurus* has been analyzed using allozyme (Wright 1983), immunological (Lopez *et al.* 1992), and mitochondrial DNA (Heise 1998; Kizirian *et al.* 2004) data. The allozyme and mtDNA data suggest that the islands were colonized at least twice, with one founding population giving rise to the San Cristóbal and Marchena species (*T. bivittatus* and *T. habelii* respectively) and a second population giving rise to all other species. Lopez *et al.* (1992) argued for at least three founder events based on their immunological analyses; however, they also admitted that their results showed an unusually high diversity in the *Tropidurus* species they tested. Heise (1998) commented that this high diversity could be the cause of the discrepancy between the immunological studies and his own mtDNA work.

Two primary colonizations of the archipelago must have been followed by intra-Galápagos colonizations of the remaining islands. Presumably, one colonization went from San Cristóbal to Marchena, bypassing Santa Cruz and Baltra. Several colonization events are required to account for the origin of the remaining Galápagos species. Regardless of the precise number, inter-island colonizations leave some data unexplained. For example, Wright (1983) interpreted the distinctiveness of allozymic signatures among the extant species as evidence against recent inter-island immigration. Instead, Wright hypothesized that the Galápagos were at one time a single island, which subsequently subsided into the existing islands, which is not supported by geological data (Cox 1983). The existence of separate species isolated on separate islands suggests that they arose not by natural selection but rather by genetic drift (Carpenter 1966). It is unclear how the inter-island transport occurred in the first place.

A second anomaly regarding the origin of the lava lizards is Heise's (1998) argument, based on a mtDNA clock, that the Galápagos species are older than the islands they presently inhabit. Heise calibrated his clock by the presumed separation of South American lava lizard lineages at 10.5 million radiometric years by the uplift of the central Andes Mountains, but he did not show that the cytochrome *b* mtDNA sequence he used behaved in a clock-like manner in lava lizards. For the creationist, then, these dates must be evaluated in a strictly qualitative fashion and cannot be referred to any absolute chronology. Despite strong evidence from Wright (1983) that the Galápagos species arose allopatrically on separate islands, Heise placed only one divergence, that between *T. albemarlensis* (from Isabela and Fernandina) and *T. pacificus* (from Pinta) at less than the presumed radiometric age of the archipelago. Heise dated the origin of four lava lizard lineages (*duncanensis*, *delanonis*, *grayi*, and *albemarlensis/pacificus*) earlier than the age of the islands. To explain these results, he proposes that the divergence into separate lineages may have taken place on islands that are presently subsided, but that would be difficult to reconcile with the biogeographical distribution of the present species. Heise's speciation model would require the separate colonization of each island in the archipelago by separate species, without any permanent intermingling. Allopatric speciation on separate islands seems a simpler hypothesis.

An explanation of these anomalies within the creation model might be found in Wise and Croxton's (2003) post-Flood rafting hypothesis, which proposes that rafting after the Flood was much easier than it is now because of the amount of debris from the Flood left floating in the water. Such a hypothesis would be consistent with the present distribution of Galápagos *Tropidurus* species, in that they colonized the archipelago on post-Flood debris but have not intermingled since that initial colonization period. Since the Galápagos lava lizards are not monophyletic, however, their colonization of the islands requires at least two separate events. While this could be accommodated in a post-Flood rafting scenario, it seems it would be at least as *ad hoc* as conventional rafting explanations. Post-Flood rafting also does not explain the discrepancy between the age of the islands and the age of the lava lizard species, but since Heise's (1998) clock needs more study, it would be premature to draw any firm conclusions.

Future creationist research in iguanids could focus on confirming or modifying the hypothesis of a single iguanid holobaramin. The family Iguanidae is quite diverse and (as noted above) has been referred as high as the rank of order. Such diversity might imply the presence of a discontinuity, even though the present dataset supports the conclusion of only continuity within the family. Future research could focus on interspecific hybridization or the application of Wood and Murray's (2003, p. 95) modified discontinuity matrix.

## 4.4. Weevils

**4.4.1. Introduction.** After introducing the concept of natural selection in chapter four of *Origin*, Darwin proceeded in chapter five to discuss "Laws of Variation" and how they could relate to natural selection. In this context, Darwin commented on Wollaston's study of the beetles of Madeira. According to Darwin, the fact that "beetles in many parts of the world are very frequently blown to sea and perish" provided a selective advantage to wingless beetles on islands (Darwin 1859, p. 135). He noted that more than 75% of endemic beetle genera found on Madeira are "so far deficient in wings that they cannot fly" (Darwin 1859, p. 135). Furthermore, particular beetle groups that depend heavily on flight are either absent or poorly represented on Madeira. From these observations, he concluded that natural selection favored beetles deficient in flying ability on windy, island environments.

Although this appears to be an excellent example of natural selection and was even endorsed as such by Wieland (1997), Darwin himself suspected that his interpretation may have been an oversimplification. In *Natural Selection*, Darwin recognized that insect species in many parts of the world are polymorphic in flying ability, suggesting that the source of flightlessness is more complex than his selectionist interpretation (Stauffer 1975a, p. 293). Post-Darwinian ecologists have confirmed his doubts. In a review of flightlessness in carabid beetles, Darlington (1943) concluded that Darwin's explanation was too simple. Instead, he noted a correlation between altitude and flightlessness in some insects, and he proposed that the stability of the species' environment is important in maintaining flightless forms. Insect species that live in unstable, temporary environments use flight to relocate as local environments disappear (Darlington 1943).

Roff (1990) reviewed Darlington's environmental-stability hypothesis and found a correlation between altitude and flightlessness and between latitude and flightlessness. Despite the appeal of Darwin's original hypothesis of wind-blown insects being selected against in an island environment, Roff rejected the idea. As Roff points out, the number of insects being blown into the ocean would depend not on the area of the island but on the ratio of the area to the perimeter. On a large island like Madeira, it is unlikely that any insects except those nearest the shore would be blown into the ocean at such a rate as to have an appreciable selective impact on the winged state of the species. Roff's statistical analysis supports his hypothetical analysis; the fraction of flightless insect species is not significantly greater on islands than on the mainland.

Most genera of Galápagos beetles (Coleoptera) were described by Van Dyke (1953) as having a reduction in wing size, superficially supporting Darwin's original hypothesis. Van Dyke's list of Galápagos beetles included 199 species in 103 genera and

37 families. More recent species counts by Linsley and Usinger (1966) and Linsley (1977) put the number at 40 families, 123 genera, and 222 species. One of the larger families on the islands is Curculionidae, the weevils. In particular, the weevil genus *Galapaganus* (tribe Entimini) (Lanteri 1992) provides an interesting test case for insect dispersal and dispersal polymorphisms. The genus consists of fifteen described species, ten of which are endemic to the Galápagos. The remaining five species are not found in the islands but in mainland Peru and Ecuador.

Among the Galápagos beetle genera, *Galapaganus* is known principally for Sequeira *et al.*'s (2000) proposal that the species found in the Galápagos pre-date the formation of the islands and appear to have colonized more than once. Based on the cladistic analysis of Lanteri (1992), at least three colonizations are necessary to account for the species in the Galápagos. Since multiple colonizations have been observed in other closely-related animal groups in the Galápagos (Wyles and Sarich 1983; Lopez *et al.* 1992), it might be unremarkable to find it in a genus of insects, except that these insects are flightless. Obviously, as Lanteri stated (1992), "the possibility of active dispersal to the islands [*i.e.* by flying] has to be discarded." The colonizations of the Galápagos by the *Galapaganus* ancestors must have been passive, by rafting or by attachment to other animals.

To evaluate the biogeography of *Galapaganus* within the creation model, the weevil species must first be placed in the context of their baramin. I obtained a published dataset consisting of 115 morphological characters scored for 82 curculionid species and 21 outgroup taxa representing eight additional beetle families (Marvaldi *et al.* 2002). The curculionid species represent 27 different subfamilies. The dataset is comprised of 37 larval and 78 adult characters. I subjected this dataset to baraminic distance analyses using the distance correlation test (Robinson and Cavanaugh 1998a) and MDS (Wood 2004; see Appendix). With the results of these analyses, I will attempt to interpret the baraminology of the weevils and place dispersal polymorphism into a creationist perspective.

**4.4.2. Results.** At a relevance cutoff of 0.95, nine characters were omitted from the dataset, leaving 106 for calculation of baraminic distances. The results of the baraminic distance correlation analysis (Figure 27) reveal two very distinct groups. The first group contains all curculionid taxa plus the brentid species *Antliarhinus zamiae*, *Apion* sp., and *Ithycerus noveboracensis*. The second group consists of fifteen outgroup taxa of families Nemonychidae, Anthribidae, Belidae, Attelabidae, Megalopodidae, and Cerambycidae. Each group is defined by significant positive correlation between each possible species pair. Taxa from different groups exhibit mostly significant negative baraminic distance correlation.

Two species, *Caenominurus topali* (Caridae) and *Aporhina australis* (Brentidae), are positively correlated with members of both groups. *Caenominurus* is positively correlated with all outgroup taxa (Brentidae species of the first group and all members of the second group) but no members of the Curculionidae. *Aporhina* correlates positively with all curculionid taxa and nine outgroup taxa of the families Brentidae, Caridae, and Attelabidae. *Caenominurus* correlates negatively with 29 curculionid taxa, and *Aporhina* correlates negatively with eight outgroup taxa of families Anthribidae, Nemonychidae, Megalopodidae, and Cerambycidae.

I performed classical MDS on the baraminic distances as described previously (Wood 2004; see Appendix). Stress for the uncorrected baraminic distance matrix at three-dimensional MDS was 0.084. The baraminic distances were then corrected by addition of the maximum baraminic distance (0.621) to render the matrix metric, resulting in a 3D MDS stress of 0.537. As in previous studies of baraminic distance MDS, I utilized the uncorrected distances (as calculated by BDIST) for the MDS descriptions of the curculionid baraminic distances in this report. The minimal stress for the uncorrected dataset was 0.045 at six dimensions. The low stress for the three-dimensional MDS and the low dimensionality of the minimal stress implies that the 3D MDS pattern is a reasonable representation of the taxic clustering.

The taxic pattern revealed in the 3D MDS reveals a tight cluster of core curculionid taxa with at least three outlying groups from the same family. The remaining eight beetle families form a curvilinear structure with one end (representing the family Brentidae) close to the central curculionid cluster (Plate 7). The three outlying curculionid groups are subfamilies Dryophthorinae, Erirhininae + Ocladiinae, and Scolytinae + Platypodinae. *Ocladius* is the closest curculionid taxon to a non-curculionid, the brentid *Ithycerus*.

**4.4.3. Discussion.** The baraminic distance correlation

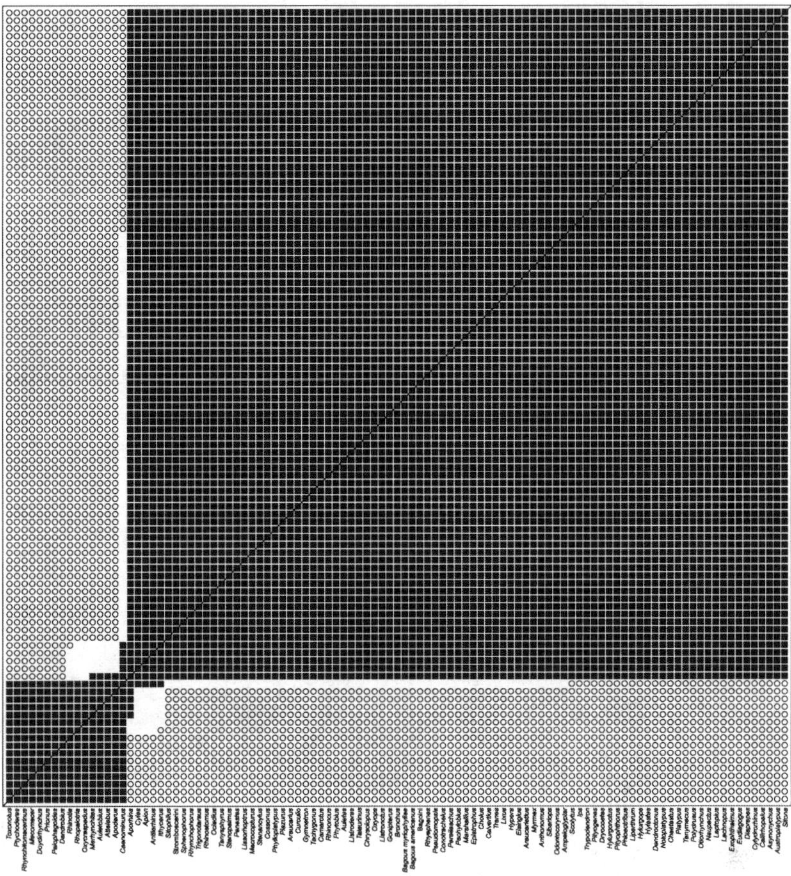

Figure 27. Baraminic distance correlation for the weevil dataset of Marvaldi *et al.* (2002). Taxa with significant ($p<0.05$) positive correlation are indicated as filled squares. Taxa with significant ($p<0.05$) negative correlation are indicated as open circles.

and MDS results agree very well with the phylogenetic analyses of Marvaldi *et al.* (2002). Marvaldi *et al.* performed parsimony analysis on the morphological data, bayesian and parsimony analysis on 18S rDNA sequences from the same taxa, and parsimony analysis on a combined morphological + molecular dataset. The 3800 bayesian rDNA trees leave most relationships unresolved within the Curculionidae, but they do tend to support the inclusion of Brentidae and Caridae within the curculionids. Similarly, an earlier analysis of mitochondrial 16S rDNA by the parsimony method showed that the curculionids were polyphyletic; although a neighbor-joining analysis of the same data showed a monophyletic Curculionidae (Wink *et al.* 1997). These findings are consistent with my baraminic distance correlation analysis that shows the brentids correlated positively with the curculionids and *Caenominurus* (Caridae) correlated positively with members of the curculionids.

Marvaldi *et al.*'s (2002) parsimony analysis of the rDNA dataset produced 29 most parsimonious trees, the consensus of which again supported a paraphyletic Curculionidae. As in the bayesian analysis, the carid *Caenominurus* and the brentids form a monophyletic clade with all the curculionids except *Ocladius*. Again, this pattern agrees with the general findings of my baraminic distance analyses, which place *Ocladius*, *Caenominurus*, and the Brentidae at the interface between the curculionids and non-curculionids. In contrast to my findings, however, the consensus rDNA parsimony tree shows *Ocladius* forming a monophyletic clade with the Anthribidae, which is not supported by my findings. Nevertheless, considering the differences between the clustering techniques employed (baraminological vs. phylogenetic) and between the datasets used (morphological vs. molecular), the degree of congruence between the results is striking.

Marvaldi *et al.*'s (2002) parsimony analysis of the morphological dataset used in this study produced only four most parsimonious trees. Based on the strict consensus tree, the tree of the major taxa in the dataset branch in the following order: ((Megalopodidae, Cerambycidae), ((Nemonychidae, Anthribidae), (Belidae, (Attelabidae, (Caridae, (Brentidae, (Ocladiinae, (Erirhininae, (Dryophthorinae, (other curculionids, (Scolytinae + Platypodinae )))))))))). As can be seen in the 3D MDS results (Plate 7), the order of branching in the consensus tree is almost exactly congruent with the ordering of taxa in the three-dimensional taxic pattern.

The only differences are the ordering of the Chrysomeloidea (families Megalopodidae and Cerambycidae) and Nemonychidae, the separation between Nemonychidae and Anthribidae seen in the 3D MDS, and the position of the Dryophthorinae. In the consensus parsimony tree, the Dryophthorinae are basal to all curculionids except the Erirhininae and Ocladiinae; whereas in the 3D MDS they are at least as distant from the non-curculionids as the Scolytinae + Platypodinae.

As for the baraminic classification of these taxa, the baraminic distance correlation and 3D MDS do not seem to indicate any discontinuity among any of the beetles in this dataset. The baraminic distance correlation analysis reveals a pattern of positive correlation that connects all taxa in the dataset, and the pattern of negative correlation does not warrant the conclusion of discontinuity (as noted in previous analyses in this monograph). In the 3D MDS results, it is tempting to classify the taxic pattern as a biological trajectory in the sense of Wood and Cavanaugh (2003); however, the absence of a clear chronological trend in the taxa prevents that conclusion. Assuming that too many outgroup taxa might be interfering with the detection of discontinuity around the Curculionidae, I performed a dataset reduction as I did with the turtles (see Section 4.2.5). I recalculated baraminic distance correlation for just the Curculionidae and Brentidae, but the results (not shown) revealed significant, positive correlation between curculionid and brentid species. In addition to these traditional baraminological considerations, the striking congruence between the baraminic distance results and the parsimony analyses of the morphological dataset and of an independent molecular dataset strongly argue for a continuity between all taxa in the present sample.

If I were to conclude that the beetle families analyzed herein form a single monobaramin representing nearly 60,000 species by Marvaldi *et al.*'s (2002) count, it would be the largest monobaramin by 600% described to date. Furthermore, if the absence of discontinuity within this group implies that the holobaramin to which the weevils belong encompasses the entire order Coleoptera, or some large subset thereof, this would be an astonishing number of species within a terrestrial animal holobaramin. Wood and Murray (2003, pp. 71-72) suggested that the family rank is a reasonable approximation of the holobaramin. Even though this approximation was based on a very small sampling of vertebrate and plant baramins, it is still a good guide to baraminology. What then should we conclude about the weevil baramin? One possibility is that the focus of the present study is too large by far. Supporting this idea is the high degree of similarity exhibited by the weevil taxa. All curculionid taxa have the same character state for 52 of the 115 characters in the Marvaldi *et al.* (2002) dataset. This results in an average baraminic distance for curculionids of 0.098 and a maximum of 0.236. Thus, Marvaldi *et al.* (2002) have chosen their characters to emphasize similarities and differences between Curculionidae and its closest evolutionary relatives. It is possible that a morphological dataset emphasizing differences and similarities within the Curculionidae might reveal an unambiguous discontinuity. Consequently, I withhold judgment on the baraminic status of the weevils, except to proceed with the assumption that the curculionid tribes are probably monobaraminic.

Lanteri's (1992) description of genus *Galapaganus* included ten Galápagos species and five native to mainland Ecuador and Peru, now classified in the subfamily Entiminae and tribe Entimini. The closest relative to *Galapaganus* in the dataset would be *Naupactus peregrinus*, subtribe Naupactina. I will assume that the *Galapaganus* weevils belong to the same monobaramin as other mainland Curculionidae, and probably share a true common ancestor with mainland species. Based on her morphological analysis, Lanteri (1992) recognized two groups of *Galapaganus* species. The first group, the *femoratus* group, contains only two species found on the mainland. The *darwini* group consists of the remaining 13 species found both in the Galápagos and on the mainland. The groups are distinguished by characters of antennae, hind legs, and male genitalia.

How then did *Galapaganus* species come to the Galápagos? Lanteri (1992) concluded from her cladistic analysis that the present Galápagos Islands were colonized by a minimum of two *Galapaganus* ancestors, placing the origin of the genus itself on the mainland. The mitochondrial DNA phylogeny produced by Sequeira *et al.* (2000) suggested that the divergence of the *femoratus* and *darwini* group occurred 7 million radiometric years ago, which antedates the radiometric date for the origin of the extant islands. Sequeira *et al.* calibrated their clock by reference to a general survey of arthropod mtDNA, rendering their clock estimates somewhat suspect. Nevertheless, Lanteri's (1992) and

Sequeira et al.'s (2000) phylogenies are congruent, and Lanteri's phylogeny reveals that the Galápagos species are polyphyletic with mainland species, implying that at least some lineages originated prior to colonization of the islands. Considering these results together, I would conclude that the species presently found in Galápagos did not originate there. I propose that the diversification of the genus probably occurred on the mainland.

Lanteri's (1992) cladogram suggested that either the Galápagos were colonized once by the *Galapaganus* ancestor with at least two recolonizations of the mainland or that (as Lanteri concluded) the islands were colonized only once by the *darwini* group with a single recolonization of the mainland. Sequeira *et al.* (2000) did not include mainland species in their mitochondrial DNA phylogeny, so the results of the morphological analysis cannot be confirmed. Nevertheless, because the prevailing South Equatorial Current runs from the mainland to the islands, it is difficult to imagine any recolonization of the mainland by rafting. Consequently, I conclude that the most likely locale for the origin of the Galápagos *Galapaganus* species is the mainland, with separate rafting events accounting for the colonization of the Galápagos. This conclusion is mitigated by the possibility of secondary dispersal by sea birds, which could potentially explain recolonization of the mainland.

**4.4.4. Diversification and Biological Change.** Properly understood, mediated design is a hypothesis to explain the emergence of a complex phenotype during intrabaraminic diversification (Wood 2003a). Wood (2003a) proposed that mediated design could be detected in a baraminic population that exhibited discrete variation between forms that possessed and forms that lacked a particularly complex phenotype, especially if the phenotype is homoplastic. The first proposed example of mediated design was the occurrence of $C_4$ photosynthesis in the composite subtribe Flaveriinae (Wood and Cavanaugh 2001), and the scarcity of $C_4$ plants in that monobaramin (Wood and Cavanaugh 2001; Cavanaugh and Wood 2002) supports the conclusion of mediated design. An alternative proposal is that some variation is degenerative from a previously perfect state (Wieland 1991; Wood 2001, 2002c). One can imagine the difficulty of distinguishing mediated design from degeneration in cases where many members of a baramin vary in the presence or absence of a complex trait.

Consider for example a hypothetical baramin that contains 100 species, only 5 of which possess a highly-complex phenotype. Because the remaining 95 species lack the phenotype, the simplest interpretation would be that the ancestors of the baramin lacked the phenotype. In contrast, if 50 of the 100 species in our hypothetical baramin possessed a complex phenotype, and these fifty species were not closely-allied, what would the most likely condition of the ancestor be? An ancestral population that lacked or possessed the phenotype would be equally probable. If the ancestral population lacked the phenotype, we would attribute the origin of the phenotype to mediated design. If the ancestral population possessed the phenotype, we would attribute absence of the phenotype to degenerative changes. Insect dispersal polymorphisms illustrate this problem of distinguishing degeneration from mediated design.

As noted in the introduction to this section, flying insects can vary in their wing development, often within the same species (e.g. Jackson 1928). If we place these species in their probable baramins, it becomes obvious that the ability to fly has either appeared or disappeared numerous times during the diversification of insect baramins. If the ability to fly were the result of mediated design, we would expect the majority of species within an insect baramin to be flightless, but such is probably not the case. If, however, flightlessness arises from genetic degeneration, we might expect the majority of species to be flighted and the flightless species to be incapable of producing individuals with the ability to fly. As we shall see, neither of these options adequately describes insect dispersal polymorphism, leaving the unanswered question: From where do flight polymorphisms arise?

In surveying flight polymorphisms, Zera and Denno (1997) observed that the determination of wing morphology can be entirely genetic (as in the weevil *Sitona hispidula*), environmental (as with planthoppers, aphids, and crickets), or both. Environmentally-determined phenotypes are not properly attributed to natural selection, since they are not heritable. Within the Curculionidae, Jackson's (1928) comprehensive study is one of the few that reveal a genetic cause of winglessness. She discovered that the presence of macropterous wings in *Sitona hispidula* was a Mendelian recessive trait. Because of the occurrence of macropterous individuals with substantially reduced wing muscles in the metathorax, she suspected that the flight muscles were also under control of a separate Mendelian recessive trait (at least one mating of a brachypterous individual and a macropterous individual with reduced wing muscles produced an individual with normal wing muscles). Thus, in *Sitona hispidula*, the ability to fly is controlled by at least two genes and varies within a single species.

*Sitona* might seem to be a clear example of degeneration by "loss of genetic information," but to generalize this conclusion to all curculionids, and in particular to *Galapaganus*, would be premature, since winglessness can have advantages over the ability to fly, and should therefore not be considered a degenerated condition. In discussing dispersal polymorphisms, researchers generally agree that the ability to fly is maintained in species that inhabit unstable environments where the potential for local extinction is high (Harrison 1980). The energetic tradeoff between using energy to fly and to reproduce in turn maintains the flightless forms (Zera and Denno 1997). Thus, flightless forms actually have an advantage over flying forms in certain circumstances. Why then, in the unpredictable environment of the Galápagos do *Galapaganus* species not exhibit flight polymorphisms?

One answer would be simply that the ancestors of *Galapaganus* were permanently flightless and thus were their progeny. There may be other reasons, as yet unexplored, for the favoring of the flightless weevils in the arid environment of Galápagos. As Jackson (1928) noted in her dissections, in *Sitona* forms with reduced wing muscles, the space in the metathorax otherwise occupied by flight muscles was filled with fat. Extra fat could be an advantage during periods of poor food supply. Furthermore, Lanteri and Normark (1995) noted that parthenogenesis in Entimini is correlated with winglessness; e.g., only two parthenogenetic curculionids are not wingless. Although *Galapaganus* is not known to be parthenogenetic (Lanteri 1992; Lanteri and Normark 1995), its general advantage for colonizing islands would seem to be obvious.

In the case of the *Galapaganus* weevils, the origin of flightlessness by degenerative changes to the genome would seem to be well-supported. Nevertheless, lack of definitive evidence precludes firmly accepting winglessness as a degeneration, especially since winglessness and parthenogenesis are correlated in related species. The complexity required to reproduce by parthenogenesis should not be attributed to degeneration, and since winglessness seems to be a condition preliminary to the development of parthenogenesis, perhaps winglessness in curculionids is not necessarily a degeneration either. Further research into the baraminology and diversification of the curculionids should elucidate the mechanisms behind the dispersal polymorphisms. A new morphological dataset should be created for the analysis of diversity within the family Curculionidae using baraminic distance methods. This new dataset will help creationists to understand the continuity and discontinuity of the weevils, and will therefore assist in understanding the diversification of the weevil baramin(s).

### 4.5. Darwin's Finches (Geospizini)

**4.5.1. Introduction.** Darwin's finches comprise 13-15 different species, classified variously as family Geospizidae (Swarth 1929, 1931), subfamily Geospizinae (Bowman 1961), and most recently as tribe Geospizini (Sato *et al.* 2001). Approximately thirteen species are endemic to the Galápagos archipelago, with one species (*Pinarolloxias inornatus*) found on Cocos Island 450 miles to the northeast. Tribe Geospizini is currently classified in the subfamily Emberizinae and family Fringillidae (Sibley and Monroe 1990). Drably colored birds, the Galápagos species have been studied extensively as a classic case of natural selection and adaptive radiation (e.g. P.R. Grant 1999). The famous "beak of the finch" can be small and narrow or large and blunt, often reflecting the bird's preferred diet. Work by Peter and Rosemary Grant over the past two decades has shown that the average beak depth of Ground Finch populations on Isla Daphne Major increases or decreases in response to environmental changes (and thus probably diet), particularly to severe climatic events (P.R. Grant and B.R. Grant 1987).

Lack (1947, pp. 14) recognized four groups, which he classified as genera: the ground finches (*Geospiza*), the tree finches (*Camarhynchus*), the warbler finch (*Certhidea*) and the Cocos finch (*Pinarolloxias*). Bowman (1961) questioned Lack's common names and recognized two additional genera, *Platyspiza* and *Cactospiza*, both originally classified in Lack's tree finch group. Modern DNA sequence analyses (Freeland and Boag 1999a, 1999b) supported the recognition of Lack's original four groups plus an additional monospecific genus, *Platyspiza crassirostris*. I will return to the results of these and additional molecular studies below.

The diet of the ground finches (*Geospiza*) and *Platyspiza* is primarily vegetation with a varying percentage of insect prey, and the tree finches (*Cactospiza* and *Camarhynchus*) feed mostly on insects with some plant material. The warbler finch (*Certhidea olivacea*) eats insects exclusively (Bowman 1961). On Isla Wolf, the sharp-beaked ground finch (*Geospiza difficilis*) exhibits a remarkable behavioral variation by parasitizing boobies. *G. difficilis* individuals peck at the wings and tails of Nazca and red-footed boobies on Isla Wolf and drink their blood. They are also known to steal and consume booby eggs by a cooperative egg-rolling behavior involving several individual finches (Köster and Köster 1983). The woodpecker finches, *Cactospiza pallida*, exhibit a different behavioral modification in that they use bits of wood as tools to pry dead wood apart and to obtain insects otherwise unreachable by the bill alone (Merlen and Davis-Merlen 2000).

**4.5.2. Previous Creationist Response.** Considering the Marshian interpretation of speciation as variation within a created kind, it should come as no surprise that creationists rarely discuss the finches of the Galápagos in publications. As Morris and Morris (1996, p. 238) claimed, most creationists explain Darwin's finches with essentially an evolutionary scenario: Modern species of finches derive from a single ancestor by "variation" (like most creationists, they will not call it evolution). Classifying Darwin's finches in the same baramin (or equivalent systematic category) is extremely common among creationists (e.g. Lammerts 1966; Coffin 1983b, p. 398; Wieland 1992; Cumming 1997).

Creationist Walter Lammerts (1966), though a rose breeder by training, gained access to the finch collection of the California Academy of Sciences and made measurements on several hundred specimens. Lammerts was much impressed with the seemingly uninterrupted intergradation from one species to another (see Figure 28). Like many creationists who would follow, he suggested that the finches might more realistically be classified as subspecies of a single species. He relegated the differences in the subspecies (or "races" as he also called them) to "chance arrangement of their original variability potential" (Lammerts 1966). Lammerts (1966) commented, "If species are to be erected on such minute norms, then indeed we will be burdened with an almost infinite number of names." Other creationists writing on the finches have also argued that the finches are too similar to constitute separate species (Coleman 1986; Wieland 1992, 1995; Cumming 1997). Despite this near universal skepticism regarding the number of species, no creationists have proposed an alternative classification. Most merely recommend recognizing the currently-accepted species as subspecies or races.

Although creationists accept the common ancestry of Darwin's finches, they differ significantly on their interpretation of the origin of the modern species. Lammerts (1982), Coleman (1986), and Helder (1996) questioned the role of natural selection in producing the differences between the finch species. Lammerts (1982) argued that environmental fluctuations known to produce morphological changes in finch populations do not endure long enough to produce a directional change to a different species. Instead of selection, these authors emphasized the influence of genetic drift or proposed no alternative mechanism for the origin of the modern finch diversity.

In contrast to the selection critics, Wieland (1992, 1995) accepted the role of natural selection in the origin of the finches,

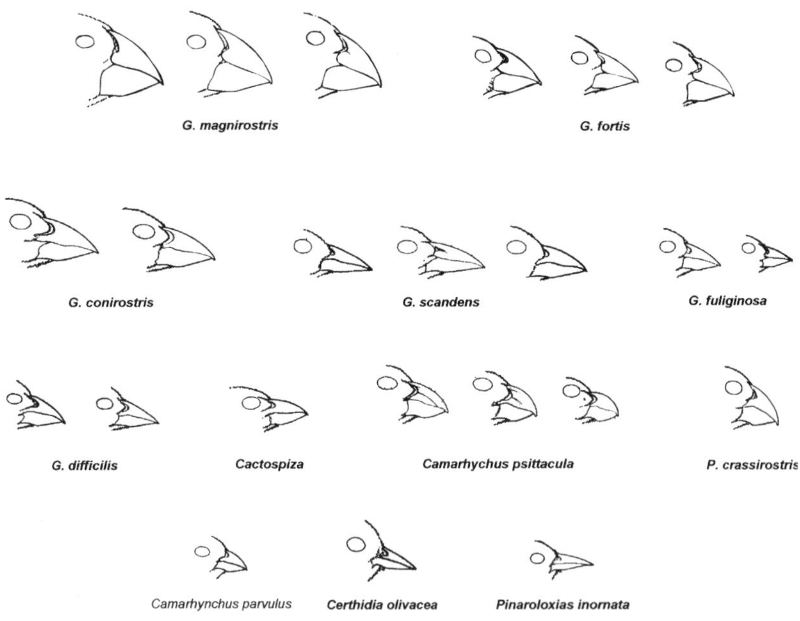


Figure 28. A selection of finch diagrams adapted from Swarth (1931).

possibly because it is consistent with his belief that speciation is the sorting of previously-existing allelic potential (Wieland 1991), called elsewhere heterozygous fractionation (Wood 2002a). In Wieland's view, species originate from previously-large gene pools, but the change is always a degenerative one: genetic information is necessarily lost during the fragmentation of the gene pool required to produce new species. Not surprisingly, Ruse has sharply criticized this view of degeneration from perfection, arguing that the correspondence between finch beaks and diet could hardly be called a "degeneration" (Ruse 1982). Popular works speculated that recombination (Batten *et al.* 2000) or mutation (Ham 1984) might play a role in the origin of the modern finches. As with genetic drift, none of these hypotheses have been tested.

**4.5.3. Noncreationist Critiques.** The adaptive radiation of Darwin's finches has occasionally come under criticism by noncreationists. Harper (1980) argued that all the species of Darwin's finches could have come to the Galápagos (and Cocos) via an irruptive migration from Central America, in much the same form that we find them today. In his initial presentation, Harper showed that if finches are assumed to have irrupted from mainland Central America, then the number of species per island correlates well with the "target width," the size of the island as seen by a bird flying from the mainland (Harper 1980).

Harper's proposal was subsequently criticized by Galbraith *et al.* (1984), who at times mischaracterized Harper's original work. For example, Galbraith *et al.* (1984) claimed that Harper used credibility as a criterion for accepting his theory, when Harper used *comprehensibility* to argue for utilization of his theory as a classroom exercise in critical thinking (Harper 1980). This misunderstanding is especially ironic since the Galbraith *et al.* (1984) paper summarized arguments devised in an undergraduate classroom using Harper's original paper as an exercise in critical thinking. Despite the shortcomings of their article, however, Galbraith *et al.* (1984) correctly noted that the relationship between island size and species density is a feature common to many organisms that could not possibly irrupt (e.g. plants, see Connor and Simberloff 1978). Harper's response provided a more detailed mathematical justification of his hypothesis, but did not address the basic question of the biogeographical relationship between species density and island size, other than to claim that the finches "are an anomaly" (Harper 1985).

As we shall see below, Harper's concept of irruption, while possibly helpful for understanding the migration of the finch ancestor(s) to the Galápagos, neither anticipated nor explained important new data on the classification of the finches. Harper's (1980) original article, initially published in the *Journal of Biological Education*, was reprinted in a 1981 issue of *Creation Research Society Quarterly* and cited once by Reiss (1986) in the British journal *Biblical Creation*. Few other creationists have referenced his work, possibly because it seems to reject the common ancestry of the finches, an acceptable concept to many creationists writing on the subject. Furthermore, it does not explain how the species that irrupted to the Galápagos and Cocos just happened to be the most similar to one another and left no close relatives on the mainland.

In *Icons of Evolution*, Wells (2000) devoted a chapter to Darwin's finches. Wells's comments are strongly reminiscent of creationist thought on the subject. Like Cumming (1997), Wells noted that hybridization between species of Darwin's finches might suggest that the species boundaries have been drawn too narrowly. Wells cited Peter Grant's (1993) discussion of finch hybrids and suggested that perhaps only six species of Darwin's finches exist rather than fourteen. His critique of Grant's natural selection research echoes that of Lammerts (1982) and Helder (1996). While Wells acknowledged the impact of drought on finch bill depths, he questioned the importance of this observation because bills returned to their pre-drought depths in subsequent wetter years.

**4.5.4. Baraminological Considerations.** Creationist speculation about the species status of Darwin's finches can be significantly clarified and tested utilizing baraminological methods. It is impossible to evaluate claims of adaptive radiation in the finches (e.g. Lack 1947, chap. 16; Bowman 1961) if their ancestry in a creationist model is ambiguous or merely accepted on an intuitive basis, as seems to be the case with most creationist writers (e.g. Morris and Morris 1996). Furthermore, baraminological analysis may further elucidate species classification in the finches, potentially clarifying the persistent suggestion that Darwin's finches are not true species. Finally, if Darwin's finches constitute a monophyletic monobaramin, the disagreement between creationists who accept natural selection (e.g. Wieland 1992) and those who question it (e.g. Helder 1996) could be resolved by reference not only to ongoing studies of finches but also to creationist theories of post-Flood diversification (e.g. Wood 2003b).

Unlike the tortoises and iguanids, I have been unable to locate a published morphological dataset suitable for baraminic distance and MDS analyses. Consequently, the finches will be the first of two bird groups (including the Galápagos hawks) that I will discuss in context of other proposed baraminology techniques, including hybridization (e.g. Scherer 1993b). Despite this limitation, the finches provide excellent evidence of continuity among themselves. The evidence from morphology that so impressed Lammerts (1966) has already been presented, but the more recent, and somewhat more surprising, evidence from molecular studies will constitute the bulk of the following discussion.

By the criterion of hybridization, all ground finches (*Geospiza*) represent a single monobaramin because all possible hybrid combinations are known (P.R. Grant and B.R. Grant 1992; P.R. Grant 1993). This monobaramin includes six of the thirteen finch species native to the Galápagos. Although hybridization among the tree finches has also been suggested (e.g. Lack 1947, p. 98), I could find no definitive reports of such hybrids. Furthermore, intergeneric finch hybrids have also not been reported. Thus, hybridization evidences continuity only within a single genus (*Geospiza*) of Darwin's finches.

In the absence of direct evidence of hybridization, we may also turn to indirect evidence, for example of introgression, to argue for continuity of species. The possibility of introgression brings us to molecular analyses intended to distinguish species of Darwin's finches. In all sequence analyses (Freeland and Boag 1999a, 1999b; Petren *et al.* 1999; Sato *et al.* 1999; Sato *et al.* 2001; Burns *et al.* 2002), Darwin's finches always form a monophyletic clade; however, identification of monophyletic species lineages is not as consistent. The difficulty of distinguishing species of Darwin's finches is also seen in early studies of finch allozymes (Ford *et al.* 1971; Polans 1983).

Allozyme electrophoresis studies initially revealed an extreme homogeneity among the finches (Ford *et al.* 1971; Polans 1983). In a sample of 257 individuals constituting 12 species of finches, Polans (1983) found that 241 from all 12 species shared the same alpha-glycerophosphate dehydrogenase banding pattern and 253 from all 12 species shared the same esterase banding pattern. Interspecific Nei distances calculated from the banding patterns of ground finch species range from 0.001 to 0.028 and average 0.013. Interspecific Nei distances among the tree finch species were more diverse, ranging from 0 to 0.129 and averaging 0.051. Between the tree and ground finch species, the Nei distances ranged from 0.008 to 0.127 and average 0.038.

Polans's (1983) allozyme work was later confirmed by Freeland and Boag's (1999a; 1999b) mitochondrial and nuclear DNA analyses. Using 16S rRNA and control region sequences, Freeland and Boag (1999b) found that among the tree finches and warbler finch, only *Platyspiza crassirostris* was monophyletic in their sample. The warbler finch *Certhidea olivacea* exhibited two divergent lineages, corresponding to subspecies *olivacea* from Santa Cruz, and subspecies *fusca* + *mentalis* + *cinerascens* from Marchena, Española, and Genovesa. Taken together, however, the two lineages were paraphyletic. The divergence in *Certhidea* lineages was confirmed in Petren *et al.*'s (1999) microsatellite analysis. In Freeland and Boag's (1999b) analysis, the tree finches were monophyletic with respect to *Certhidea*, but within the group, only one species (*P. crassirostris*) was monophyletic. Of the sequences from two *Camarhynchus psittacula* individuals, one was identical to a *C. parvulus* sequence and the other clustered with *Cactospiza pallida* (Freeland and Boag 1999b).

Freeland and Boag's (1999a) results from their DNA analysis of the ground finches revealed still more diversity. Of 55 *Geospiza* control regions sequenced, they found 20 haplotypes that did not correspond to recognized species or geographical regions. For example, haplotype 1 occured in specimens referred to *G. conirostris* and *G. difficilis* from Genovesa, *G. fortis* from Daphne and Santa Cruz, *G. fuliginosa* from Santa Cruz, and *G. magnirostris* from Marchena, Santa Cruz, and Genovesa. In the maximum-likelihood phylogeny, none of the previously-recognized species formed monophyletic clades, and no clades corresponded strictly to birds of particular islands. Freeland and Boag (1999a) also found little concordance between mitochondrial haplotypes and nuclear alleles of the internal transcribed spacer (ITS) of rRNA. These results are consistent with Grant *et al.*'s (2000) failure to find microsatellite support for a monophyletic *Geospiza difficilis*.

**4.5.5. Continuity with Non-geospizines.** Based on gross similarity to other finches, it seems reasonable to conclude that Darwin's finches belong to a larger holobaramin. DNA analyses consistently place the geospizines as a sister group of or nested within the tanager tribe Thraupini (Sato *et al.* 2001; Burns *et al.* 2002). Sato *et al.* (2001) identified the dull-colored grassquit (*Tiaris obscura*) as the closest relative of Darwin's finches, but Burns *et al.*'s (2002) more extensive study revealed a monophyletic clade consisting of Darwin's finches and species of *Tiaris, Coereba, Euneornis, Loxigilla, Melopyrrha, Loxipasser,* and *Melanospiza*. All of these species nest in domed nests rather than the more common cup-shaped nests, hence the Latin name Tholospiza (Burns *et al.* 2002).

Based on the large number of hybrids known from fringillid subfamily Carduelinae (Fehrer 1993), we might predict that hybrids would be at least equally common among the Emberizinae if a comprehensive survey of reproductive compatibility was conducted. Aside from the *Geospiza* hybrids from Galápagos, reports of hybrids involving members of the Emberizinae are rare. Gray (1958) listed eight intergeneric hybrids involving twelve emberizine genera. No reported crosses involve an emberizine and any species of Darwin's finches.

**4.5.6. Discussion.** As I noted above, suggestions that the Darwin's finches are not true species persist among creationists (Lammerts 1966; Coleman 1986; Cumming 1997). As Lammerts (1966) noted firsthand, the finch specimens can be arranged to form an almost perfect gradation from large- to small-billed forms. His observation is in keeping with others who have also examined finch specimens, including Darwin himself (1845, pp. 379-380). Voicing his dissent, Bowman (1961, p. 262) claimed, "there is no 'perfect' gradation between genera and between species of the Geospizinae if *shape* of the bill and other cranial features are considered carefully." Still, he was unwilling to classify certain individual specimens because of their resemblance to more than one species (Bowman 1961, p. 263). I interpret Bowman's comments in terms of a (mostly) continuous frequency distribution, with certain shapes occurring at greater frequencies. These high-frequency shapes correspond to true species, but individuals with low-frequency bill shapes do in fact occur between them. These low-frequency bill shapes give the impression of a continuous gradation, but recognition of the frequency of particular bill shapes supports the classification of the finches into different species.

Morphological similarity has been used as a criterion for

identifying members of a common baramin in the past (Wood *et al.* 2003). Marsh (1947, pp. 172-173) himself implicitly used morphology to infer baraminic relationship. Considering the unanimity of those who have examined Darwin's finch specimens (Swarth 1931; Bowman 1961; Lammerts 1966; P.R. Grant 1999), I conclude that the finches do indeed represent a diverse but also a morphologically continuous group of birds. That certain shapes and forms occur with higher frequency than others does not detract from the morphological similarity of the population as a whole.

If I had only the morphological similarity data, I would hesitate to assign members of the Galápagos finches to a single monobaramin; however, when considered in concert with the molecular results, the case for a geospizine monobaramin appears particularly strong. Given the morphological identification of species, of which Bowman (1961) was so certain, I find it especially surprising that Freeland and Boag (1999a, 1999b) were unable to identify monophyletic mitochondrial lineages among the finches they examined. Freeland and Boag attributed the polyphyletic finch "species" to either introgression or incomplete lineage sorting. Incomplete lineage sorting occurs when organisms are examined while in the process of speciation, at which point genetic lineages have not yet resolved into monophyletic lineages that match the species divergence. The more recent the species ancestor, the more likely that a molecular phylogeny will be unable to resolve the species lineages. Incomplete lineage sorting would be supported by the unusual level of microsatellite polymorphisms in the finches (Petren 1998).

I would argue that introgression must also contribute, possibly significantly, to the sequence homogeneity of Darwin's finches. The oscillating stress induced by El Niño is well-known, and its impact on Darwin's finches has already been mentioned. B.R. Grant and P.R. Grant (1996a) found that the survival and breeding of interspecific hybrids increased after the 1982-1983 El Niño. Thus, while introgression after a single El Niño would be very small, over the course of as little as one century, introgression at specific geographic localities could be quite high. Indeed, P.R. Grant and B.R. Grant (1997a) suggested that *G. fuliginosa* has failed to establish a larger population on Daphne Major because of hybridization with *G. fortis* and unidirectional introgression into the *fortis* population. If introgression was the sole cause of the poor correlation between morphological species and mitochondrial DNA haplotypes, I would expect instead to see a strong geographical clustering of the DNA haplotypes. Since that is not the case with the present sampling (Freeland and Boag 1999a, 1999b), both introgression and incomplete lineage sorting contribute to the independence of mitochondrial haplotypes and morphological species.

In the context of baraminology, both introgression and incomplete lineage sorting would be evidence of true continuity as defined by Wood *et al.* (2003). Introgression results from the production of fertile $F_1$ hybrids, which Wood *et al.* (2003) accept as evidence of continuity. Incomplete lineage sorting could only occur if the species truly shared a common ancestor, which would imply a genetic continuity among the offspring. In the case of the Darwin's finches, evidence of continuity from incomplete lineage sorting is reinforced by the morphological gradation between the species. Given these evidences, I see no credible objection to including all of Darwin's finches in a single monobaramin, even though intergeneric hybrids have not been reported.

What then is the relationship of the geospizine monobaramin to other finches of Emberizinae or Fringillidae? The evidence here is less clear. An hypothesis of continuity among at least twelve genera of emberizine species (excluding Geospizini) could be inferred from the intergeneric hybrids mentioned above, although the twelve genera involved are a poor sample of the subfamilial diversity. More interesting in this regard are inter-subfamilial and interfamilial hybrids listed by Gray (1958). Such hybrids, if accurately reported, might imply that the holobaramin is at the level of the order Passeriformes. Fehrer (1993) rejected the reports of interfamilial and inter-subfamilial hybridization and places subfamilies Carduelinae and Fringillinae in separate basic types. Since, however, basic types are not identified by considering evidence of discontinuity, it is possible that Fehrer's basic types (monobaramins) belong to a larger holobaramin.

Presently, the connection of Geospizini to any larger holobaramin could only be hypothesized based on the molecular affinity between Darwin's finches and *Tiaris* (Sato *et al.* 2001) and the Tholospiza (Burns *et al.* 2002) and on claims of morphological similarity (e.g. Swarth 1931). As Wood (2002b) argued, molecular evidence can distort baraminological inferences, and morphological similarity should be quantified in order to test baraminic hypotheses. Consequently, although my intuition suggests that the geospizines belong to a larger holobaramin, lack of evidence prevents my definitive judgment on such a hypothesis.

**4.5.7. Diversification of the Finches.** Regardless of whether or not the Geospizini monobaramin belongs to a larger holobaramin, we may still hypothesize on the nature and origin of the extant species of Darwin's finches. Before considering the origin of bill diversity in Darwin's finches, we must first ascertain the identity of the actual species of Darwin's finches. Specifically, what of the creationist contention that these species are too similar to be true species? That high frequencies of individual birds cluster in specific morphological types is observational data (e.g. Swarth 1931; Bowman 1961). Because these morphological types exhibit different feeding habits (Bowman 1961), mating calls (Bowman 1983; Podos 2001), bill morphology (Bowman 1961; P.R. Grant 1999), and a propensity to choose a mate from within their own group (Lack 1947; P.R. Grant 1999), there should be little doubt that these morphological types are true species by the biological species concept. Nevertheless, the failure of biochemical analysis (Ford *et al.* 1971; Polans 1983) and of mitochondrial and nuclear DNA analysis to confirm the genetic identity of these species (Freeland and Boag 1999a, 1999b) raises legitimate doubts about the validity of these species.

If Freeland and Boag (1999a, 1999b) were correct in proposing both incomplete lineage sorting and introgression in Darwin's finches, should we consider the finch species as true species? At the very least, Freeland and Boag's results support recognition of genetically-distinct genera, but the species question has not yet been answered satisfactorily. The fact that the intrageneric morphological types appear and even behave as true biological species is certainly curious in the light of a lack of genetic differentiation or high rate of introgression. Leaving aside the question of species identity in this group, I will instead address the (deceptively) simpler question of the origin and maintenance of the diversity of bill shape and size.

The high degree of similarity among the finch species and the high variability of bill size proved mysterious for nearly a century after Darwin's initial visit. In *Origin*, Darwin discussed the mockingbirds rather than the finches. The three mockingbird species are isolated on different islands, providing an obvious explanation within Darwin's evolution theory. The slightly differing environments of the two islands provided opportunity for allopatric speciation. In contrast, multiple finch species coexist on most of the larger islands, implying a more complex model of sympatric speciation or allopatric speciation followed by secondary contact by immigration.

The final report on the extensive California Academy of Sciences collection of 5000 finch specimens, written by Harry Swarth (1931), provided no clear evolutionary explanation of the origin and persistence of the morphological diversity of the finch species. Since the species occupied the same environment, he disallowed natural selection as an option. The only other option was random variation. The modern theory of finch adaptive radiation was originally devised by David Lack (1947). He proposed that the differences between the finch species arose and were maintained because the species differed by diet. Lack (1947) rejected the role of selection in explaining variation within species, preferring instead interspecific competition. In a preface written for a 1960 reprint of his finch book, Lack (1947, p. iii) claimed that intraspecific variations were not viewed as adaptive in the 1940s but during the 1950s came to be explained nearly exclusively by natural selection. Bowman (1961), following that trend, endorsed selectional explanations for the bill variation he observed within and between species.

The ongoing field work of Peter and Rosemary Grant (e.g. P.R. Grant 1999), particularly on Isla Daphne Major off the north coast of Santa Cruz (Plate 1), has certainly done more to reveal evolutionary trends in Darwin's finches than anything else. For 30 years, they have banded and tracked nearly all *Geospiza fortis* and *G. scandens* individuals on Daphne Major, measuring bill dimensions and reproductive characteristics (P.R. Grant and B.R. Grant 2002a). They have repeatedly observed directional selection in response to El Niño (Boag and Grant 1981; B.R. Grant 1985; Gibbs and Grant 1987; B.R. Grant and P.R. Grant 1989, 1993). Other studies reveal evidence that is consistent with past competition and character displacement (B.R. Grant and P.R. Grant 1982; P.R. Grant 1983; Schluter *et al.* 1985; Abbott *et al.* 1977) and natural selection (B.R. Grant and P.R. Grant 1983). Rather than review the entirety of their work, I will describe just two examples of competition and selection studies as representatives of their research.

When two bird species that exploit similar resources for food or nesting are sympatric, competition may occur but is very difficult to observe. Rather than directly observing competition, researchers instead look for potential results of competition, including competitive exclusion (absence in a locality of a species that is otherwise expected to be present) and character displacement (evolution of different morphologies to exploit slightly different resources to avoid competition). Schluter *et al.* (1985) found evidence of character displacement in populations of *G. fortis* and *G. fuliginosa*. On Santa Cruz and other islands where the two species are sympatric, their bills are divergent, reflecting the use of different seeds for food. On Daphne Major, where *G. fuliginosa* is almost absent, and Los Hermanos, where *G. fortis* is absent, the bill dimensions of the resident *fortis* and *fuliginosa* populations approach the intermediate condition of the sympatric populations. Schluter *et al.* (1985) interpreted the differences in bill dimensions on islands with sympatric populations as character displacement, resulting from competition for similar food sources.

Natural selection in the finches is clearly seen in an example from Isla Genovesa (B.R. Grant and P.R. Grant 1989). During the 1982-1983 El Niño, the *Opuntia* population in the study site on Isla Genovesa crashed and did not begin to recover until 1986. During the years 1984-1986, *Opuntia* flowers and fruits were largely unavailable as food for the resident finches, *G. conirostris* and *G. magnirostris*. Each of these species responded differently to this selectional pressure. Bills of *conirostris* became significantly shorter and bills of *magnirostris* became significantly deeper. Because *conirostris* feeds directly on *Opuntia* flowers and fruits using a long bill, long bills were selected against during the absence of *Opuntia* plants. In contrast, *magnirostris* uses its deep bill to crush the hard seeds of *Opuntia* and the harder seeds of *Cordia*. When the *Opuntia* plants disappeared, the only food left for *magnirostris* were the very hard seeds of *Cordia*, selectively eliminating finches with smaller bills incapable of cracking *Cordia* seeds.

Critics of the Grants' work on natural selection point out that El Niño is an oscillating phenomenon, producing alternating periods of abundant rain and extreme drought (Lammerts 1982; Helder 1996). Although a single environmental stress might produce a directional selection for particular bill traits, the result of an oscillating environment should be an oscillating selection, without a net change in any particular direction (Wells 2000, p. 169). While this is intuitively correct, it is not born out by the long-term research of P.R. Grant and B.R. Grant (2002a). Despite the recurrence of droughts and El Niños, their observations of *G. scandens* and *G. fortis* on Daphne Major have revealed long-term directional changes in body size, bill depth, and bill shape. Wells (2000, pp. 168-169) correctly pointed out that during the years following the 1982-1983 El Niño, bill depths in *fortis* returned to their smaller, pre-Niño values (Gibbs and Grant 1987). Since then, however, they have continued to get progressively smaller, resulting in a net linear change from large to small over the thirty years of the Grants' research (P.R. Grant and B.R. Grant 2002a). P.R. Grant and B.R. Grant (2002a) attributed these trends to unpredictable, long-term interactions between the climate, the finches, and the plants and animals that serve as food for the finches.

The modern model of the origin of the finch species invokes progressive allopatric speciation (P.R. Grant and B.R. Grant 1996, 1997b, 2002b; P.R. Grant 2001). Lack (1940; 1947, pp. 118-122) developed this model, and Dobzhansky (1951, p. 206) succinctly explained it, "The species have become differentiated on the different islands of the archipelago." P.R. Grant and B.R. Grant (2002b) explained the model in three steps with notable variations: First, the ancestors of the modern finches, perhaps as few as 30 individuals (Vincek *et al.* 1997), arrived on at least one of the islands and became adapted to its environment. Second, some of the original population spread to other islands in the archipelago and became adapted to their peculiar environment. The second stage can happen several times and is responsible for the evolution of new species. In the third stage, formerly allopatric species come into contact again by migration of one species to an island already inhabited by another species. The result of secondary contact of species can be absorption of one by hybridization and introgression as in the case of *G. fuliginosa* on Daphne Major (P.R. Grant and B.R. Grant 1997a) or character displacement as in the case of *G. fortis* and *G. fuliginosa* on Santa Cruz (Schluter *et al.* 1985). Alternatively, the third phase of sympatry might not occur at all, as in the case of the genetic varieties of *Certhidea olivacea* on Marchena/Española/Genovesa and Santa Cruz (Freeland and Boag 1999b). The allopatric finch speciation model is supported by the morphological, genetic, and vocalization differences between allopatric populations of *G. difficilis* (Grant *et al.* 2000), and by the single species of Darwin's finch on the lone Cocos Island.

As a creationist, I agree in general with Wieland (1992) that evidence of natural selection is not contradictory to a creationist perspective. I do not agree with Wieland's (1992) attribution of the diversity of the modern finches to a degeneration, nor would I attribute the initial variation of modern finches to random mutation, as P.R. Grant (2001) suggests. My interpretation of the finches arises from three important issues: First, random mutation cannot generate beneficial mutations fast enough for selection to act to produce new species. Instead, Haldane's dilemma (ReMine 1993, chap. 8) predicts that deleterious mutations will cause the extinction of a population before a beneficial allele can be fixed by selection and a new species produced, unless the entire process proceeds *very* slowly (much more slowly than the age of the Galápagos would allow).

Second, the individual finches are difficult to classify unambiguously in a particular species, either by morphological analysis (Bowman 1961; Lammerts 1966) or genetically (Freeland and Boag 1999a, 1999b). At the same time, what appear to be morphological species do exhibit tendencies to mate with other members of their own species (B.R. Grant and P.R. Grant 1996a). Mating preference appears to be determined by a blend of visual appearance (plumage and morphology) and vocalization (B.R. Grant and P.R. Grant 1987). Since vocalization is culturally inherited (sons learn their song from their fathers) (B.R. Grant and P.R. Grant 1996b), it need not vary directly with genetics, which may explain how species identifiable by mating preference and morphology do not correspond with monophyletic genetic lineages. Because errors can occur in the transmission of song, interspecific hybridization can occur (B.R. Grant and P.R. Grant 1996b). The morphological diversity of the finches, then, is maintained partly by natural selection and partly by mating choice (which admittedly can also be influenced by selection, e.g. B.R. Grant and P.R. Grant 1987; Podos 2001).

The third issue important to my interpretation of Darwin's finches are the peculiar feeding specializations of certain populations. As I have already mentioned, *G. difficilis* on Isla Wolf feed by parasitically pecking at the flesh of boobies and drinking their blood and by stealing eggs and cracking them open (Köster and Köster 1983). Additionally, the finches of the Cocos Island (*Pinarolloxias inornata*) exhibit a wide variety of intraspecific feeding "adaptations," that are culturally inherited (Werner and Sherry 1987). These variations illustrate the opportunistic feeding behavior of finch populations. There is little doubt that finch populations will eat what they can, not merely foods for which they are morphologically "adapted." Thus, *G. difficilis*, instead of feeding on seeds on Isla Wolf, exploits a different food source altogether. Similarly, the *P. inornata* population is supported by subpopulations behaviorally exploiting different food sources.

The latter two observations are not inconsistent with the allopatric model of the persistence of bill variation in Darwin's finches by natural selection (P.R. Grant 2001; P.R. Grant and B.R. Grant 2002b), but Haldane's dilemma suggests that natural selection plays little role in the origin of the species. I explained above that post-Flood diversification was rapid and unlike speciation changes occurring today. The rate of morphological change was much higher after the Flood and produced more diversity than any selectional changes do today. With the concept of diversification in mind, I would argue that Darwin's finches illustrate the final stages of the diversification period. The morphological variation exhibited in the finches sufficed to separate the different varieties into apparent "species," but was not nearly comparable to morphological changes observed earlier in the post-Flood period. For example, the morphological diversity of the felids (Robinson and Cavanaugh 1998b) or equids (Cavanaugh *et al.* 2003) easily overshadows the diversity of Darwin's finches.

Many creationists have proposed that the Flood was followed by a period of rapid speciation (Woodmorappe 1996, p. 182; Brand 1997, p. 304-305; Tyler 1997; Sarfati 2002, p. 79; Wood 2002a), which Wood and Murray (2003, p. 170) call diversification. Since rapid speciation of the same scale is no longer occurring, diversification must have ended at some point. As mentioned above, I informally refer to this period after the Flood during which diversification occurred as the "diversification period." Although creationists have discussed diversification frequently, the nature and manner of its cessation has not been a primary focus. Many possible scenarios are imaginable (e.g., linear decay, immediate cessation, etc.), but the simplest is an exponential decay in the production of new species. If this is the correct model for the cessation of diversification, we might expect that species produced at the end of the diversification period would be 'imperfectly' formed. For example, we might predict that late-produced species would be difficult to distinguish or completely interfertile. If Darwin's finches originated at the end of the diversification period, the imperfect species-formation could explain the observation of morphologically-distinguishable populations of finches (e.g. Bowman 1961) that do not correspond to genetic lineages (Freeland and Boag 1999a, 1999b). Today we find finch varieties that look and behave like true species but which are poorly-differentiated genetically and capable of producing fertile, interspecific hybrids.

Alternatively, we might hypothesize that diversification itself is not strictly confined to a period of history but instead is triggered by some form of environmental stress. The resulting diversification could be proportional to the magnitude of stress which triggered the changes. Thus, after the Flood, when the environment was in such a state of upheaval, diversification was extreme, producing the appearance of a specific period of diversification. After the residual catastrophism from the Flood settled down, additional stressors in the environment could trigger new episodes of diversification of much less magnitude than those immediately following the Flood. In this hypothesis, the similarity of Darwin's finches and the failure to recognize species genetically could result from a minor pulse of diversification induced by a very small environmental stress. Whichever model of diversification is correct, Darwin's finches appear to be readily explicable within the creation biology model.

The most important question to my perspective on diversification is the origin of the shape and size variation today observed in the finches. Burns *et al.* (2002) showed that bill depth and length is highly conserved among congeneric fringillid species, except in the Tholospiza, which includes Darwin's finches. Within the non-geospizine Tholospiza, bill depth and width (and feeding habits) can vary between species almost as much as between the geospizine species. Although the actual genetic elements that controls finch bill size or shape are unknown (P.R. Grant 2001), the heritability of bill morphology is generally high (Boag 1983). Schneider and Helms (2003) showed that neural crest cells are involved in the development of interspecific variation in beak morphology, and Smith (1993) found that an intraspecific polymorphism in bill morphology in the black-bellied seedcracker of Cameroon (*Pyrenestes ostrinus ostrinus*) is caused by a single gene. Thus, it appears that in the Tholospiza variation in bill size could have originated by very few genetic changes that influence neural crest cells.

The importance of this variation to diversification is apparent when compared to fossil horses. MacFadden (1992, pp. 102-103) notes that specimens referred to *Merychippus* and *Parahippus* are highly variable and heterogeneous. Cavanaugh *et al.*'s (2003) research has shown that both genera are transitional between subfamilies in the horse baramin. Thus, the origin of a completely new family might be accompanied by an increase in variation in a single genus, and diversification may operate by a sudden and substantial increase in variability that is later sorted out by natural selection, mating preferences, etc. If the finches do represent a late-stage diversification event, they may be a stage of diversification "frozen" by either their geographical isolation or by the general cessation of diversification. A study of the genetic origins of bill variation in finches could reveal the specific mechanisms that cause such variability. Consequently, I suggest that the Tholospiza finches could become a very important creationist model of diversification.

### 4.6. Galápagos Penguins

**4.6.1. Introduction.** Because we often associate penguins with the cold of the Antarctic, the Galápagos penguin (*Spheniscus mendiculus*, Figure 29) seems strangely out of place living on the equator. Such is not the case, however, since penguins such as the Humboldt penguin (*S. humboldti*) are known to live far north of the Antarctic (Bingham 2001, p. 65). It is merely the popular perception of penguins that associates them with snow and frigid temperatures. Since the Humboldt current runs along the coastal Peru (where the Humboldt penguin lives) then through the Galápagos Islands, it is easy to imagine how the ancestors of the Galápagos penguin could find themselves following the current by rafting and/or swimming with the raft, and subsequently settling in the newly-formed Galápagos archipelago. That they did not simply swim to the islands would be implied by no modern observations of penguin migration to the archipelago.

Far more important than the equatorial heat to the Galápagos

Figure 29. The Galápagos penguin *Spheniscus mendiculus*. Photo courtesy Corel Corporation.

penguin's survival is the unpredictability of the Galápagos climate. With breeding populations restricted to Isabela, Fernandina, and Floreana (Boersma 1979; Vargas *et al.* 1997), the Galápagos penguins rely on the Cromwell Current to bring cold water to the islands, which provides them with food (Boersma 1974). Severe disruptions in water temperature during El Niño result in high penguin mortality, from which the populations are slow to recover (Valle 1986; Rosenberg and Harcourt 1987; Valle *et al.* 1987). Because of the environmental unpredictability, the Galápagos penguin is an opportunistic species, eating a wide range of food sources and laying an unusual number of eggs (Boersma 1974, p. 196-197). Galápagos penguins can breed year-round and may produce three times as many eggs as other penguins and seabirds during any given year (Boersma 1974, p. 197; Bingham 2001, p. 68).

Creationists have mentioned penguins only rarely and then only in the context of celebrating God's design (e.g. Doolan 1992; Moxie 1996). A consideration of their baraminological relationships will aid in understanding the nature of this design and their diversification. I obtained a published dataset compiled by Giannini and Bertelli (2004) and consisting of 70 integumentary and behavioral characters. I analyzed this dataset using baraminic distance and classical MDS. Using the baraminological relationships of penguins as an interpretive framework, I will discuss methods that the Galápagos penguin uses to cope with heat and the relationship of those methods to adaptation and design.

**4.6.2. Baraminology.** The extant penguins consist of eighteen species endemic to the southern hemisphere. Penguins are classified not only in their own family Spheniscidae (Reilly 1994, p. 9) but also in their own order Sphenisciformes (Carroll 1988, p. 356). The evolutionary sister group of the penguins is generally agreed to be order Procellariiformes, the petrels and albatrosses (Carroll 1988, p. 367; Cooper and Penny 1997). Despite this general agreement, an unambiguous stratomorphic intermediate between flying birds and penguins has not yet been described. The earliest penguin fossils are from the Eocene and exhibit specializations characteristic of the Spheniscidae (e.g. see Jenkins 1974; Carroll 1988, p. 356-357; Myrcha *et al.* 2002; Clarke *et al.* 2003). Bird and bird-like fossils stratigraphically lower than the lowest penguin fossils exhibit a confusing array of morphologies, as illustrated by ongoing feathered dinosaur research (e.g. Xu *et al.* 2003).

Giannini and Bertelli (2004) examined penguin phylogeny using 70 integumentary and behavioral characteristics. The dataset consisted of eighteen penguin species and twelve outgroup species. The outgroup species were the common loon (*Gavia immer*) and eleven species of procellariiformes. Of the seventy characters, 34 were scored as inapplicable to all outgroup species and were eliminated from this analysis. These characters (25-58 in Giannini and Bertelli 2004) scored attributes of adult and juvenile plumage. The remaining characters scored attributes of the bill, iris, feathers, natal plumage, feet, and breeding. These characters (0-24 and 59-69 in Giannini and Bertelli 2004) will be referred to here as the "reduced dataset" for purposes of analysis by baraminic distance correlation and classical MDS.

Baraminic distances were calculated from the reduced dataset using BDIST as described previously (Wood 2002b). At a relevance cutoff of 0.95, three characters were eliminated from the analysis, leaving 33 characters for calculation of baraminic distances. The baraminic distance correlation results are summarized in Figure 30. Three distinct groups of penguins are distinguishable from the results. The first group consists of the two species of genus *Aptenodytes*. The second group contains *Eudyptula minor* and the genus *Spheniscus* (including the Galápagos penguin). The genera *Eudyptes* and *Megadyptes* and two species of *Pygoscelis* comprise the third group. The precise placement of the chinstrap penguin *Pygoscelis antarctica* into one of these groups is difficult to judge, since *P. antarctica* correlates positively with all other penguins except the genus *Aptenodytes*. The outgroup taxa correlate positively with each other but negatively with all members of the penguin group three. In addition, the black-eyebrowed albatross (*Diomedea melanophrys*) and the southern giant petrel (*Macronectes giganteus*) correlate negatively with members of penguin group two. *Pachyptila desolata* correlates negatively with one member of penguin group two, namely *Eudyptula minor*. Members of group one (genus *Aptenodytes*) correlate positively with each other but not with any other penguins.

I calculated classical MDS of the baraminic distances calculated from the reduced dataset of Giannini and Bertelli (2004) as described previously (Wood 2004, see Appendix). The results for the unscaled baraminic distances revealed a minimal

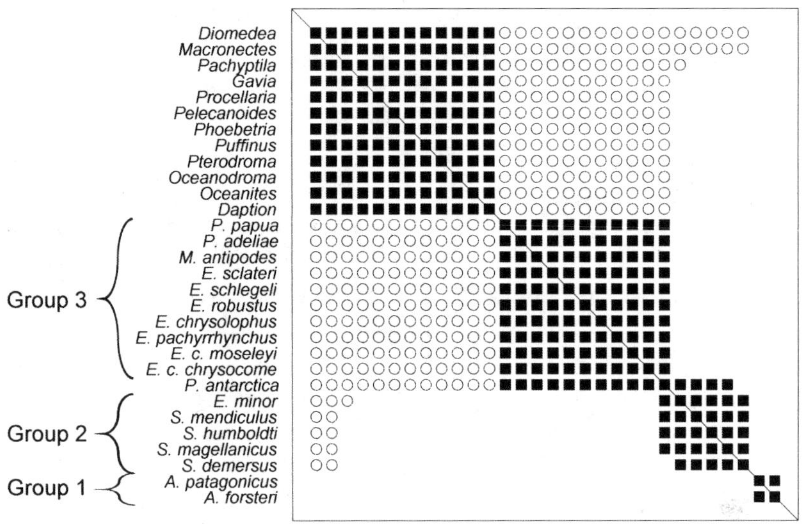


Figure 30. Baraminic distance correlation for the penguin dataset of Giannini and Bertelli (2004), reduced to eliminate non-relevant characters as described in text. Taxa with significant ($p<0.05$) positive correlation are indicated as filled squares. Taxa with significant ($p<0.05$) negative correlation are indicated as open circles.

stress of 0.045 at five dimensions and a stress of 0.10 at three dimensions. Minimal stress of the scaled baraminic distances was 0.26 at 14 dimensions, with a stress of 0.40 at three dimensions. The 3D MDS pattern for the unscaled baraminic distances reveals a notable separation between the three groups of penguins with *P. antarctica* located adjacent to penguin group three (Figure 31). The penguins and the outgroup species are also clearly separated. The closest outgroup species to the penguins is the loon *Gavia immer*.

The baraminic distance correlation and MDS results support the general features of Giannini and Bertelli's (2004) cladistic analysis using the full seventy characters. The three groups of penguins identified here correspond to three clades of penguins. According to Giannini and Bertelli's (2004) consensus tree (their figure 1), the *Eudyptula* + *Spheniscus* clade forms the sister taxon to all other penguins. Within the remaining species, *Aptenodytes* forms the sister taxon to *Pygoscelis*, *Megadyptes*, and *Eudyptes*.

Although these clades are supported in the baraminic distance analysis of the reduced dataset, there is no particular arrangement of clades that would be supported by the present results. It is possible that a more detailed arrangement of penguin genera could be determined if the full dataset was used without the outgroup taxa. Since the detailed relationships of penguins are beyond the scope of this review, that analysis is left to future researchers.

Given the baraminic distance correlation and MDS results, I provisionally propose that the Spheniscidae comprise a holobaramin. The continuity within and between groups one and two is established by the significant, positive correlation between the chinstrap penguin and all other penguins of groups one and two. Continuity of of the two *Aptenodytes* species is established by significant positive correlation with each other, but their lack of positive correlation with other penguins makes their inclusion in the penguin holobaramin based solely on an intuitive evaluation of their morphological similarity. Indeed, that there

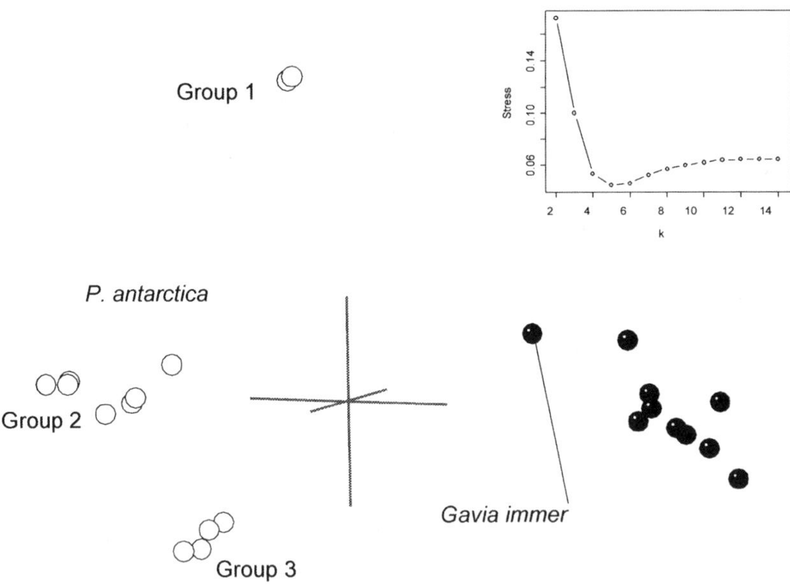


Figure 31. Three-dimensional classical MDS applied to uncorrected baraminic distances of the penguin dataset and the stress of *k*-dimensional classical scaling on the same baraminic distance matrix plotted as a function of the number of dimensions (*k*). Penguins (white) and outgroups (black) are distinguished.

might be a discontinuity separating some species of penguins does seem to strain credibility, and future analysis of the penguin species should support my inference of continuity between all penguins. Thus, I conclude that all penguin species belong to the same monobaramin, which is supported by the strong positive correlation observed between most pengiun species.

A penguin holobaramin must also be discontinuous from all other species, which can be argued in two ways, by discontinuity criteria and by the statistical analysis presented here. First, penguins fulfill several of the discontinuity criteria of Wise (1992) and Wood and Murray (2003, p. 95). The penguin ancestral taxon is unknown (Wood and Murray's question 10); the earliest known penguin fossils already exhibit penguin specializations (Jenkins 1974; Myrcha *et al.* 2002; Clarke *et al.* 2003). Furthermore, the phylogeny and chronology of the avian orders are poorly known in the evolutionary model (e.g. van Tuinen and Hedges 2004), implying true discontinuities exist between the orders. Specifically for the Sphenisciformes, morphological evidence suggests that the Gaviiformes is the sister taxon to the penguins (e.g. O'Hara 1989), while molecular sequence data implies a close relationship to the Procellariiformes (e.g. van Tuinen *et al.* 2001). This disagreement could imply the presence of a true discontinuity.

The apparent discontinuity implied by the difficulty of inferring the penguins' nearest ancestors is confirmed by the baraminic distance analysis. Baraminic distance correlation between the outgroup taxa and the penguins in the Giannini and Bertelli (2004) reduced dataset is mostly negative. Of the 216 possible comparisons between a penguin and an outgroup species, 143 show significant negative baraminic distance correlation, implying discontinuity. All outgroup species and members of penguin group three are negatively correlated. Considering the general evidence of discontinuity (from discontinuity criteria) and the statistical support for significant negative baraminic distance correlation between penguins and non-penguins, I conclude that a discontinuity surrounds the penguins. As a group that shares continuity within and discontinuity with outgroups, the penguins therefore fulfill the definition of a holobaramin.

**4.6.3. Galápagos Penguins and Design.** As noted above, creationists marvel at the anatomical and behavioral features of penguins that allow them to survive the cold of the Antarctic. Such features are attributed to God's design (Moxie 1996). The

Galápagos penguin must survive the opposite problem, the relentless heat of an equatorial home. Though not anatomically altered in any particular way to cope with the heat, *S. mendiculus* exhibits a number of behavioral traits for keeping cool. Like the South American Humboldt penguins, Galápagos penguins nest in burrows or crevices to shield themselves from the sun (Bingham 2001, pp. 63, 69). Galápagos penguins also pant and swim to cool off (Reilly 1994, pp. 135-136). Because heat can be lost through the feet or the area under the flippers, Galápagos penguins can often be observed hunched over with their flippers extended to the sides to shade their feet and sides from the equatorial sun (Reilly 1994, p. 135).

These behavioral traits highlight the general lack of diversification in the penguins. In contrast to the finches (see above), the Galápagos penguin exhibits very little adaptation that might be attributed to natural selection. Some groups (e.g. the finches) diversify greatly in a harsh environment, while others (e.g. penguins) do not. Such diversity in diversity does not yet have an explanation in the evolution or creation models. In evolution, it is generally considered a consequence of "chance." Within the creation model, we can attribute the penguins' success in either hot or cold environment ultimately to a wise Designer, but the lack of diversity in the penguins does raise the intriguing question of why some groups diversify while others do not. In the case of the penguin, these birds are obviously well-adapted to a variety of environments without major anatomical modifications. Thus, the penguins might not have diversified as much as the fringillids because the penguins can survive without such modifications as the fringillids have experienced. Such an answer is ultimately unsatisfying, though, since the fringillid diversity seems so extravagant. It might be possible that diversification is not always related to changes in environment. In fact (as in the case of evolution), it may turn out to be simply a matter of chance.

Related to the question of their adaptation to the variability of the Galápagos environment is the question of how the penguins came to the islands in the first place. The general concept of post-Flood rafting (Wise and Croxton 2003) seems the most reasonable explanation with the present data. We know that extant penguins are capable of swimming hundreds of kilometers on foraging trips (Kooyman 2002), but there is no evidence that South American penguins (e.g. *S. humboldti*) have swum to Galápagos in historical times. Furthermore, long-range migration of Galápagos penguins is also unknown. Thus, it is necessary to hypothesize that either the dispersability of the Galápagos penguin ancestor was higher in the past or that the Galápagos penguin ancestor came to the islands via a post-Flood debris raft. Since we expect that rafts of Flood debris would have existed after the Flood, movement of penguins on debris rafts seems the more reasonable explanation.

In the future, creation biologists can focus on confirming continuity among all extant penguins. An osteological dataset would allow the inclusion of fossil taxa in the baraminic distance analysis. An osteological dataset would also clarify the discontinuity surrounding Spheniscidae. Such discontinuity should also be examined using Wood and Murray's (2003, p. 95) modified discontinuity matrix or Robinson's (1997) molecular sequence techniques.

## 4.7. Pelecaniformes

**4.7.1. Introduction.** The traditional avian order Pelecaniformes includes approximately 66 extant species (Hedges and Sibley 1994), of which eight are found in the Galápagos Islands (Swarth 1931) (see Figure 32). The order is characterized by a totipalmate foot, in which all toes are webbed; a gular pouch, most developed in the pelicans; and salt glands in the orbits of the eyes (Carroll 1988, p. 355; Feduccia 1999, p. 187). Pelecaniforms are organized into six extant families: Phaethontidae (tropic birds, 1 genus, 3 spp.), Fregatidae (frigatebirds, 1 genus, 5 spp.), Sulidae (gannets and boobies, 3 genera, 9 spp.), Phalacrocoracidae (cormorants, 1 genus, 38 spp.), Anhingidae (anhingas, 1 genus, 4 spp.), and Pelecanidae (pelicans, 1 genus 8 spp.) (Feduccia 1999, p. 188). Present on Galápagos are members of five of these families: three booby species (*Sula sula*, *S. nebouxii*, and *S. granti*), two frigatebirds (*Fregata minor* and *F. magnificens*), the brown pelican (*Pelecanus occidentalis*), the red-billed tropicbird (*Phaethon aethereus*), and the flightless cormorant (*Phalacrocorax harrisi*) (Swarth 1931; Thornton 1971) (Figures 32 and 33). In this section, I will discuss the baraminic positions of the pelicans, cormorants, and boobies; the frigatebirds and tropicbird will be left to future research.

Whereas discontinuity is technically defined as "significant, holistic difference" (Wood *et al.* 2003), evidence of discontinuity is often derived from a failure of phylogenetic methods to account

Figure 32. Pelicaniform species native to the Galápagos Islands, A. blue-footed booby (*Sula nebouxii*), B. Nazca booby (*Sula granti*), C. red-footed booby (*Sula sula*), D. magnificent frigatebird (*Fregata magnificens*), E. brown pelican (*Pelecanus occidentalis*). Not shown: Flightless Cormorant (*Phalacrocorax harrisi*, see Figure 33), Great Frigatebird (*Fregata minor*), and Red-billed Tropicbird (*Phaethon aethereus*). Photos courtesy Corel Corporation (A, C, D, E) and NOAA (B).

Figure 33. Nesting flightless cormorants *Phalacrocorax harrisi*. Photo courtesy Corel Corporation.

for a group's origin. For example, Wise (1992) included evidence of ancestral groups in his discontinuity matrix, which Wood and Murray (2003, p. 95) retain. With this in mind, it can be helpful to review evidence of the phylogeny as a prelude to baraminology of the pelecaniforms. According to Feduccia (1999, p. 187), the sister group of the Pelecaniformes might be Procellariiformes, but this relationship is not "obvious." Romer (1945, p. 268) reported a Cretaceous Pelecaniform fossil, but the assignment to Pelecaniformes is no longer considered to be reliable (Feduccia 1999, p. 187). The stratigraphically-lowest fossil form is the Eocene *Prophaethon* from England, assigned to its own family Prophaethontidae (Carroll 1988, p. 355; Feduccia 1999, p. 187).

Cracraft's (1985) cladistic analysis of 52 morphological and ethological characters strongly supported the monophyly of the order, but DNA evidence suggested that the order is composed of at least three different groups (Hedges and Sibley 1994). Based on DNA/DNA hybridization, the pelicans appear closely related to the shoebill (*Balaeniceps rex*), the frigatebirds to the penguins and procellariiforms, and the remaining pelecaniform families form a paraphyletic assemblage. Hedges and Sibley's (1994) ribosomal RNA analysis confirmed the relationship of pelicans and the shoebill, but placed the frigatebirds on a monophyletic branch with the condors, and placed the tropicbirds, boobies, and cormorants on a monophyletic branch by themselves. Kennedy and Spencer's (2004) analysis of 1756 nucleotides of mitochondrial DNA supported a sister relationship of the tropicbirds and albatrosses. Though Feduccia (1999, p. 187) commented that the molecular evidence is unreliable, Hedges and Sibley (1994) expressed similar doubts about the morphological evidence. More recently, a morphological study by Mayr (2003) supported the polyphyly of the pelecaniforms. Mayr's (2003) most parsimonious trees separated the tropic birds from the remaining pelecaniforms. A resolution of this conflict has not yet been published.

**4.7.2. Baraminology.** Because of the molecular/morphological conflict, the baraminic position of these birds is difficult to predict. Whereas the ambiguity of the sister group might suggest that the pelecaniforms are surrounded by a discontinuity, the molecular results imply that some pelecaniforms could be related to non-pelecaniform birds. The morphological characters of this order (totipalmate foot, gular pouch, orbit salt gland) could imply a common baraminic origin, but again the conflicting molecular data and more recent morphological analyses could be interpreted as indicative of discontinuities within the Pelecaniformes.

Important to any consideration of baraminology is the occurrence of hybrids as evidence of continuity. Gray (1958, p. 2-3) listed several putative hybrids between pelecaniforms, but all are intrageneric. Most significant of these are the pelican hybrids (genus *Pelecanus*); Gray lists three hybrids involving three of the eight species (37.5% of the family). In addition, Gray also lists putative hybrids between the masked booby (*S. dactylatra*) and the brown booby (*S. leucogaster*) and between the long-tailed cormorant (*Phalacrocorax africanus*) and the pygmy cormorant (*P. pygmeus*). Based on these hybrids, I would propose that genus *Pelecanus* is a monobaramin. The booby and cormorant hybrids represent too few species from which to draw baraminic conclusions of any reliability.

To clarify the baraminic position of the cormorants, I performed a baraminic distance correlation test on a published morphological dataset consisting of 137 characters from 36 taxa (Siegel-Causey 1988). The taxa in the dataset represent 35 species of *Phalacrocorax* and one species of *Anhinga*. To clarify the baraminic position of the booby family Sulidae, I constructed a composite dataset consisting of the 124 morphological characters from Warheit (1990), 25 ethological and ecological characters from Friesen and Anderson (1997), and 38 morphological and ethological characters from Cracraft (1985). The composite dataset covers all nine sulid species and an outgroup species (pelagic cormorant, *Phalacrocorax pelagicus*). To supplement the baraminic distance correlation test, I also calculated 3D classical MDS for the baraminic distances of each dataset.

**4.7.3. Results.** Beginning with the full Siegel-Causey (1988) cormorant dataset, I elected to omit *P. ranfurlyi* from the analysis because the states of 60 of the 137 characters were unknown for that taxon. With the 35 remaining taxa, only one character scored below 0.95 relevance and was subsequently eliminated from the baraminic distance calculations. The resulting pattern of baraminic distance correlations reveal two clear groups, which correspond to Siegel-Causey's subfamilies Leucocarboninae and Phalacrocoracinae + Anhingidae (Figure 34). All members of each group share significant, positive baraminic distance correlation with all other members, and most members of either group show signficant, negative correlation with members of the other group.

Following the recommendations of Wood (2004; see appendix), I calculated 3D MDS using the cormorant baraminic distance matrix and a version of the baraminic distance matrix corrected by the addition of the maximum baraminic distance. For the cormorant dataset, the maximum distance calculated is 0.452, between three pairs of taxa: *P. sulcirostris* and *P. chalconotus*, *P. capillatus* and *P. chalconotus*, and *P. carbo* and *P. chalconotus*. Three-dimensional MDS on the baraminic distance matrices yielded a stress of 0.110, while 3D MDS on the corrected distance matrix yielded a stress of 0.422. Because of the much lower stress for the uncorrected distance matrix, I will limit my description of the 3D pattern to the baraminic distances as calculated by BDIST (Wood 2002b) (Figure 35).

MDS of the cormorant baraminic distance matrix for all possible dimensions revealed a minimum stress of 0.020 at eight dimensions. Though much higher, the stress at three dimensions is still quite low and consequently the 3D pattern should be a good depiction of the eight-dimensional structure. The 3D taxic

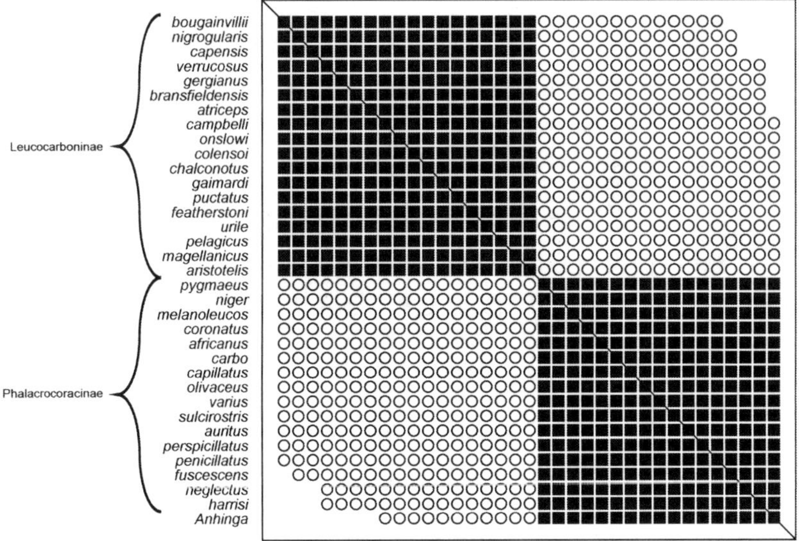


Figure 34. Baraminic distance correlation for the cormorant dataset of Siegel-Causey (1988). Taxa with significant ($p<0.05$) positive correlation are indicated as filled squares. Taxa with significant ($p<0.05$) negative correlation are indicated as open circles.

pattern reveals a complex geometry, with five distinct groups (Figure 35). The first group, consisting solely of the anhinga, occupies the central-most position in the pattern. The remaining four groups may be divided into two sets, which correspond to Siegel-Causey's (1988) subfamilies Leucocarboninae and Phalacrocoracinae. The two leucocarbonine groups consist of (A) *gaimardi*, *featherstoni*, *urile*, *aristotelis*, *pelagicus*, *magellanicus*, and *punctatus*; (B) *onslowi*, *colensoi*, *chalconotus*, *campbelli*, *atriceps*, *bransfieldensis*, *georgianus*, *capensis*, *bougainvilli*, *nigrogularis*, and *verrucosus*. The two phalacrocoracine groups consist of (A) *coronatus*, *niger*, *africanus*, *melanoleucos*, and *pygmaeus*; (B) *fuscescens*, *neglectus*, *harrisi*, *varius*, *penicillatus*, *perspicillatus*, *olivaceus*, *auritus*, *sulcirostris*, *capillatus*, and *carbo*. If the four phalacrocoracid groups are viewed according to the subfamilies, such that the groups of the same subfamily were joined by an imaginary axis, the axes would be orthogonal.

After filtering the composite sulid dataset at a relevance cutoff of 0.95, 186 of the 187 characters were used to calculate

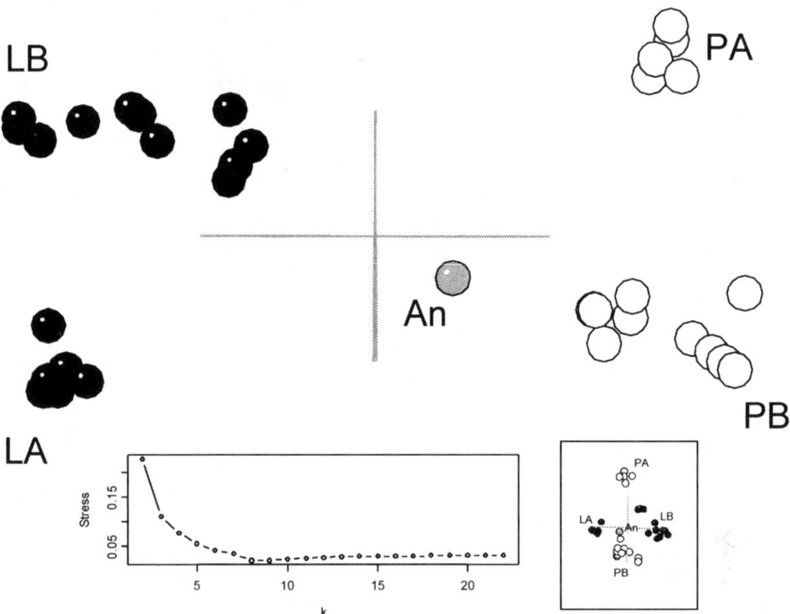


Figure 35. Three-dimensional classical scaling applied to uncorrected cormorant baraminic distances (top) and the stress of n-dimensional classical scaling on the same baraminic distance matrix plotted as a function of the number of dimensions (n). Taxa shown are Leucocarboninae (black), Anhingidae (grey), and Phalacrocoracinae (white). Also shown in inset is an alternative perspective of the clustering, illustrating the orthogonal relationship of taxa.

baraminic distances. The results of the baraminic distance correlation on the composite Sulidae dataset are shown in Figure 36. Significant positive correlation is found among members of the same genus, but positive correlation between the genera does not occur. Some significant negative correlation exists between the gannets (genus *Morus*) and the boobies (genus *Sula*), but no negative correlation exists between the outgroup cormorant and any of the ingroup species.

I performed MDS on the sulid baraminic distance matrix and on the distance matrix corrected by addition of the maximal distance (see Appendix). For this matrix, the maximal distance of 0.554 was observed twice, between the blue-footed booby (*Sula nebouxii*) and the pelagic cormorant (*P. pelagicus*) and between *P. pelagicus* and the Peruvian booby (*Sula variegata*). The stress for a three-dimensional classical MDS of the uncorrected distance matrix was 0.042 and for the corrected distance matrix was 0.352. As in all previous cases (Wood 2004), the stress is much less for the uncorrected baraminic distances, and all calculations and descriptions contained herein will refer to the uncorrected distance matrix. The minimal stress for the baraminic distance matrix was 0.022, calculated for a four-dimensional MDS. The three-dimensional MDS pattern should then be a good approximation of the optimal 4D structure.

The taxic pattern calculated in a 3D MDS reveals a nearly-regular tetrahedral shape, with the four genera of the dataset at the vertices (Figure 37). The three gannet species (*Morus bassanus*, *M. capensis*, and *M. serrator*) are clustered very tightly, indicating their near identity to each other. In contrast, the five booby species of genus *Sula* are more diffuse in the 3D pattern. The regular tetrahedral shape of the 3D pattern implies that with the present composite dataset, each genus is approximately equidistant from the other three genera. This is supported by merely taking the average intergeneric distance for all taxa in the

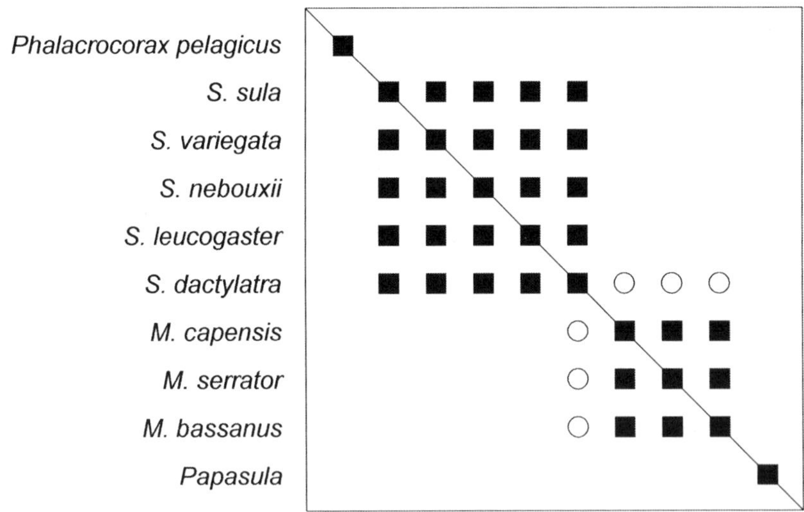


Figure 36. Baraminic distance correlation for the Sulidae dataset constructed for this study as described in text. Taxa with significant ($p<0.05$) positive correlation are indicated as filled squares. Taxa with significant ($p<0.05$) negative correlation are indicated as open circles.

dataset, which ranges from 0.433 (between *Sula* and *Papasula*) and 0.521 (between *Sula* and *Phalacrocorax*).

**4.7.4. Discussion.** The two phalacrocoracid groups distinguishable in the baraminic distance correlation results correspond roughly to the subfamilies recognized by Siegel-Causey (1988), with the exception of the placement of *Anhinga*. The groups within the subfamilies, which are recognizable only in the 3D MDS results generally correspond well to clades in Siegel-Causey's cladistic analysis. Phalacrocoracinae groups A and B correspond exactly to monophyletic lineages in Siegel-Causey's phylogeny. Group A consists of Siegel-Causey's genus *Microcarbo*, and group B consists of Siegel-Causey's genera *Compsohalieus*, *Hypoleucos*, and *Phalacrocorax*. Leucocarboninae group A corresponds to a monophyletic lineage which Siegel-Causey

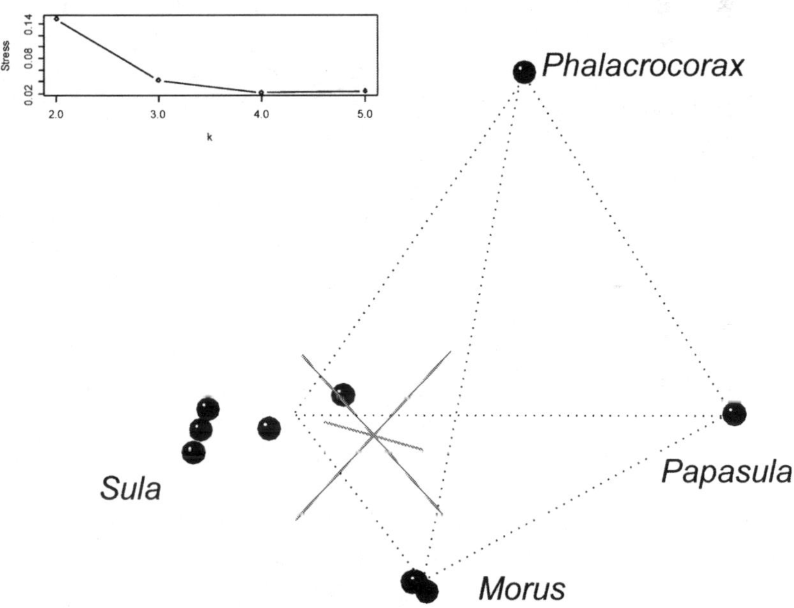


Figure 37. Three-dimensional classical MDS applied to uncorrected Sulidae baraminic distances (top) and the stress of *k*-dimensional classical scaling on the same baraminic distance matrix plotted as a function of the number of dimensions (*k*). Tetrahedral shape adopted by the four genera of the dataset is noted by dotted lines.

places in the genus *Stictocarbo*. Only Leucocarboninae group B is not monophyletic and consists of Siegel-Causey's genera *Euleucocarbo*, *Nesocarbo*, *Notocarbo*, and *Leucocarbo*. The close correspondence between such different methods (cladistics and 3D MDS) suggests that both techniques are recovering real taxic clustering patterns from this dataset.

Considering past disagreements over their classification, the position of *Anhinga* is of special interest. Siegel-Causey (1988) recommended recognizing family Anhingidae, following the majority of classifications reviewed by Johnsgard (1993, pp. 7-9). Cracraft (1985) by contrast was unique in placing water turkeys in subfamily Anhinginae within family Phalacrocoracidae. The baraminic distance results suggest that Cracraft is correct and that anhingas are not only members of Phalacrocoracidae but also members of the existing subfamily Phalacrocoracinae. While generally supporting the inclusion of *Anhinga* within the Phalacrocoracidae, the 3D MDS results would not support inclusion of *Anhinga* within either recognized subfamily. Thus, taken together, the baraminic distance correlation and 3D MDS analyses support Cracraft's (1985) inclusion of subfamily Anhinginae within Phalacrocoracidae.

The strong negative baraminic distance correlation observed between the two phalacrocoracid subfamilies is good evidence for discontinuity between the two subfamilies, *i.e.* that the two subfamilies constitute apobaramins. This assignment would be consistent with the findings of other baraminology studies, which often place the baraminic boundaries at the family or subfamily level. In the case of the cormorants, however, previous classification of the family might warrant a closer examination of their baraminic status. Although Siegel-Causey classifies the cormorants in nine different genera, they have historically been classified in only one genus *Phalacrocorax* or two genera *Phalacrocorax* (cormorants) and *Leucocarbo* (shags) (Johnsgard 1993, pp. 10-13). Johnsgard (1993, p. 13) treated the nine genera of Seigel-Causey as subgenera of the traditional genera *Phalacrocorax* and *Leucocarbo* (corresponding to subfamily Phalacrocoracinae and Leucocarboninae respectively).

If the Phalacrocoracidae is composed of two separate baramins, we might expect a broader recognition of this by a generally-accepted classification of the two baramins into separate taxonomic groups. Alternatively, if the cormorants represent a single baramin, what could be the cause of the near-universal negative baraminic distance correlation between the subfamilies? The 3D MDS reveals that the pattern of positive and negative correlation is heavily biased by the unsual orthogonal geometry between the leucocarbonines and the phalacrocoracines. Because of this unusual geometry, I do not judge the negative baraminic distance correlation observed in this dataset to be evidence of discontinuity. Instead, I recommend that the dataset be expanded to include another outgroup taxon, such as a pelican or booby, and that the baraminic distance correlation analysis be repeated.

Interpreting the baraminic distance correlation and MDS results of the composite sulid dataset is difficult. As noted above, significant positive correlation is typically interpreted as evidence of continuity, and significant negative correlation is interpreted as discontinuity. Since no significant correlation – positive or negative – is found between the cormorant and the Sulids, it is not possible to infer anything about the baraminic relationship of sulids to other pelecaniforms. The negative correlation between *Morus* and *Sula* would suggest discontinuity between the genera, but this would be unprecedented in vertebrate baraminology. As noted above, vertebrate baramins and basic types identified to date are larger than a single genus. Unless substantial errors have occurred in the classification of the Sulidae, continuity between the three genera *Sula*, *Morus*, and *Papasula* should be expected.

Since attempts at classifying sulids by morphology and DNA sequence are in good agreement (Friesen and Anderson 1997), I reject the idea that the sulids are improperly classified. Given good classification of the Sulidae, the baraminic distance correlation results imply that the sulid genera comprise separate baramins or that the data somehow has been biased towards distinguishing the genera of sulids. Considering Warheit's (1990) data, which constitute the majority of the data in the composite dataset, was selected to resolve relationships within the Sulidae, I tend to favor the latter interpretation. The results of the 3D MDS of the sulid baraminic distance matrix support this interpretation. Unlike other multi-generic datasets in this monograph, the genera in the composite sulid dataset are approximately equidistant, resulting in a tetrahedral pattern in 3D MDS. As with the peculiar geometry of the cormorant taxa, the tetrahedral shape of the sulids probably contributes to the peculiar pattern of baraminic distance correlation.

**4.7.5. Summary.** To summarize, the hybridization of pelican species suggests that genus *Pelecanus* is a monobaramin. The baraminic distance results from the cormorants and the sulids suggests that the following groups are also monobaramins: *Sula*, *Morus*, Leucocarboninae, and Phalacrocoracinae + *Anhinga*. Evidence of discontinuity from the same studies is ambiguous. Strong evidence for discontinuity occurs between the cormorant subfamilies, but confirmation from traditional classification is lacking. Weak evidence for discontinuity occurs between the gannets (*Morus*) and boobies (*Sula*), but a baramin consisting of just one genus from a larger family would be unprecedented. The 3D MDS results for both of these genera reveal unusual geometries which undoubtedly bias the baraminic distance correlation results.

Returning to the Galápagos species, the three boobies represent members of a single monobaramin and likely descended from a common ancestor present on the Ark. The flightless cormorant (*Phalacrocorax* (*Compsohalieus*) *harrisi*) belongs to the monobaramin Phalacrocoracinae + *Anhinga* and is genetically related to flighted species. The brown pelican also belongs to a monobaramin, but since this species' distribution is widespread, I will not discuss it further here. The relationships of the booby and cormorant baramins provide unique opportunities to study what I have previously termed "biological imperfection" (Wood and Murray 2003, chap. 10). Briefly defined, a biological imperfection is any biological phenomenon that appears to be contrary to our understanding of the nature or intentions of the Creator. Biological imperfections have been attributed to degeneration of an originally perfect creation (Wood 2002c; Mace *et al.* 2003), but as we shall see in the Galápagos cormorant and boobies, our own imperfect perceptions of the Creator or His creation can also be at fault.

A common position in creationism is that loss of traits is easily explained within the creation model as degeneration from a more perfect state (Stambaugh 1991; McCoy 1992; Wood 2001). Some creationists take this idea to an extreme by attributing *all* biological change to degeneration (Wieland 1991), which I have argued is unlikely to be correct (Wood 2002a). In this light, it is not surprising to find that Batten *et al.* (2000, p. 123) attribute flightless species that are cobaraminic with flighted species to "loss of genetic information." The flightless cormorant provides an excellent opportunity to evaluate this claim.

According to Livezey (1992), the anatomical modifications that lead to *P. harrisi*'s flightlessness are heterochronic. The great size of *P. harrisi* also contributes to its predisposition to flightlessness, since it is presumably near the upper-limit of flight capability for phalacrocoracids. Flighted cormorants fly to reach nests and for migratory purposes. Nesting sites in the Galápagos are readily available without flying and are adjacent to a steady food supply. Because the Galápagos environment exhibits long-range unpredictability (Boersma 1974), the need for a seasonal migration in response to regular changes in food supplies is negated (insect flight polymorphisms are advantageous in situations of short-term environmental instability rather than long-term seasonal changes). These conditions render flight unnecessary in *P. harrisi*. From these considerations, we can agree that the Galápagos cormorants appear to have lost a trait common to all other cormorants, with a relaxed natural selection for flight possibly contributing to the survival of the flightless cormorants.

Should we attribute this loss of flight in the cormorant to loss of genetic information or degeneration? There is presently no way to know, but it seems unnecessary. Whatever genetic information is necessary to build a wing is present in the flightless cormorant, as indicated by not only the presence of wings but also the presence of the same number of flight feathers as found in flighted cormorants (Livezey 1992). A more likely explanation would be that the developmental mechanisms in *P. harrisi* have changed in some way, resulting in an altered developmental rate for the pectoral limbs.

Should we attribute this change to "degeneration" or "imperfection?" Since both of these concepts carry with them the connotation of a lower quality of life from a previously better existence, this too seems unwarranted, since there is no evidence that *P. harrisi* is suffering from a lower-quality existence than flighted cormorants. Although *P. harrisi* populations are decimated by severe alterations in their food supply (coinciding with El Niño), the population numbers recover very rapidly, much faster than Galápagos penguins (Valle *et al.* 1987). Thus, although one could argue that *P. harrisi* would survive better if individuals could fly to new food sources during El Niño, their population recovery indicates that even severe El Niños have little lasting effect. Rather than being a degeneration or imperfection,

*P. harrisi* appears quite suited to its harsh environment.

Boobies present a second example of putative imperfection. Three species of boobies occur in the Galápagos: the Nazca booby (*Sula granti*, formerly *S. dactylatra*, see Pitman and Jehl 1998), the red-footed booby (*S. sula*), and the endemic blue-footed booby (*S. nebouxii*) (Figure 32). Reproduction in the Nazca booby is obligately siblicidal. Although Nazca boobies usually lay two eggs, the elder-born chick must kill its younger sibling or both will die (see J.B. Nelson 1978, p. 365). Apparently, food resources are only sufficient to raise a single chick. The clutch size of two eggs may be an "insurance" mechanism: in cases when the first-born chick dies, the second-born can be raised instead (Clifford and Anderson 2002). The practice of siblicide is correlated with hormonal differences between the chick siblings, particularly in corticosterone and progesterone levels (Tarlow *et al.* 2001).

A long-held tenet of the creation model is that animal death did not occur before the Fall (Clark 1947, p. 40; Marsh 1950, pp. 261-263; Whitcomb and Morris 1961, p. 461-464), yet animals that cannot survive without killing other animals are common. Usually such animals are parasites or carnivores, causing the suffering or death of others by consuming their bodies. In the case of the Nazca booby, the victim is ejected from the nest but not eaten. Of interest to the creationist is the intrabaraminic variation. Although *S. granti* is obligately siblicidal, *S. nebouxii* and *S. sula* are not. Female red-footed boobies (*S. sula*) regularly lay only a single egg (J.B. Nelson 1978, p. 685), and *S. nebouxii* is one of two sulids that raise more than one chick (J.B. Nelson 1978, p. 525). Studies of siblicide in sulids can help us to understand the origin of this peculiar habit and may give insight into the origin of biological imperfection in general.

Pelecaniforms represent a rich source for future creationist research. Of foremost importance is the determination of the baraminic status of the order and the families traditionally referred to it. Once these baraminological questions have been resolved, creationists can with greater confidence turn to issues of imperfection as reflected in siblicide in the boobies or flightlessness in the flightless cormorant.

## 4.8. Galápagos Hawk

**4.8.1. Introduction.** The Galápagos archipelago is home to a single endemic species of hawk, *Buteo galapagoensis* (Ferguson-

Lees and Christie 2001, pp. 667-668) (Figure 38). Once present on fourteen of the islands, the hawk today survives on only nine, with the majority living on Santiago and Isabela (DeVries 1975). In 1970, DeVries (1973) estimated there were only 130 pairs living in the islands. Settlers in the Galápagos exterminated them because they perceived the hawk as a threat to their chickens. Typical hawk prey includes lava lizards, marine iguanas, centipedes, rats, doves, and Audubon's shearwaters (Thornton 1971, p. 151; DeVries 1973), but Galápagos hawks will take whatever food sources they can get (DeVries 1975; Ferguson-Lees and Christie 2001, p. 668). In 1975, DeVries recorded a population of only 130 pairs (DeVries 1975), but more recently the population has increased to 500 adults and 400 juveniles (Ferguson-Lees and Christie 2001, p. 668).

Hawks and buzzards of the genus *Buteo* are presently classified in the family Accipitridae and the order Falconiformes. Swarth (1931) claimed that the most similar species morphogically is Swainson's hawk, *Buteo swainsoni*. Voous and de Vries (1978) conducted a more detailed analysis of the Galápagos hawk and concluded that it most closely resembled the red-backed hawk (*B. polyosoma*) and the white-tailed hawk (*B. albicaudatus*). More recently, Riesing *et al.* (2003) published a mitochondrial DNA analysis of the genus *Buteo*. Based on both neighbor-joining and parsimony trees, the sequences most similar to the Galápagos hawk's came from Swainson's hawk, confirming Swarth's morphological observations. According to the same mtDNA phylogenies, *B. polyosoma* and *B. albicaudatus* are only distantly related to *B. galapagoensis*.

**4.8.2. Baraminology.** The baraminology of birds of prey has been commented on twice in creationist literature. Culp's (1994) review of North American birds of prey drew baraminic boundaries very narrowly by placing the 36 species into 33 baramins. Zimbelmann (1993) reviewed interspecific hybridization within the Falconiformes and proposed that the subfamilies Accipitrinae and Buteoninae together constituted a basic type (monobaramin), consisting of greater than 70 species. Considering the many baraminology studies that have shown baramins with great numbers of species, Culp's (1994) circumscription of 33 bird of prey baramins, each with very few species, is unlikely to be correct. Zimbelmann's (1993) hypothesis of a Buteoninae + Accipitrinae monobaramin is more consistent with baraminology

Figure 38. Galápagos Hawk *Buteo galapagoensis*. Photo courtesy Corel Corporation.

research on other groups.

Unlike other basic types that are identified based on many examples of interspecific and intergeneric hybrids (e.g. Fehrer 1993), Zimbelmann's (1993) Buteoninae + Accipitrinae basic type is based on only five intrageneric hybrids and two intergeneric hybrids. Four of these hybrids involve species of the genus *Buteo*: *B. buteo* × *B. lagopus*, *B. buteo* × *B. jamaicensis*, *B. buteo* × *Accipiter gentilis*, and *B. buteo* ×

*Parabuteo unicinctus.* Assuming that a family is the closest approximation of a holobaramin, Zimbelmann's circumscription of monobaramin Buteoninae + Accipitrinae omits 58 confamilial genera encompassing approximately 165 species (Ferguson-Lees and Christie 2001) A review of the current literature on accipitrid hybrids supports the inclusion of a few additional genera in the Buteoninae + Accipitrinae monobaramin (Figure 39), but these genera still do not encompass the majority of possible taxa. Other baraminological analyses must be applied to confirm the Buteoninae + Accipitrinae monobaramin.

Wise (1990) proposed that organisms that fall within the range of similarity of hybridizing organisms should be considered in the same baramin as those that hybridize. In his study of turtle baraminology, Robinson (1997) used Wise's criterion to extend the monobaramin of hybridizing turtles by including species that were more similar to either of the hybridizing species than the hybridizing species were to each other. With recently-published mitochondrial *nd6* and pseudocontrol region DNA sequences from *Buteo* species (Riesing *et al.* 2003) supplemented with additional sequences from GenBank, a more conclusive estimate of the monobaramin can be made using the hybrids listed by Zimbelmann (1993).

Since *Buteo jamaicensis* and *Parabuteo unicinctus* are capable of hybridizing, I used *B. jamaicensis* as a standard of comparison to determine if the Galápagos hawk (*Buteo galapagoensis*) belongs to the same monobaramin. Figure 40 shows the mtDNA distances between four samples of *B. jamaicensis* and 29 samples from 21 other species (see Table 4). The distances were calculated from a 921-nucleotide CLUSTALW (Thompson *et al.* 1994) alignment of the $tRNA^{Pro}$, *nd6*, $tRNA^{Glu}$, and pseudocontrol regions using the DNADIST program of the Phylip package (Felsenstein 1993). The horizontal lines indicate the distances between the four samples of *B. jamaicensis* and the three samples of *P. unicinctus*. Points below the lines represent taxa that are more similar to *B. jamaicensis* than *B. jamaicensis* is to *P. unicinctus*.

The results of this mtDNA analysis indicate that *B. jamaicensis* is more similar to nearly all of the sampled *Buteo* species than to *P. unicinctus*. This would confirm Riesing *et al.*'s (2003) phylogeny and the separation of *P. unicinctus* in a separate genus. Baraminologically, the *Buteo* species *jamaicensis, ventralis, regalis, japonicus, lagopus, albigula, galapagoensis, swainsoni,*

| | | *Accipiter* | *Buteo* | *Circus* | *Gyps* | *Aegypius* | *Milvus* | *Parabuteo* |
|---|---|---|---|---|---|---|---|---|
| *Accipiter* | 47 | ■ | ■ | | | | | |
| *Buteo* | 28 | ■ | ■ | | | | ■ | ■ |
| *Circus* | 13 | | | ■ | | | | |
| *Gyps* | 7 | | | | | ■ | | |
| *Aegypius* | 4 | | | | ■ | | | |
| *Milvus* | 3 | ■ | | | | | ■ | |
| *Parabuteo* | 1 | ■ | | | | | | |

Figure 39. Intra- and intergeneric hybridogram of the Accipitridae, constructed from Gray's (1958) list of interspecific hybrids, updated with interspecific hybrid reports from Corso and Forsman (1997), Schreiber *et al.* (2000), Zimbelmann (1993). The number of species in each genus as classified by Ferguson-Lees and Christie (2001) are indicated next to the genus name. Genera not known to hybridize with other genera are omitted from the diagram.

*lineatus, hemilasius, rufofuscus, augur, auguralis, albonotatus, platypterus, polyosoma, albicaudatus*, and *magnirostris* can all be included in a single monobaramin because they all fall within the range of similarity of the hybridizing species *B. jamaicensis* and *P. unicinctus*. The white-rumped hawk *B. leucorrhous*, the great black hawk *Buteogallus urubitinga urubitinga*, and the savannah hawk *Buteogallus meridionalis* are consistently more dissimilar from *B. jamaicensis* than *B. jamaicensis* is from *P. unicinctus*. These three species cannot be included in the present delineation of the *Buteo* monobaramin by this particular continuity criterion.

Since *B. jamaicensis* is also known to hybridize with *Accipiter gentilis* and *P. unicinctus* (Zimbelmann 1993), we can also include these species in the *Buteo* monobaramin. A mitochondrial DNA analysis of other *Accipiter* species may confirm Zimbelmann's (1993) original proposal of monobaramin Accipitrinae + Buteoninae. A search of NCBI's GenBank reveals that no publically-available sequences from *B. jamaicensis* and *A.*

Table 4. *Buteo* sequences used in this study (GenBank GI number and taxon).

| | |
|---|---|
| 29569511 | *Buteo japonicus japonicus* |
| 29569513 | *Buteo hemilasius* |
| 29569515 | *Buteo rufofuscus* |
| 29569517 | *Buteo augur* |
| 29569519 | *Buteo augur* |
| 29569521 | *Buteo auguralis* |
| 29569523 | *Buteo lagopus kamtschatkensis* |
| 29569525 | *Buteo regalis* |
| 29569527 | *Buteo jamaicensis* |
| 29569531 | *Buteo jamaicensis borealis* |
| 29569533 | *Buteo jamaicensis borealis* |
| 29569535 | *Buteo jamaicensis borealis* |
| 29569537 | *Buteo ventralis* |
| 29569539 | *Buteo albigula* |
| 29569541 | *Buteo galapagoensis* |
| 29569543 | *Buteo swainsoni* |
| 29569545 | *Buteo swainsoni* |
| 29569547 | *Buteo albonotatus* |
| 29569549 | *Buteo lineatus elegans* |
| 29569551 | *Buteo lineatus lineatus* |
| 29569553 | *Buteo platypterus platypterus* |
| 29569555 | *Buteo polyosoma polyosoma* |
| 29569559 | *Buteo polyosoma poecilochrous* |
| 29569561 | *Buteo albicaudatus colonus* |
| 29569563 | *Buteo albicaudatus hypospodius* |
| 29569565 | *Buteo magnirostris saturatus* |
| 29569567 | *Buteo leucorrhous* |
| 29569569 | *Parabuteo unicinctus harrisi* |
| 29569571 | *Parabuteo unicinctus unicinctus* |
| 29569573 | *Parabuteo unicinctus unicinctus* |
| 29569575 | *Parabuteo unicinctus unicinctus* |
| 29569577 | *Buteogallus meridionalis* |
| 29569579 | *Buteogallus urubitinga urubitinga* |

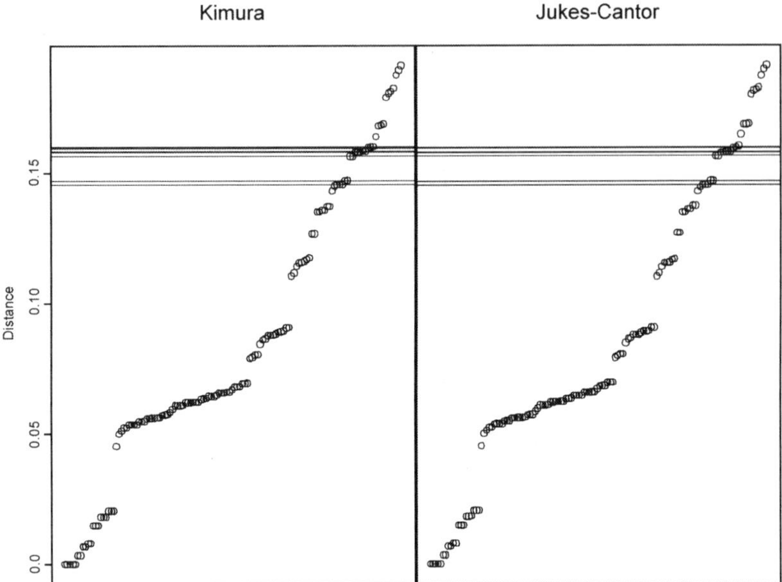


Figure 40. DNA distances between four samples from *Buteo jamacaiensis* and 29 samples from 21 other species, calculated from a 348-nt alignment of 35 sequences from the Riesing *et al.* (2003) dataset (see text for taxa list). DNA distances were calculated using the DNADIST program of the Phylip package (Felsenstein 1993), based on the Kimura and Jukes-Cantor DNA distance models. Horizontal lines represent the distances between sequences from three*Parabuteo unicinctus* samples and the four *B. jamaicensis* samples. Points above the highest horizontal line represent taxa more dissimilar to *B. jamaicensis* than *P. unicinctus*. These taxa are *Buteo leucorrhous, Buteogallus urubitinga urubitinga*, and *Buteogallus meridionalis*.

*gentilis* come from the same region of the mitochondrial genome. Until such sequences become available, the precise relationship of other *Accipiter* species to the *Buteo* monobaramin cannot be ascertained. The present results confirm that *B. galapagoensis* belongs to a monobaramin that includes most *Buteo* species, *Parabuteo unicinctus*, and at least some *Accipiter* species as well. Since each of the proposed closest relatives of *B. galapagoensis* – namely *B. swainsoni* (Swarth 1931), *B. polyosoma* (Voous and DeVries 1978), and *B. albicaudatus* (Voous and DeVries 1978) – is included, *B. galapagoensis* probably shares a common ancestor with a hawk still living on the American mainland.

**4.8.3. Diversification and Biogeography.** Swainson's hawk (*B. swainsoni*), a close relative of the Galápagos hawk, is a migratory species, wintering primarily in northeastern Argentina and spending the summer in the Great Plains and Rocky Mountains (Ferguson-Lees and Christie 2001, p. 663). The migratory route follows the Central American isthmus and may require as much as 40 to 50 days to complete. There is some speculation that Swainson's hawks fast during migration, although there is little evidence to support this contention (Goldstein *et al.* 1999). The ability to fast for long periods during migration would aid the ancestors of *B. galapagoensis* during their flight to the islands.

In contrast to its intercontinental-migrating cousin, the Galápagos hawk is extremely sedentary. Although the hawks appear on multiple islands, there are no recorded interisland movements (Ferguson-Lees and Christie 2001, p. 667), and the islands from which the hawks were exterminated by settlers have not been naturally repopulated (Swarth 1931; DeVries 1975). Their present sedentary ways obviously contrast not only with their sister taxon *B. swainsoni* but also with their ancestors, who must have at least once successfully completed a 600-mile migration over water.

Further curiosities of interest to the creationist are manifested in the Galápagos hawk's social and behavioral habits. Like most other animals of the archipelago, the hawks are not alarmed by the presence of humans (DeVries 1975). As Thornton observes (1971, p. 151), since all hawks normally lack predators, the tameness of the Galápagos species cannot be attributed to a lack of predators in the archipelago. Since God Himself placed the fear of man in animals (Gen. 9:2), the Galápagos hawk could provide an interesting opportunity to determine how that fear is maintained biologically.

Finally, the cooperative polyandry of the Galápagos hawk sets it apart from other members of the *Buteo* monobaramin and indeed from birds of prey in general. DeVries (1973) noted that the only other polygamous bird of prey is the hen harrier (*Circus cyaneus*), but in that species polygyny, when it does occur, is deleterious. Galápagos hawks breed in groups of one female and two to three males (Ferguson-Lees and Christie 2001, p. 668). Each male mates with the female and assists in the care of the offspring and defense of the nesting territory. Much has been written on the origin of morphological or DNA diversity within a baramin

(Wieland 1991; Wood 2002a), but intrabaraminic behavioral variation, though possibly common, is rarely considered. The Galápagos hawk provides an excellent test case for understanding behavioral variations, which should be especially interesting to the baraminologist in light of Schloss's (1998) use of altruistic animal behavior as evidence of intelligent design.

Of greatest importance to future creationist research on the Galápagos hawk is the identification of the baramin to which the species belongs. A good morphological dataset of the birds of prey will undoubtedly assist creationists in understanding the baraminology of hawks, eagles, and buzzards. Behavioral and diversification issues can then be examined with greater confidence.

## 4.9. Plants

**4.9.1. Introduction.** Serious study of the Galápagos flora began with the 1825 collection made by English naturalists David Douglas and John Scouler, and Darwin himself collected the first large sampling of the flora during his five-week visit in 1835 (Wiggins 1966; Porter 1980). Although Darwin did not consider himself competent in botany, he dutifully collected plants from South America and the Galápagos Islands with the encouragement of Cambridge professor John Stevens Henslow (Porter 1980). Modern research in Galápagos systematics has yielded an exhaustive description of the vascular plants (Wiggins and Porter 1971) with recent updates (Porter 1983; Lawesson *et al.* 1987). According to the most recent checklist (Lawesson *et al.* 1987), the vascular plant members (species, subspecies, or varieties) number 749, of which 216 (28.8%) are endemic, 271 (36.2%) are indigenous but not endemic, and 262 (35.0%) are introduced exotics.

Wiggins and Porter (1971) produced a widely-accepted description of six vegetative zones of the islands, which arise from a combination of water availability, temperature (both of which depend on an interaction of elevation and climate), slope face, and soil characteristics. Beginning from the shore and working inland, their zones are (1) the Littoral Zone, (2) the Arid Zone, (3) the Transition Zone, (4) the *Scalesia* Zone, (5) the *Miconia* Zone, and (6) the Fern-Sedge Zone. The Littoral Zone occurs along the shorelines of most of the islands and is dominated by four different mangrove species. The Arid Zone extends inland from the Littoral

Zone to an elevation of 80-120 meters. Due to the extensive lava fields surrounding most of the central volcanic cones of the western-most islands, the Arid Zone occupies the largest area of the five zones. The three cactus genera of Galápagos (*Opuntia*, *Brachycereus*, and *Jasminocereus*) and the small deciduous trees of the incense and spurge families (*Bursera* and *Croton*, respectively) dominate this zone. The Transition Zone marks the band of elevation where water availability improves. As a consequence, the species found in this zone are a mixture of species from the Arid and *Scalesia* Zones. At 180-400 m elevation, the *Scalesia* Zone is the region of highest rainfall in the islands and is named for the endemic Asteraceae genus *Scalesia*. Trees are common in this zone. Above this elevation, rainfall is limited to cloud mist. Thus, the *Miconia* Zone, dominated by dense shrubs, is a region of lower water availability with infrequent occurrence of trees. The zone possesses a slightly acidic soil. The Fern-Sedge Zone, with bog-like soils, is the highest region of elevation and occurs on all of the larger islands. Except for the tree fern *Cyathea weatherbyana*, the majority of plants in this zone are perennial sedges (Wiggins and Porter 1971, pp. 17-30).

Because of the relevance to diversification research, I will focus my discussion here primarily on endemics. Among the flowering plants, seven endemic genera in three different families occur in the islands. Endemic genera of the Asteraceae are *Darwiniothamnus* (2-3 sp.), *Lecocarpus* (3 spp.), *Macraea* (1 sp.), and *Scalesia* (11-15 spp.) (Wiggins and Porter 1971, pp. 342-344, 353-361; Porter 1983; Lawesson *et al.* 1987). Endemic genera of the Cactaceae are *Brachycereus* (1 sp.) and *Jasminocereus* (1 sp.) (Wiggins and Porter 1971, pp 534-537), and the remaining cactus genus found on the islands, *Opuntia*, consists of entirely endemic species. The final endemic genus is the monotypic *Sicyocaulis* of the family Cucurbitaceae, which for brevity's sake I will not discuss further. Because of its potential importance in photosynthesis research (Kennedy *et al.* 1980; Wood and Cavanaugh 2001), I will also review the endemic species of the genus *Mollugo* (Molluginaceae). Undoubtedly other members of the Galápagos flora will occasion many more opportunities for baraminological research.

**4.9.2. Asteraceae.** The family Asteraceae contains nearly 20,000 species (Bremer 1994), with such familiar members as daisies, sunflowers, and marigolds. The vast number of species makes the family a valuable test case for research in baraminology and the limits and nature of diversification (Wood and Cavanaugh 2001; Cavanaugh and Wood 2002). Most recently, Cavanaugh and Wood (2002) published a baraminological analysis of the Asteraceae tribe Heliantheae *sensu lato*. They concluded that species referred to Heliantheae *sensu stricto*, Helenieae, and Eupatorieae constitute a single monobaramin. Based on a lack of evidence for discontinuity, they also speculated that tribe Senecioneae might belong to the same monobaramin. These four tribes together would comprise 40-45% of the Asteraceae (Cavanaugh and Wood 2002). Wood's (2004) re-analysis of the same dataset using MDS supports their general conclusions.

Although Cavanaugh and Wood (2002) included no endemic Galápagos taxa in their analysis, their results are nevertheless significant to the present discussion because three of the four endemic genera, *Lecocarpus*, *Macraea*, and *Scalesia*, are classified in tribe Heliantheae *s. str.* (Bremer 1994, pp. 595, 604, 611). Because of the previous baraminological analysis of Heliantheae *s. l.*, it would be reasonable to hypothesize that these three genera belong to the monobaramin identified by Cavanaugh and Wood (2002), pending confirmation by further baraminological analysis.

*Scalesia* species are shrubby or arborescent (Plate 8) and are found on most of the major Galápagos Islands, with the exception of Islas Darwin, Marchena, Genovesa, Rábida, and Española (Eliasson 1974). The majority of species are pioneer plants on recent lava flows or cinder and ash deposits (Wiggins and Porter 1971), and studies of the demography of three *Scalesia* species reveal a high mortality and turnover rate (Hamann 2001). Although *Scalesia* is considered to be the most successful species radiation of all endemic plants (McMullen 1999, p. 21), populations of several species are currently threatened by grazing feral goats (Mauchamp 1996; Mauchamp *et al.* 1998).

In considering the systematics and phylogenetic affinities of *Scalesia*, most authors concur that the genus belongs to the tribe Heliantheae and subtribe Helianthinae (Eliasson 1974; Robinson 1981; Bremer 1994). This classification is based on morphology, cytology (Eliasson 1974), and chloroplast DNA restriction sites (Schilling *et al.* 1994). The chemosystematics suggests a slightly different interpretation, since the presence of various sesquiterpenes in *Scalesia* is unique in the Helianthinae (Spring *et al.* 1997; Spring *et al.* 1999). The sister taxon of *Scalesia* has generally been considered to be *Helianthus* or *Viguiera* (Eliasson 1974; Porter 1983), but chloroplast DNA restriction data place *Scalesia* in close relationship with *Pappobolus* (Schilling *et al.* 1994). Even though it suggests a different sister group, the chloroplast DNA restriction sites still reveal a close relationship with *Viguiera*. Although Karis and Ryding (1994) omitted *Scalesia* from their cladistic analysis of the Heliantheae, they did include the closely-related *Helianthus*. Consequently, Cavanaugh and Wood's (2002) baraminological analysis of their dataset would allow us to provisionally place *Scalesia* in the same baramin as *Helianthus*.

As noted above, *Scalesia* species represent the most diverse endemic plant genus in the Galápagos Islands. Their arrival on the islands, however, remains enigmatic. We can say with some certainty that *Scalesia* is most closely-related to South American species (Porter 1983; Schilling *et al.* 1994), and thus must have arrived on the islands from the east. Although Porter (1983) claimed that the *Scalesia* ancestor probably arrived by birds, it is not clear from the present seed characteristics how this might have occurred. *Scalesia* achenes are smooth and generally lack a pappus that would allow for epizoic transport (Eliasson 1974). The possibility of endozoic transport by avian consumption of *Scalesia* achenes is possible, but this apparently does not occur today, since natural transport between islands is rare (Eliasson 1974). Lack of an obvious transport mechanisms for *Scalesia* achenes might indicate that speciation has altered this characteristic from the ancestral condition, which was presumably more amenable to dispersal.

The species of *Scalesia* are variable, and Wiggins and Porter (1971, p. 353) claimed that hybridization has been proposed to account for some of the variability. While Wiggins and Porter (1971) recognized only eleven species, Eliasson's (1974) most commonly-cited circumscription cited fourteen species. The recent description of *S. gordilloi* (Hamann and Andersen 1986) brings the number of species to fifteen, which agrees with the count in Lawesson *et al.* (1987). Not surprisingly, this multiplicity of species in an endemic genus has been called an "adaptive radiation" (e.g. McMullen 1999, p. 21), even though actual evidence of adaptation in *Scalesia* has not been forthcoming. Nielsen *et al.* (2002) argued that the presence of ray florets in

*S. affinis* is correlated with an increase in pollinator visitation frequency and number of achenes produced when compared to the rayless *S. pedunculata*. Nielsen *et al.* (2002) interpreted this correlation as an adaptive advantage, but since most *Scalesia* species lack ray florets, this trait cannot account for the entirety of the *Scalesia* radiation. Since eleven of the fifteen *Scalesia* species occur on single islands or two adjacent islands, it is tempting to conclude that founder effect and drift may have played a stronger role than selection in producing the *Scalesia* species.

Two other endemic Asteraceae genera are classified in tribe Heliantheae: *Lecocarpus* and *Macraea*. Both are shrubs, but only *Macraea laricifolia* is found throughout the archipelago (Wiggins and Porter 1971; Lawesson *et al.* 1987). According to Adsersen's (1980) description, each of the three *Lecocarpus* species are found on separate islands. *L. pinnatifidus* is found on Floreana; *L. lecocarpoides* occurs on Española, and *L. darwinii* is on San Cristóbal. The separation of species on separate islands admits allopatric speciation as an explanation for the diversity within the genus. Robinson (1981) placed *Lecocarpus* in the subtribe Melampodiinae. Researchers generally agree that the closest relatives to *Lecocarpus* are *Acanthospermum* and *Melampodium* (Wiggins and Porter 1971; Adsersen 1980; Porter 1983). Karis and Ryding's (1994) inclusion of *Melampodium* in their dataset allowed Cavanaugh and Wood (2002) to place this genus in the Heliantheae monobaramin. Consequently, I would predict that *Lecocarpus* belongs to the same monobaramin.

The affinities of the monotypic genus *Macraea* are less clear. Robinson (1981) placed *Macraea* in subtribe Ecliptinae, and Porter (1983) claimed that the genus is most similar to the tropical American genus *Wedelia*. Panero *et al.*'s (1999) chloroplast DNA restriction site phylogeny placed *Macraea* nearest the pantropical weedy genus *Sphagneticola* and placed two species of *Wedelia* at a much more distant position. As with *Scalesia* and *Lecocarpus*, Karis and Ryding (1994) excluded *Macraea* from their Heliantheae dataset, and as a result, Cavanaugh and Wood's (2002) baraminological analysis of the dataset may be applied to the question of *Macraea*'s baraminic position only by reference to closely-related taxa. Regardless of the exact affinity, I would predict that *Macraea* would belong to the Heliantheae monobaramin, because both *Eclipta* and *Wedelia* are included in Cavanaugh and Wood's (2002) description of the Heliantheae *s.l.*

monobaramin.

The remaining endemic composite genus *Darwiniothamnus* belongs to tribe Astereae. *Darwiniothamnus* is highly variable and occurs widely throughout the archipelago. Experts disagree on the precise classification of this variability. Wiggins and Porter (1971, pp. 325-327) listed one species, Porter (1983) and McMullen (1999, pp. 101-102) listed two species, and Laweson *et al.* (1987) listed three. *Darwiniothamnus* is referred to tribe Astereae, one of the larger tribes (~170 genera and almost 3000 species) of Asteraceae (Bremer 1994). Porter (1983) claimed that *Darwiniothamnus* is most closely related to *Erigeron* (see also Wiggins and Porter 1971, p. 326). Since Astereae has not been analyzed using baraminology methods, I performed a baraminic distance correlation analysis and MDS on a published dataset (Xiaoping and Bremer 1993). The dataset consists of 26 characters, the majority of which are morphological. Taxa included in the dataset are 24 Astereae genera, including *Erigeron* and the outgroup tribe Anthemideae.

After filtering for 0.95 relevance, three characters were eliminated from the baraminic distance calculations. The results of the baraminic distance correlation are shown in Figure 41, and imply that no strong discontinuity separates these taxa. Significant negative correlation is sparse, and significant positive correlation connects all taxa in the dataset. Most important to the present discussion, *Erigeron*, the close relative of *Darwiniothamnus* (Wiggins and Porter 1971; Porter 1983), shows correlation with nine other taxa in the dataset, including the outgroup Anthemideae.

I calculated three-dimensional MDS for the uncorrected baraminic distance matrix and a distance matrix corrected by addition of the largest distance (see Appendix). The largest distance in the matrix, 0.696, occurs between *Bellis* and *Gutierrezia*. Stresses for the 3D MDS of the corrected and uncorrected distance matrices were 0.218 and 0.488 respectively. Once again, the stress for the uncorrected distance matrix was substantially lower than for the corrected distance matrix, and the uncorrected distance matrix will be used for the MDS described here. The stress for the 3D MDS is quite high (0.218), and the minimal stress for the Astereae dataset is 0.070 at seven dimensions. These statistics indicate that the taxic structure of Astereae inferred from this dataset is quite complex and may be poorly represented in only three dimensions. The 3D MDS pattern is a diffuse structure with no obvious taxic groupings (Figure 42). The pattern consists of a main "cluster" of taxa and at least two distinct outlying groups. One outlier consists of the genera *Chiliotrichum* and *Hinterhubera*. *Conyza*, *Archibaccharis*, and *Psiadia* comprise the second outlying group. *Bellis*, *Chaetopappa*, and *Boltonia* form one end of the main cluster, with *Grindelia* and *Gutierrezia* at the other end. The outgroup Anthemideae is located within the main taxic cluster.

The 3D MDS pattern does not corroborate the findings of Xiaoping and Bremer (1993). Their parsimony analysis revealed 319 most parsimonious trees, the strict consensus of which shows three clear clades that they classify as subtribes. The first tribe Grangeinae, consisting of the single genus *Grangea*, is basal to

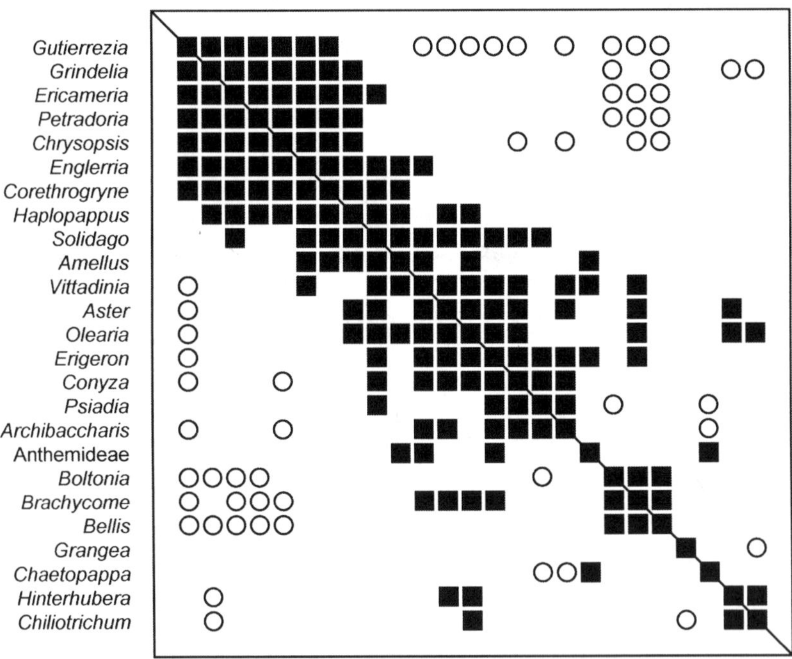


Figure 41. Baraminic distance correlation for the Astereae dataset of Zhang and Bremer (1993). Taxa with significant ($p<0.05$) positive correlation are indicated as filled squares. Taxa with significant ($p<0.05$) negative correlation are indicated as open circles.

the remaining Astereae taxa. In the 3D MDS results, *Grangea* is neither particularly distinct from the main cluster of taxa nor closely allied to the outgroup Anthemideae. The remaining two subtribes (Solidagininae and Asterinae), while separated in the 3D MDS pattern, do not form distinct taxic clusters.

The peculiar baraminic distance correlation results reveal a mixture of positive and negative correlation throughout the pairs of Astereae sampled. The pairs of taxa with significant positive correlation outnumber those with significant negative correlation nearly three to one (78 vs. 27 respectively). Except for the frequent negative correlation, the positive correlation could be interpreted as continuity throughout the group. As we have repeatedly seen in baraminic distance studies, though, significant negative baraminic distance correlation can occur in two different cases. Negative correlation can indicate the presence of two significantly different

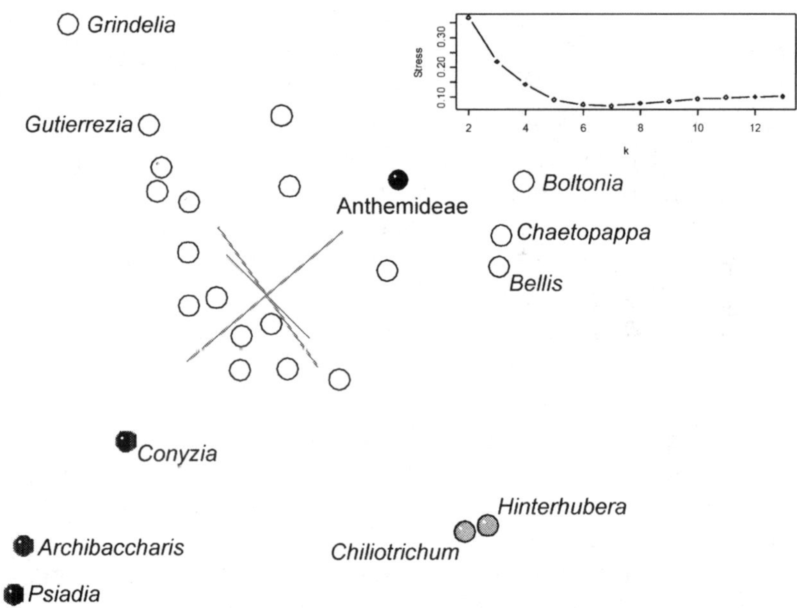


Figure 42. Three-dimensional classical MDS applied to uncorrected Astereae baraminic distances and the stress of *k*-dimensional classical scaling on the same baraminic distance matrix plotted as a function of the number of dimensions (*k*). The outgroup tribe Anthemideae is indicated in black, and the two outlying groups are also indicated (grey and striped).

groups (e.g. Robinson and Cavanaugh 1998b; Wood 2002b) or may simply reveal an underlying complexity of the geometric distribution of taxa in biological character space (Cavanaugh *et al.* 2003; this monograph). In this case, the complexity of the character space geometry is revealed by the relatively high 3D MDS stress and the minimal stress occurring at seven dimensions. The 3D MDS does not reveal the existence of two obvious groups, and the outgroup taxon Anthemideae occurs within the cluster of Astereae taxa. Considering all the available evidence, I conclude that the negative baraminic distance correlation is the result of a peculiar geometry of the taxa in character space and that there is no evidence of discontinuity between the taxa in the dataset.

Based on these results, I would predict that all Astereae species belong to a single monobaramin, and that this monobaramin is not discontinuous with the Asteraceae tribe Anthemideae. To summarize Asteraceae baraminology (Figure 43), Wood and Cavanaugh (2001) concluded that subtribe Flaveriinae constituted a monobaramin but was not discontinuous with other closely-related subtribes. Cavanaugh and Wood (2002) expanded this monobaramin to include tribes Heliantheae *s. str.*, Helenieae, and Eupatorieae, and they did not find evidence of discontinuity between these tribes and Senecioneae. Wood (2004) confirmed these results using MDS. Cavanaugh and Wood (2002) also argued for discontinuity surrounding the Asteraceae, but the evidence for such discontinuity is not statistical. In the present study, I find another Asteraceae monobaramin, Astereae, which is not discontinuous with the tribe Anthemideae. Thus the hypothesized apobaramin Asteraceae (Cavanaugh and Wood 2002) contains at least two monobaramins, Astereae and Heliantheae *s.l.* + Eupatorieae.

As noted above, the Asteraceae genera endemic to the Galápagos probably belong to the two Asteraceae monobaramins described here (Astereae) and by Cavanaugh and Wood (2002) (Heliantheae *s.l.* + Eupatorieae). Even though I refer three of the endemic genera to one Asteraceae monobaramin (Heliantheae) and one endemic genus to another Asteraceae monobaramin (Astereae), it is important not to assume that all of these taxa derived from only one ancestor that arrived on the archipelago. The close affinities between the endemic Galápagos genera and genera that occur outside of the islands imply that each endemic genus probably had a separate dispersal to the islands and a separate diversification history.

**4.9.3. Cactaceae.** Cacti are familiar desert succulents mostly native to the western hemisphere. Leaves of cacti are much reduced compared to other plants, and the stems are the primary photosynthetic organs. Most cacti photosynthesize using the Crassulacean Acid Metabolism (CAM) pathway, although substantial photosynthetic variation occurs in many cactus taxa. As with $C_4$ photosynthesis (see below), intermediates between $C_3$ and CAM plants exist (Monson 1989). The cactus family consists of less than 2000 species in 75-90 genera (Wiggins and Porter 1971, p. 535). Apart from brief comments by Klotz (1972) and Harris (1976) and an essay by Howe and Austin (2002) on the saguaro, no creationist researchers have ever examined the cacti from a baraminological or even general creationist perspective.

Howe and Austin (2002) speculated that the presence of spines in the cacti originated as part of the curse of thorns and thistles (Gen. 3:18). Botanically speaking the connection between cactus spines and "thorns and thistles" is tenuous, since the context of the curse is clearly agricultural and since spines are technically neither thorns nor thistles. Nevertheless, creationists have traditionally attributed deleterious or undesirable biological

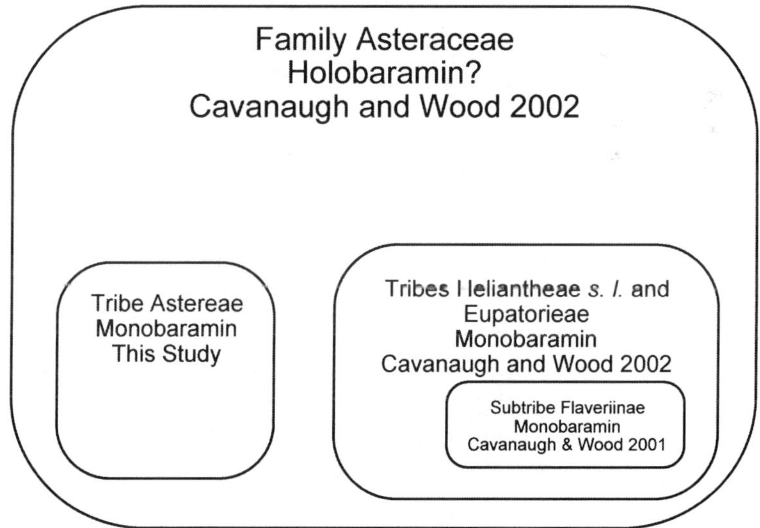


Figure 43. Schematic diagram illustrating previous and present baraminic hypotheses for the composite family Asteraceae.

phenomena to the Curse (e.g. Wood 2001), so it is unsurprising that cactus spines would be so attributed. However, we must be careful not to blame the Curse for any and every aspect of creation that we find personally distasteful or undesirable. Cactus spines illustrate this concept very well. Since spines are found on all species of Cactaceae, we have no evidence of variation which might suggest a spineless ancestor. Attributing cactus spines to the Curse therefore relies only on a personal decision on whether spines are harmful. Before any firm conclusions can be drawn, more work is needed to develop criteria for distinguishing created conditions from those resulting from the Curse and to understand the historical development of spines within Cactaceae.

Foundational to future creationist work in the Cactaceae is a good baraminological analysis of the family. By identifying the cactus baramin(s), we can begin to understand the cactus's natural variability and what changes may have occurred during their history. Because I was unable to locate a suitable morphological dataset for baraminological analysis, I will limit my comments to a brief presentation of current thinking on the phylogeny of the Cactaceae. The cactus family is widely regarded as monophyletic, and this has been confirmed in molecular analyses (e.g. Nyffeler 2002). Cactaceae is a member of the portulacaceous "cohort" (Applequist and Wallace 2001) or "alliance" (Hershkovitz and Zimmer 2000), a clade of four families (Cactaceae, Portulacaceae, Basellaceae, and Didiereaceae) in the order Caryophylales. Molecular analyses of the portulacaceous cohort and the Caryophylales has shown that the Cactaceae clade is nested in a paraphyletic Portulacaceae (Applequist and Wallace 2001), closely allied with the genera *Portulaca* and *Talinum* (Applequist and Wallace 2001; Cuénoud *et al.* 2002). Within the cactus clade, the genus *Pereskia* forms a basal grade in the analysis of Nyffeler (2002). The remaining cactus subfamilies (Cactoideae and Opuntioideae) form distinct clades, but the high degree of similarity between the taxa suggests a recent origin of cactus diversity (Nyffeler 2002).

Although monophyly is not a criterion for membership in a monobaramin (*sensu* Wood *et al.* 2003), a monophyletic group can be a starting point for baraminological analysis. Beginning then with the monophyletic Cactaceae, we can ask whether evidence of discontinuity separates the family from other plants. The possibility of paraphyly with Portulacaceae warrants further investigation for evidence of discontinuity between cacti and *Portulaca* and *Talinum*. Within the cactus family, the cactus subfamilies should be examined for evidence of continuity, and potential discontinuity between the subfamilies should also be tested. For the purposes of this monograph, I will proceed with the assumption that the genus *Opuntia* (possibly with *Pereskiopsis* which may be paraphyletic with the *Opuntia* species, see Nyffeler 2002) forms a monobaramin.

The indigenous Galápagos cacti are entirely endemic and are classified into three genera: the endemic and monotypic genera *Jasminocereus* and *Brachycereus*, and the non-endemic and widely-ranging *Opuntia* (prickly pear). *Brachycereus nesioticus* is a short, barrel-shaped cactus that forms large colonies on lava flows (Wiggins and Porter 1971, p. 534; McMullen 1999, p. 321). *Jasminocereus thouarsii* is an arborescent, "candelabra" cactus common to the Arid Zone (Wiggins and Porter 1971, pp. 535-537). Howell (1933) classified both of these endemic genera in the genus *Cereus*, but Dawson (1966) claimed that *Jasminocereus* and *Brachycereus* are most similar to the Ecuadorean species *Monvillea maritima* and *Armatocereus cartwrightianus*, respectively, rather than to any members of *Cereus*. Any of these claims of close affinity could serve as the basis for future baraminological analyses.

Species of the genus *Opuntia* occur in two basic forms: arborescent and prostrate (Figure 44). Predominantly arborescent forms are *O. insularis*, *O. saxicola*, four varieties of *O. echios*, three varieties of *O. megasperma*, and one variety of *O. galapageia*. The shrubby, low-growing forms are *O. echios* var. *zacana*, *O. galapageia* var. *profusa*, and *O. helleri* (Wiggins and Porter 1971, pp. 539-546). The origin of the arborescent *Opuntia* species has been a subject of speculation and disagreement. The most common explanation involves natural selection by grazing tortoises. The alternative theory cites competition with trees for sunlight.

Dawson (1964, 1966) first invoked tortoise grazing as an explanation for the evolution of arborescent *Opuntia* in the Galápagos. According to this theory, arborescent *Opuntia* evolved as a defense against grazing tortoises. Presumably, on islands with heavy tortoise grazing, the development of an arborescent form would move the fleshy pads of the *Opuntia* out of the hungry tortoises' reach. In support of this theory,

Dawson (1964) notes that the sprawling *Opuntia* species occur on islands that apparently never had tortoise populations (Wolf, Darwin, Genovesa, Marchena, and Seymour). Islands that have (or had) tortoise populations possess primarily arborescent forms; although as we noted in the tortoise section, this correlation is not statistically significant. Both Harris (1976, pp. 88-89) and Klotz (1972) presented this theory favorably in their writings on Galápagos, although Harris (1976, p. 86) mistakenly claimed that arborescent forms of *Opuntia* occur exclusively on Galápagos. As we have already seen in the tortoise section, correlation between the occurrence of saddleback tortoise populations and arborescent prickly pears is statistically insignificant.

In 1973, Arp proposed a substantially different explanation for the distribution of arborescent *Opuntia* species. He argued that competition with surrounding trees for sunlight is the major factor in the evolution of the arborescent *Opuntia* species (Arp 1973). Arp gave three reasons to support his idea. First, if tortoise grazing were the primary factor in the evolution of *Opuntia*

Figure 44. Galápagos *Opuntia* species of arborescent (*O. echios*, I. Santa Cruz, left) and shrubby (*O. saxicola*, I. Isabela, right) forms. Photos courtesy Roger Sanders.

height, we should expect the cacti to grow just beyond the reach of the tortoises and then stop. In reality, several of the arborescent forms can grow more than ten meters tall (Howell 1933; Wiggins and Porter 1971). Second, he believed that the height of the arborescent *Opuntia* species was positively correlated with the height of surrounding trees, an observation that has since been corroborated by more careful studies (Nobel 1981; Hicks and Mauchamp 2000). Third, he noted that arborescent forms of *Opuntia* are not limited to the Galápagos. By his count, 97 of the 250 *Opuntia* species are arborescent. What of the low-growing, prostrate forms on tortoise-less islands? These islands are also very windy, providing a selective advantage for growing along the ground.

What then is the origin of the endemic *Opuntia* species in the Galápagos? This question is difficult to answer since we lack important information about Galápagos prickly pears. For example, are the Galápagos *Opuntia* species monophyletic? If so, is their common ancestor younger or older than the projected age of the extant archipelago? These questions would significantly impact our understanding of the origin and potential adaptive significance of the Galápagos *Opuntia* species. Nevertheless, the occurrence of arborescent *Opuntia* species outside of the Galápagos warrants discussion, because it suggests an origin of the form by mediated design (Wood 2003a). Wood (2002a) previously proposed that diversification might have happened so quickly that form actually preceded function. In other words, the various possible forms that a baramin can adopt are "programmed" into their created progenitors (Wood 2003a). At later points in time, apparently new forms emerge within a baramin, simply as an outworking of their created potential. In this view, function is important to the *maintenance* of form but does not participate in the *origin* of form. In support of this perspective, Wood and Cavanaugh (2001) cited the occurrence of $C_4$ photosynthesis in the genus *Flaveria*.

With respect to *Opuntia* then, I would propose that tortoise grazing, adjacent trees, and wind velocity could contribute to the maintenance of prostrate and arborescent forms, but the observation of non-Galápagos arborescent *Opuntia* species supports my claim that such forms are not primarily caused by their function or adaptive significance. Indeed, the occurrence of sprawling and arborescent varieties within the same species (*O.*

*echios* and *O. galapageia*) further demonstrate the flexibility of members of this baramin in changing their growth habit. Future baraminological research in the Cactaceae should illuminate these questions further.

**4.9.4. Molluginaceae.** In numerous plant species, the common $C_3$ photosynthetis is modified to a $C_4$ pathway, wherein $CO_2$ fixation and the Calvin-Benson cycle are spatially separated in the leaf. $CO_2$ fixation occurs in the mesophyll cells of the leaf, yielding one of several $C_4$ acids depending on the particular type of $C_4$ photosynthesis. These acids are then transported to the Bundle Sheath Cells (BSCs) surrounding the veins of the leaf, where the acids are metabolized and the $CO_2$ enters the Calvin-Benson cycle (for a more complete treatment of $C_4$ photosynthesis, see Edwards and Walker 1983; Sage and Monson 1999). Specific advantages of $C_4$ photosynthesis involve the reduction of photorespiration (Monson *et al.* 1984), rendering $C_4$ photosynthesis advantageous in hot, arid climates such as the Galápagos Islands (Ehleringer *et al.* 1997). $C_4$ photosynthesis occurs sporadically in isolated species of numerous plant families. In an early creationist commentary on $C_4$ photosynthesis, Murphy and Howe (1975) ask a very important question: "how probable is it that 100 plant genera from over 10 different families would undergo these complex evolutionary changes independently?"

Answering Murphy and Howe's question became slightly more complicated in 1974, when Kennedy and Laetsch (1974) reported the first evidence of a plant (*Mollugo verticillata*) with characteristics intermediate between $C_3$ and $C_4$ photosynthesis. Subsequent research revealed numerous examples of plants possessing a photosynthesis pathway intermediate between $C_3$ and $C_4$ (hereafter referred to as "$C_3$-$C_4$ intermediate plants") (Monson *et al.* 1984; Monson 1989; Monson and Moore 1989). Wood and Cavanaugh (2001) were the first to analyze $C_3$-$C_4$ intermediate plants of the genus *Flaveria* (Asteraceae) within a creationist context. They argued that all species of *Flaveria* were derived from a single ancestral stock that was most likely $C_3$. Based on the presence of $C_4$ genes in $C_3$ species (Lipka *et al.* 1994), they concluded that God created the ancestors of the modern baramin with the genetic potential for $C_4$ photosynthesis, to be expressed at a later date. Wood (2003a) recently used the term "mediated design" to refer to the creation of a genetic potential for a complex trait that is later revealed in a phylogenetically convergent manner. Mediated design resolves Murphy and Howe's (1975) question of how a complex biochemical pathway could appear in many different plant families by attributing its ultimate origin to God and its historical origin to mechanisms of intrabaraminic diversification.

*Mollugo* species provide an opportunity to refine our understanding of the mechanism of mediated design. In addition to the $C_3$-$C_4$ intermediate plant *M. verticillata* (Kennedy and Laetsch 1974; Sayre and Kennedy 1977), *M. pentaphylla* and *M. lotoides* exhibit morphological traits of $C_4$ plants, and *M. nudicaulis* has a photorespiration rate intermediate between $C_3$ and $C_4$ plants (Kennedy *et al.* 1980). The Galápagos Islands are home to five of the twenty *Mollugo* species, four of which are endemic (Wiggins and Porter 1971, p. 217-218). Like the species of *Flaveria*, the Galápagos *Mollugo* species exhibit a range of growth habits. Of the four subspecies of *M. flavescens*, three are annual and one is perennial. Of the three subspecies of *M. floriana*, one is annual and two are perennial. The remaining endemics, *M. crockeri* and *M. snodgrassii*, are both perennial.

Stebbins (1966) recommended further study of the endemic *Mollugo* species to determine whether the annual forms were primitive or derived in the genus. I agree with Stebbins's recommendation, with the added proposal that the Galápagos *Mollugo* endemics also be examined for traits of $C_3$-$C_4$ intermediate photosynthesis. To my knowledge, of the five *Mollugo* species found in the Galápagos, only the pantropical *M. cerviana* (an annual species) has been evaluated in this fashion and found to be thoroughly $C_4$ (Kennedy *et al.* 1980). In *Flaveria*, the presence of $C_4$ photosynthesis is strongly correlated with an annual, herbaceous habit, and woody $C_4$ plants are recognized to be unusual (Kennedy *et al.* 1980). Since the growth habit of the Galápagos *Mollugo* endemics varies, it may be that they vary in photosynthesis type as well, possibly within a single species.

Especially intriguing in this regard is *M. nudicaulis*. Leaves of *M. nudicaulis* progress from $C_3$ to $C_4$ as they age (Raghavendra *et al.* 1978). This photosynthetic variation in a single plant, correlated to the age of the leaf, implies that the $C_4$ phenotype is controlled by more than just Mendelian genetics. In considering the causes of intrabaraminic diversification, creationists have often relied heavily on the neodarwinian mechanism of allele sorting via natural selection (e.g. Marsh 1947; Wieland 1991). The tight control of the $C_4$ trait in *M. nudicaulis* would be strong evidence against a simple sorting of allelic information. The concept of mediated design, with its emphasis on unexpressed genetic potential, would be more consistent with the photosynthetic variety seen in *Mollugo*.

## 4.10. Biogeography

**4.10.1. Introduction.** The importance of Galápagos to the formation of evolutionary biogeography has already been explored in Chapter 2, but here I will develop that theme further. When Darwin visited the islands, species stasis still dominated biological thinking. A dominant model in British science at the time was natural theology, the belief that God created organisms in a state of perfect adaptation to their environments. Thus, geographic ranges were explained by appeal to "centers of creation," hypothetical areas into which God created species and from which they spread (unchanged) to their modern ranges. As I noted in Chapter 2, Darwin's observation of the similarity of species from different Galápagos islands, particularly the mockingbirds, precipitated an intellectual crisis. If the mockingbirds were merely variants of the same species, then the "centers of creation" would be preserved: God created a single species which spread throughout the archipelago. Because the mockingbirds were judged to be different species, Darwin wondered why they came to occupy adjacent islands. In other words, why would there be a relationship between species similarity and geographic proximity? These observations led Darwin to accept the notion of species transmutation. Believing that the mockingbird species originated from a single species, the descendants of which dispersed throughout the islands, was a simpler hypothesis than believing that God created very similar species in adjacent habitats for unknown or perhaps arbitrary reasons.

In contrast to natural theologians of Darwin's younger days, today's creationists affirm a single creation event and a single global catastrophe with recolonization of the earth by land animals from Ararat. The young-earth creationist framework precludes re-creation of species, "centers of creation" for modern organisms, and even species stasis. Thus, the species of the Galápagos were not created in the islands nor in any nearby center of creation. Instead, the Galápagos were certainly devoid of life immediately after the Flood (Gen. 7:21-23), whether the islands formed during or after the Flood. The ancestors of Galápagos plants probably sprouted from propagules that formed large vegetation mats during and after the Flood. The land animals must have sprung from ancestral stock that survived the Flood on the Ark, explaining their affinities with South and Central American species. In modern creationism, the question of how animals colonized the islands remains an important issue to be addressed.

Some researchers (e.g. Baur 1891a, 1891b, 1897; Hemsley 1895; Van Dyke 1953) have suggested that the Galápagos Islands are continental islands, once connected to mainland South America by a land bridge, an idea embraced even by some creationists (Brown 1995, p. 93). Sunken land masses were popular devices in the nineteenth century to explain disjointed distributions of plants and animals (Fichman 1977). Although land bridges could certainly resolve the question of how land animals dispersed to islands, such obviously *ad hoc* devices are generally deprecated in science, except in cases where external evidence (such as geology) would warrant their acceptance. In general, there is a lack of geological evidence to support the existence of sunken continents and in particular any land connection between South America and the Galápagos (Williams 1966). In addition, the disharmonic composition of organisms on the islands argues that they were always oceanic islands. Had there been a land connection, there would be a distribution of organisms more similar to that of the mainland (Stebbins 1966; Porter 1983).

As true oceanic islands, the Galápagos could be colonized by three basic ways: wind, other organisms, or rafting. Wind dispersal would be most common among the plants and birds. Indeed, high winds are often invoked to explain the original arrival of bird ancestors in the Galápagos (e.g. Thornton 1971, p. 202; Abbott and Abbott 1978). Dispersal by other organisms would primarily include accidental introductions by sea birds; although in historical times, intentional introductions by man have had a large affect on the native environment. Dispersal by rafting would be the major source of land animals in the Galápagos.

**4.10.2. Dispersal by Wind, Ocean, and Other Organisms.** Porter listed 543 indigenous vascular plant taxa (species, subspecies, and varieties), of which 231 (43%) are endemic (Porter 1983). Porter attributed nearly a third of these endemics (32%) to introduction by wind. He attributed 59% to introduction by birds, and only 8% to oceanic drift. Clearly, one cannot know for certain how a particular species arrived in the Galápagos, but attributions to particular mechanisms can be made based on the characteristics of seeds or spores. For examples, it would be reasonable to assume that plant species with seeds adapted to wind dispersal, such as most composites, probably arrived by wind. Spores, too, are well known for dispersal by wind. In this regard, it is interesting to note that the fraction of pteridophyte endemics is only 7.5% of the total indigenous pteridophyte taxa. Endemic dicots comprise 58.4% of indigenous dicot taxa (Porter 1983). The paucity of pteridophyte endemics has been noted in earlier surveys of Galápagos plants (Svenson 1938). More recent species counts yield similar ratios of endemic flowering plants (see Lawesson *et al.* 1987; McMullen 1999, pp. 20-23).

Ocean dispersal seems to be extremely infrequent in the Galápagos flora. Certainly the plants of the Littoral Zone, such as the numerous mangroves (Wiggins and Porter 1971, p. 17), would be an exception to the rule. Littoral plants normally thrive in salty or brackish water and disperse on ocean currents (Porter 1983). A few other plants could have arrived in the Galápagos by oceanic dispersal of seeds. Studies conducted by Stephens (1958, 1966) indicated that cotton seeds can survive up to two months submerged in salt water. Based on these results, he proposed that the Galápagos cotton *G. barbadense* arrived from mainland Ecuador by floating on ocean currents. The seeds of the other Galápagos cotton species *G. klotzschianum* could survive submersion in salt water, but they cannot float (Stephens and Rick 1966). Since *G. klotzschianum* is also found in Mexico, Stephens and Rick (1966) proposed that the present populations are relicts of a previously widespread species, although that idea does not explain how *G. klotzschianum* got to the Galápagos in the first place.

One case of proposed oceanic dispersal warrants special note: the tortoises. Caccone *et al.* (2002) attributed the tortoises' arrival in the Galápagos to the surprising ability of the tortoises to float (but not swim) with their heads above the water. Van Denburgh (cited in Thornton 1971, p. 127) recounted two tortoises that were captured during the 1906 California Academy expedition. While they were being loaded on a skiff for transport off the island, the tortoises were lost to the ocean after the skiff was destroyed in the surf. Much to the surprise of Van Denburgh the tortoises were discovered the next day bobbing in the ocean. This story has been repeated (e.g. Thornton 1971, p. 127; Larson 2001, pp. 135-136), often as anecdotal evidence that tortoises could survive floating in the ocean from the South American mainland.

Although wind and birds can account for the introduction of most indigenous plant species, the establishment of these species as a viable breeding population requires further considerations. For example, if the Galápagos are indeed oceanic islands, we would expect a majority of indigenous taxa to be monoecious and self-compatible (Baker 1955). McMullen's (1987) sampling of Galápagos angiosperms revealed 40 of 52 (76.9%) were self-compatible. Even in dioecious species, the rare occurrence of monoecious individuals, called "leaky dioecism," would aid in the establishment of the occasional dioecious species in the Galápagos, as seems to be the case with *Croton scouleri* (Mauchamp 1997).

It is important to note at this point that many of the species of Galápagos plants retain the traits that apparently led to their arrival. In contrast, flora of other oceanic islands, like Hawaii, have a much higher fraction of dioecious species (see Mauchamp 1997). This seems to indicate that Galápagos plants have not undergone significant diversification, despite the high fraction of endemic species. Supporting this view would be the presence of only seven endemic flowering plant genera (McMullen 1999, p. 20). Because the origin of the present Galápagos Islands probably took place near the end of the post-Flood diversification period, I would expect that the degree of diversification in Galápagos species to be small, despite obviously frequent speciation.

**4.10.3. Dispersal by Rafting.** Transport of land organisms on vegetation mats is a commonly-mentioned mechanism for the introduction of Galápagos fauna (e.g. Smith 1966; Orr 1966). Within the conventional model of the origin of the Galápagos, rafting can explain some of the biogeographical data only if long periods of time are assumed. Given the 3-5 million year age for the present archipelago, the expectation that a random rafting event would occasionally deliver terrestrial organisms to the Galápagos probably approaches certainty. Indeed, as Orr (1966) noted, large vegetation mats may still be seen floating through the Gulf of Guayaquil after heavy rains. Within the creation model, however, vast time periods for stochastic rafting events are not available. Instead, Wise and Croxton (2003) argued that debris mats from the Flood probably provided the means by which organisms (particularly land animals) reached remote islands. Wise and Croxton's biogeography model makes several specific predictions about the distribution of terrestrial organisms that are of special interest to considerations of the Galápagos.

Perhaps the most important of these predictions is that rafting success will decrease exponentially throughout the post-Flood period (Wise and Croxton 2003). As the logs and vegetation that compose the debris mats became waterlogged, parts of mats would sink, and the mats themselves would have become destabilized. In the floating log mat at Spirit Lake, Austin (1991) notes that different species of logs sink at different rates, presumably according to their density, sap content, and brittleness. As a result, debris mats acting as rafts immediately after the Flood would likely have been capable of carrying much larger creatures for much longer distances. In the decades and centuries that immediately followed the Flood, more and more logs would sink and the unstable rafts could only carry organisms that were more naturally raftable.

Another possible prediction of the model not discussed by Wise and Croxton is the affect of raft destabilization on the size of rafting organisms. As discussed previously in this Section, insular body size trends are apparent in the Galápagos, where the world's largest extant tortoises are found. It is possible that destabilizing rafts would be less likely to support very large animals, and very small animals would be more likely to be washed into the ocean. Thus, we might expect a tendency towards a "central size" in organisms rafting as the debris mats degrade. Species from baramins that normally have a large body size could only raft if they were uncharacteristically small, and vice versa. Some insular body size trends that would be consistent with this hypothesis include the tendency for dwarfism in artiodactyls and elephants and the tendency for gigantism in rodents, tortoises, and iguanas (Case 1978; Agenbroad 2001; Roth 2001). Dwarfism in lagomorphs and gigantism in bears (Case 1978) would seem to be exceptions to this hypothesis. Although a systematic evaluation of this hypothesis is beyond the scope of this present monograph, gigantism in the Galápagos Tortoise seems to be consistent with the hypothesis.

Considering the evidence at hand in the light of Wise and Croxton's (2003) rafting hypothesis, it seems likely that any rafts composed of Flood debris that might have reached the Galápagos would have been exceedingly unstable. Also, since Orr (1966) noted vegetation mats formed during modern rainstorms, I would expect a higher frequency of such smaller mats, since the total annual rainfall was probably much higher immediately after the Flood than it is now (Vardiman 1998). Considering Galápagos Tortoises' natural ability to float with their heads above water, they seem like a good candidate for rafting on post-Flood debris mats, formed either from Flood debris or vegetation associated with the extreme post-Flood rainfall. Even if they fell from an unstable mat into the water, they would probably not drown but continue their journey floating directly in the ocean.

**4.10.4. Rates.** An argument for increased organismal migration rates to the Galápagos immediately after their emergence as islands can be constructed in two different ways. First, the animal migration rate immediately after the Flood must have been much higher than now, due possibly to Wise and Croxton's (2003) hypothesized Flood debris mats. As I mentioned above, given modern rates of accidental rafting, it is reasonable that an archipelago like the Galápagos could build up its present biodiversity in millions of years. Since millions of years are not available in the creation model, the only way to account for island biodiversity in general is to infer a much higher migration rate in the past. This reasoning also applies to continents not directly connected by land to the Ararat region. Since these isolated lands have a high amount of land animal diversity, and since high rates of migration to isolated lands are not observed today, I infer that the migration rate in the past must have been much higher than today. Wise and Croxton (2003) attempted to explain this high migration rate by a mechanism (debris mats) that we know almost certainly existed in and after the Flood. Thus, for islands in general, migration rates must have been higher in the past than they are today.

The second line of evidence I would use to argue for higher past migration rates is the presence of land animals on most of the islands in the Galápagos. Although Galápagos Tortoises generally avoid the coastal regions (Merlen 1985), they are nevertheless found on most of the major islands in the archipelago, indicating past rafting activity, which presumably would necessitate a visit to the coast. The Galápagos hawk, despite being sedentary today and not known to recolonize islands from which it was eradicated (DeVries 1975; Ferguson-Lees and Christie 2001, p. 667), is also found on multiple islands and thus must have moved between them in the past. This argument could be repeated for many different land animal groups that today are not known to move between islands yet are still native to more than one island in the archipelago (e.g. Heise 1998). Since the modern sedentary species are found on more than one island yet are not known to move between islands, we can infer a higher rate of interisland movement within the Galápagos archipelago in the past.

This past higher rate of interisland movement could be caused by any of several factors. It could be related to the diversification of the Galápagos species and the loss of a migratory instinct. It could be related to environmental stresses associated with the post-Flood ice advance that could have induced organismal movement, as in Harper's (1980; 1985) irruption hypothesis. It could also be explained if the present islands are actually relicts of a previously-existing super-island that linked by land all the present islands of the Galápagos. The last hypothesis is generally not favored, since even at the low sea level of the glacial maximum, most of the major Galápagos Islands (with the exception of Isabela and Fernandina) remain separate islands (Geist 1996).

From these two different arguments (a general high rate of post-Flood animal migration and a previously high rate of interisland movement within the Galápagos), I infer a very similar conclusion: the migration rates of land animals were higher during the first few centuries after the Flood than they are today. Wise and Croxton (2003) offered one potential explanation for these high rates that is corroborated by independent evidence, including the log mat of Spirit Lake and the observation of vegetation mats in the Gulf of Guayaquil after heavy rains. To this physical hypothesis, I would add biological factors that could also contribute to animal migration, which diversification may have eliminated or masked in current populations.

**4.10.5. Sources.** Since the Humboldt Current flows north along the coast of South America and then turns west to flow past the Galápagos as the South Equatorial Current (see Figure 5), it is tempting to attribute all organisms to a South American source. Such is not the case in several important instances where detailed studies have been conducted. For example, the Tholospiza finches, of which Darwin's finches are members, center geographically on the Caribbean (Burns *et al.* 2002). Porter's (1983) review of the vascular plants of the Galápagos revealed seven pteridophyte species, four monocot species, and nine dicot species that probably originated in the Caribbean or Central America.

Although there is a minor current that occasionally flows from Central America to the Galápagos (Wooster and Hedgpeth 1966), I would argue that the migration of the iguanas and finches might warrant a different explanation. The modern current that runs from the Gulf of Panama to the Galápagos flows only from January to April, the Galápagos rainy season. The origin of the finch and iguana species, however, date to conventional periods (3 and 7 million radiometric years respectively) that coincide with or predate the emergence of the Panama Isthmus. Absence of the isthmus would alter the regional currents and would connect the waters of the Caribbean directly to the eastern Pacific. Consequently, I would argue that the altered currents (and wind patterns) before and during the emergence of the Panama Isthmus contributed to the migration of species on rafts to the Galápagos. Thus, the presence of Caribbean/Central American species in the Galápagos warrants research into alternative currents that would have existed prior to the formation of the Panama Isthmus.

# 5. Conclusions and Future Prospects

**5.1. Introduction.** After the publication of *Darwin's Finches*, David Lack converted to Christianity in 1948 (Lack 1973). According to Larson (2001, pp. 218-219), Lack's sincere devotion to the faith mystified his secular colleagues. Lack explained his views on science and faith in his 1957 book *Evolutionary Theory & Christian Belief* (Figure 45). Reminiscent of Gould's (1999) "non-overlapping magisteria" (NOMA), Lack insisted that science and faith operated in entirely separate realms and that the claims of one could have no validity in the realm of the other. Lack chided those who criticize or re-interpret evolution using Christian doctrines, and he rebuked biologists who make sweeping metaphysical claims that are obviously outside of the realm of observable science. Despite his insistence on non-interference, Lack still maintained that certain features of nature could not be explained without God. "The Christian must accept the findings of science," Lack (1961, p. 109) wrote, "and hence should accept man's evolution by natural selection. But natural selection is amoral, so cannot have produced man's moral or spiritual characteristics."

By now, it should hardly require mentioning that I strongly disagree with Lack's position. I find the NOMA principle practically unworkable. As even Lack (1961, p. 31) admitted, the straightforward reading of Genesis 1-3 contradicts the evolutionary view of origins. He believed that he solved this apparent dilemma by regarding "these chapters ... as allegorical" (Lack 1961, p. 113). Since this was well outside his area of expertise, Lack offered no criteria by which we may judge what is or is not allegorical in Scripture, presumably leaving the domain of science to set out the facts to which the Scripture must measure itself. My position is precisely the opposite: that Scripture sets out the facts to which science must measure itself.

The irony of Lack's belief is that my own position has proved

Figure 45. The dustjacket cover of David Lack's *Evolutionary Theory & Christian Belief.*

so fruitful in this review. If Lack is correct, "religion" should be utterly incapable of producing a tenable explanation of natural phenomena, much less a program for future research. I am certain that Lack would completely reject my work because I have not accepted the "fact of evolution," but it would be hard to argue that my approach has failed to explain particular aspects of Galápagos geology or biology or that my proposals could not be subjected to testing and even to falsification. In this section, I will review my findings and specify particular directions that creationist research on the Galápagos ought to proceed.

**5.2. Geology and Climate.** In my review of Galápagos geology, I argued for a post-Flood origin of the modern islands based on other creationists' opinions on formations that are of similar or older radiometric age. Recalibration of radiocarbon dates of biotic sediments from El Junco Lake indicates that the earliest biotic sediments from the lake formed within two centuries of the end of the Flood. The proximity of the formation of biotic sediments in El Junco Lake to the Flood event implies either a high rate of volcanic activity and erosion immediately after the Flood or a Flood origin of the island. Either would be consistent with the present evidence.

The uncertainty of the timing of the origin of the islands highlights the need for a method of constructing chronologies that integrate radiometric dates from $^{14}C$ and basalts, as well as general tectonic events. Obviously, such a chronology will require the generation of a method of recalibrating radiometric clocks used to date the islands' basalts. The chronology should also be closely integrated with computational models of Flood tectonics. The development of such a chronology will have broad implications for the interpretation of radiometric dating and the cessation of tectonic movement after the Flood, not to mention climate changes and changes associated with intrabaraminic diversification.

The uncertainty of the timing of the origin of the islands also highlights the need for a set of criteria by which Flood deposits may be distinguished from post-Flood deposits. Austin and Wise (1994) proposed five criteria for distinguishing the pre-Flood/Flood boundary, but no such criteria have been proposed for the Flood/post-Flood boundary. Flood phenomena which initiate at the same time tend to terminate at different times. Furthermore, the end of the Flood is difficult to identify even in the Bible. The rain stops after forty days (Gen. 7:12) and the waters prevail for 150 days (Gen. 7:24). Genesis 8:3,5 emphasize the continuous nature of the water recession. The Ark grounds on Ararat (indicating the uplift of those mountains) five months after the beginning of the Flood (Gen. 7:11,8:4), but Noah and company remained in the Ark for at least another seven months. Considering the sudden start of the Flood (Gen. 7:11), it is not surprising that sudden geologic changes would be correlated with it. Considering the more gradual cessation of the Flood, distinguishing Flood and post-Flood strata will be much more difficult.

The questions raised by plumes and hotspots will no doubt continue to be a source of active research in both conventional and creationist geology. Although catastrophic plate tectonics can account for plumes, specific application of CPT to plumes and hotspots has not been forthcoming. Modeling of Galápagos tectonics may help develop this aspect of creation geology. Until a CPT model of hotspots and plumes is developed, these data continue to be difficult to integrate into the young-earth creation model.

**5.3. Baraminology Methods.** As discussed in section 4.1, the development of novel statistical methods in recent years has resulted in a blossoming of baraminology research. Notwithstanding, neither the methods nor assumptions of baraminology have undergone serious testing. Very simple claims that could be tested are the ubiquity of discontinuity or the efficacy of baraminic distances in detecting discontinuity. With respect to these two claims, it is helpful to review the findings of the baraminological analyses performed as part of this study. Do they (and previously published studies) detect discontinuity and support assumptions about the pattern of life that are foundational to baraminology?

Table 5 summarizes the results of both baraminic distance correlation and MDS analyses from the present and previously published analyses, a total of eleven analyses (baraminic distance studies which omitted MDS were not included). The general taxonomic rank represented by the datasets analyzed ranges from genus/family (cormorants) and tribe (Heliantheae) to order (turtles). Of the eleven analyses, five (Poaceae, Spheniscidae, Iguanidae, turtles, and cormorants) reveal a taxonomic group defined by positive baraminic distance correlation and bounded by negative baraminic distance correlation with outgroup species. In four of these cases (Poaceae, Iguanidae, Spheniscidae, and turtles), I concluded that the pattern of baraminic distance correlation supports the identification of one or more holobaramins. In the case of the cormorants, I concluded that discontinuity within a genus is probably not present, and the 3D MDS seems to reveal an unusually regular taxic geometry that contributes to aberrant patterns of baraminic distance correlation.

Since five of eleven cases hardly makes discontinuity "ubiquitous," what of the other six analyses? Wood and Murray (2003, pp. 71-72) argued for a more specific discontinuity only

Table 5. Summary of all baraminic distance studies on which classical MDS has been performed.

| Taxon[1] | Rank | Taxa[2] | Relevance[3] | Characters[4] | Discontinuity? | 3D Stress (corrected)[5] | 3D Stress (calculated)[6] | Minimum stress[6] | Dimensions of minimum stress[6] |
|---|---|---|---|---|---|---|---|---|---|
| cormorant | genus/ family | 35 | 0.95 | 136 | no? | 0.422 | 0.110 | 0.020 | 8 |
| Astereae | tribe | 25 | 0.95 | 23 | no | 0.488 | 0.218 | 0.070 | 7 |
| *Tropidurus* | tribe | 27 | 0.95 | 66 | no | 0.461 | 0.104 | 0.048 | 6 |
| Heliantheae, *s.l.* | tribe | 98 | 0.95 | 139 | no | 0.583 | 0.367 | 0.049 | 20 |
| Sulidae | family | 10 | 0.95 | 109 | no? | 0.338 | 0.044 | 0.043 | 4 |
| Curculionidae | family | 103 | 0.95 | 106 | no? | 0.537 | 0.084 | 0.045 | 6 |
| Equidae | family | 19 | 0.95 | 33 | no | 0.418 | 0.089 | 0.035 | 5 |
| Poaceae | family | 66 | 0.95 | 32 | yes | 0.550 | 0.188 | 0.110 | 5 |
| Spheniscidae | family | 30 | 0.95 | 33 | yes | 0.396 | 0.100 | 0.045 | 5 |
| Iguanid | family/ order | 35 | 0.9 | 57 | yes | 0.506 | 0.235 | 0.080 | 8 |
| turtles (full dataset) | order | 30 | 0.9 | 93 | yes | 0.504 | 0.101 | 0.091 | 8 |

Notes

1. Baraminic distance and multidimensional scaling calculations for Heliantheae, Equidae, and Poaceae are described by Cavanaugh and Wood (2002), Cavanaugh *et al.* (2003), and Wood (2002b, 2004). 2. The number of taxa used for baraminic distance calculation. May differ from the number of taxa in the original dataset. 3. Relevance cutoff used for baraminic distance calculation. 4. Number of characters used for baraminic distance calculation after filtering by relevance. 5. Baraminic distances corrected by addition of maximum baraminic distance in the dataset. 6. Baraminic distances not corrected by addition of maximum baraminic distance in the dataset.

surrounding holobaramins, approximately at the taxonomic rank of family. If that argument is correct, at least three additional datasets (Equidae, Curculionidae, and Sulidae) among the eleven in Table 5 ought to exhibit discontinuity. The remaining studies are below the taxonomic rank of the family, and therefore we should not expect to find discontinuity in those datasets according to Wood and Murray's prediction. Thus, for eight of the eleven studies in Table 5, the prediction of discontinuity at or around the rank of family (and continuity for subfamilial taxa) is confirmed. I tentatively conclude therefore that the prediction of common discontinuity is supported by these baraminology studies.

The failure to detect discontinuity in three family-level datasets might be explained by lack of outgroup taxa (Equidae), unusual taxic geometry (Sulidae), or selection of characters that do not vary within the family (Curculionidae). Additionally, there may simply be a problem with the character selection for all three of these datasets. I have recently been criticized for ignoring the common practice of selecting "informative" characters for analysis (Williams 2004). In response, I claim that consciously selecting characters for a certain systematic task (such as distinguishing curculionids from noncurculionids) introduces bias, and these three datasets reveal the problems with that approach. I will argue below that the taxa and character sampling of three of the eleven datasets here discussed are inadequate for purposes of discontinuity detection.

In addition to Williams's (2004) review, several creation biologists have commented on the value of different characters and criteria. Marsh (e.g. 1941, 1947) supported hybridization as the defining characteristic of a baramin, but Scherer (1998) pointed out that failure to hybridize is ambiguous evidence. Wise's (1992) discontinuity matrix was the first attempt to systematize a useful list of discontinuity criteria, but his criteria have not been carefully examined nor even generally utilized. Using baraminic distances, Robinson and Cavanaugh (1998a) attempted to evaluate the kind of characters that reveal discontinuity using a primate dataset that included humans. Wood's (2002b) analysis of the grasses also briefly commented on the utility of molecular data. Wood *et al.* (2003) merely emphasized the importance of holistic data, although they did not give a clear definition of "holistic."

The datasets of Table 5 were all derived from the literature and analyzed with no modification (aside from filtering according to relevance). Although I find little reason to accuse the authors of these datasets, I cannot escape the suspicion that characters are selected explicitly for a pre-determined systematic opinion. As I noted above, systematists load their datasets with cladistically "informative" characters that are specific to the taxonomic task at hand. The emphasis on informative characters in datasets could explain why some datasets exhibit peculiarly regular geometry in 3D MDS (e.g. the cormorants and sulids).

Various experiments could be devised to test further the proposal that character selection inordinately influences baraminic distance correlation results. For datasets with large numbers of characters, a character sampling technique such as a bootstrap or jackknife should reveal a consistent pattern of positive and negative correlation in cases where true discontinuity exists. If the negative correlation merely derives from biased character sampling, I find no reason to expect that it would *consistently* demonstrate positive and negative correlation between taxa during character sampling. Character sampling techniques (used in a very preliminary form by Robinson and Cavanaugh 1998a) could also aid in the revision of Wise's (1992) discontinuity criteria.

The recent emphasis on holism as a requirement for detection of true baraminic relationships (Wood *et al.* 2003) seems quite reasonable based on the present sample of studies (Table 5). Although one of the baraminic distance correlation studies that revealed discontinuity sampled only 32 characters (Poaceae), much larger datasets at the tribal rank (e.g. 139 characters of the Heliantheae dataset) did not reveal discontinuity. This should be expected if discontinuity separates conventional families but not tribes. It is nevertheless intriguing that two of the smallest datasets in the eleven surveyed revealed discontinuity. Clearly, an urgent need in baraminology is the exploration and clarification of character sampling.

Closely related to character sampling is the issue of taxa sampling. Wood and Murray (2003, pp. 71-72) have argued that the baramin should be located at roughly the taxonomic rank of family or order. As a result, a dataset consisting of a wide diversity of species from a single holobaramin (ingroup) with a few apobaraminic species (outgroup) should reveal clear patterns of continuity and discontinuity. Since most datasets used in cladistics consist of a well-sampled ingroup and a few outgroup species, a skeptic might argue that baraminic distance correlation will *always* find "discontinuity" (significant negative correlation) between the ingroup and outgroup taxa, regardless of the taxonomic rank. Based on the present sample of studies (Table 5), that hypothetical opinion is not supported. The technique appears to be detecting a pattern that really exists, and it usually distinguishes between mere difference and true discontinuity.

In conclusion, I would argue that the present empirical studies support the general assumption of baraminology that true discontinuity is present roughly at the taxonomic rank of family. The questions of character and taxa sampling are certainly important issues that require further study, but they do not detract from the persuasiveness of the studies surveyed (Table 5). In addition to further study on characters and taxa sampling, additional techniques could also be developed that could provide independent confirmation of baraminic hypotheses. Specifically, the molecular techniques proposed by Robinson (1997) and the morphometric techniques of García-Pozuelo-Ramos (1998, 1999, 2002) should be further developed. With multiple techniques that use different datasets (indeed different types of data), a holobaramin hypothesis could be supported in a consilient fashion.

As for the claim that the uniquely nested hierarchy poorly describes the complexity of biological affinity (Wood and Murray 2003, p. 125), my results show that this is often true. MDS revealed complex taxic patterns in the cases of the turtles, *Tropidurus*, and Astereae, all of which were calculated from datasets that were somehow difficult to analyze (*i.e.* poor bootstrap support or many most parsimonious trees). In the case of the *Tropidurus*, the MDS results explicitly denied the results of the cladistic analysis and supported the traditional classification. The iguanid MDS also supported the traditional recognition of a discrete group of iguanid taxa (which I here classified as a holobaramin), which was unresolvable by cladistics. It seems, then, that multivariate techniques can illuminate some taxonomic problems in ways that traditional tree-based cladistics cannot.

To be fair, though, several of the present MDS analyses matched very well their cladistic counterparts. The MDS of the weevil dataset matched the order of branching on the cladistic tree almost exactly. Similarly, the groups inferred from the cormorant and sulid datasets also matched clades. Thus, cladistics is not always incapable of capturing robust systematic clustering. A topic for future research is to discover the characteristics of datasets that render them amenable to cladistic analysis or to multivariate studies like ANOPA or MDS.

**5.4. Biogeography and Diversification.** A good model of Galápagos biogeography will depend on a good model of the geological and climatological history of the area, which I already discussed above. Wise and Croxton's (2003) post-Flood rafting model provides a good theoretical foundation for constructing a general theory of post-Flood island biogeography, but regional climate and currents will no doubt require modifications to Wise and Croxton's general scheme. Of special concern to young-earth creationists will be the alterations in current flow expected during the unusual climate and geography of the immediate post-Flood period.

Diversification has been described as an unusually high rate of speciation associated with the first few centuries after the Flood (Wood and Murray 2003, chap. 11). Wood and Murray (2003, pp. 176-178) listed four properties of the mechanism of diversification: design, specificity, stability, and modern inactivity. These properties contrast with the neodarwinian model of speciation, in which random genetic variations are sifted by natural selection. The source of biological novelty in the neodarwinian model, although stable, is random, non-specific, and still active in the present. Because of these considerations, Wood (2002a) argued that neodarwinian speciation is incapable of explaining intrabaraminic diversification. Intrabaraminic diversification takes place much too quickly to be explained by the slow process of natural selection of random mutations.

As ReMine has explained (1993, chap 8), if natural selection only acts on random mutations, it cannot account for speciation even in the neodarwinian model. The problem is the occurrence of deleterious mutations, some of which can be lethal, which occur at a higher rate than beneficial mutations. Given the time required to fix an allele in a population (a necessary step in the formation of a new species), deleterious mutations would wipe out a population before selection could fix any beneficial allele. This problem, originally identified by J.B.S. Haldane, is called Haldane's dilemma. Within creationist modeling, only Wood (2002a, 2003b) has proposed a possible means of circumventing the problem by positing a higher rate of beneficial mutation by genetic elements specially-designed to beneficially alter the genome.

In the Galápagos, natural selection is an extremely common term applied to the native biota. In most cases, however, the evidence for selection is ambiguous at best. As I noted in the case of the saddleback tortoises and arborescent prickly pears, what is called "natural selection" is sometimes little more than an anecdotal observation that turns out to be wrong when examined more closely. The Grants' work with the finches do reveal true examples of natural selection, but in no case can it be said that alleles were fixed in any finch population. Furthermore, the genetic origin of variation in finch bill shape and size remains unexplained.

Closely related to natural selection is the concept of "adaptive radiation," which is frequently applied to Galápagos organisms, including the finches (P.R. Grant 1999, p. 5; P.R. Grant and B.R. Grant 2002b), tortoises (Fitter et al. 2000, p. 82), and *Scalesia* (McMullen 1999, p. 21). Identifying a precise definition of the term "adaptive radiation" is difficult however. For example, Huxley (1964, p. 486) emphasized habitat diversity in a group of closely-related organisms, while Futuyma (1986, p. 368) identified adaptive radiation with cladogenesis, without reference to habitat diversity. P.R. Grant and B.R. Grant (2002b) claimed that the evolution of all living things is an adaptive radiation, thereby identifying it with macroevolution. Carroll (1988, pp 586-587) emphasizes the invasion of habitats rendered newly-available by some change, such as the adaptive radiation of the mammals after the extinction of the dinosaurs. As Losos and Miles (2002) have pointed out, the diversity in definition and usage renders the concept of adaptive radiation impractical at best.

Recognizing these problems, Carlquist (1974) devoted extensive attention to the concept of adaptive radiation in his *Island Biology*. He listed nineteen attributes of adaptive radiation, based on common usage of the phrase in the technical literature. Some of the attributes are descriptive of adaptive radiation in general, while others could be termed criteria for identifying a case of adaptive radiation. Before discussing the specific criteria, it will be helpful to analyze the concept of adaptive radiation.

As its name suggests, adaptive radiation encompasses two different phenomena, adaptation and radiation. A taxonomic radiation is an episodic increase in both diversity and disparity.

Implicit in this concept is the idea that radiation differs from "normal" evolution in the group in question and from the evolution of close relatives. Adaptation is the process by which a taxon changes to meet the demands of its environment. Put together then, an adaptive radiation is an episodic increase in diversity and environmentally-relevant disparity. Viewed as a combination of separate concepts, we can immediately see the possibility of adaptation that is not a radiation and radiation that is not adaptive. For example, two sister taxa of extreme adaptive disparity would not constitute a radiation as the diversity is too low. Similarly, twenty closely-related species in a monophyletic group with few to no adaptive differences would be a non-adaptive radiation.

With these conceptual definitions in mind, Carlquist's list of identifying criteria can be summarized by the following criteria, which resemble the criteria of Sanders *et al.* (1987).

1. The group of taxa must occupy diverse habitats.
2. Evolution of the taxa must have occurred *in situ*.
3. The group of taxa must be monophyletic.
4. The group of taxa must be many (at least greater than two).
5. Morphological or biochemical disparity of taxa must be exceptional.

The first two criteria attempt to identify signs of adaptation. My criterion #1 correlates roughly to Carlquist's attributes 1, 2, 3, 5, 8, 10, 12, and 17. These eight attributes listed by Carlquist all deal with the issue of habitat diversity and availability, which in turn imply adaptations to different environments. Obviously, if the species in question occupy the same environment or a uniform set of environments, adaptation will be more difficult to identify (as in the case of the finches; see Lack 1947).

My criterion #2 is Carlquist's attribute #6, "Autochthonous development within a given area is virtually assumed" (1974, p. 102). The motivation for this criterion is the need to identify the specific adaptational pressures that produced the extant species. Carlquist gave Darwin's finches as an example and argued that if the species had evolved on the mainland and migrated to the islands (*i.e.* if Harper's hypothesis were true), we could not consider them an adaptive radiation. Because evolution in a different environment (followed by migration) would entail different selection pressures than those observable in the present environment, it would be impossible to determine whether the radiation occurred because of adaptation to the original environments or if adaptation occurred after the radiation was complete (presumably after migration of the parent species).

The remaining three criteria attempt to identify a radiation of species. My criterion #3 updates Carlquist's attribute #7, "A particular taxonomic group is basic to the concept of adaptive radiation" (1974, p. 102). Carlquist also suggested that radiations occur at the level of subfamily or below, specifically disregarding a suggestion that the diversity of flowering plant diversity could be attributed to an adaptive radiation. Although Carlquist regarded subspecific radiations as incipient only, I choose to consider the possibility of subspecific radiation, particularly because Carlquist himself considered the possibility of subspecific adaptive radiation in Galápagos tortoises but rejected the idea for lack of evidence of adaptation.

Paleontologists use the term "adaptive radiation" in a slightly different fashion. Carroll (1988, pp 586-587) never implied that adaptive radiation occurs in only one monophyletic lineage. Instead, the emphasis is on the removal of a barrier to evolution which allows for radiation to exploit newly-available resources. This radiation could occur in many different lineages. The paleontological usage of adaptive radiation would actually represent multiple adaptive radiations to an ecologist, who pictures one radiation event in a single lineage when speaking of adaptive radiation. In my criteria, I will follow the ecological usage of the term to be consistent with the common usage in the literature of the Galápagos Islands.

My criterion #4 equates to Carlquist's attribute #4, which stated, "most examples [of adaptive radiation] feature not a pair of divergent species, but many of them" (Carlquist 1974, p. 100). Carlquist linked the multitude of species directly to the variety of habitats they occupy, suggesting that the variety of habitats available drives the evolution of new species. In my criteria, I choose to separate the question of habitat diversity (criterion #1) and number of species, in order to distinguish adaptive and non-adaptive radiations. A large number of species fulfills the conceptual description of a large diversity and also carries with it the implication of an episodic increase of diversity and disparity. If an increase in diversity continues through time, we would not necessarily expect to find a recognizable group of closely related diverse and disparate species. That the increase in diversity was episodic is implicit in our ability to recognize the resulting taxa.

In criterion #5, I have summarized Carlquist's attributes #13 and #10. Carlquist argued that adaptive radiations involve a "strikingly different, often exceptional" disparity (1974, p. 106), and he cited the morphological variation of cichlid fish in this context. In attribute #10, Carlquist noted that island adaptive radiations are often described with reference to sister taxa on the mainland, in order to determine if the variation is somehow unusual for closely related taxa. For example, the morphology and habits of various species of Darwin's finches have been compared to six different mainland families (Carlquist 1974, pp. 200-201). This criterion also parallels the definition of adaptive radiation offered by Losos and Miles (2002), which focuses on an unusually high degree of adaptive diversity in a monophyletic group.

With reference to the Galápagos organisms discussed in this monograph, we find six groups of diverse species or subspecies that could potentially be called radiations (*i.e.* each group fulfills criterion #4), whereas other groups found on the islands consist of too few species to be considered radiations. The six groups are the finches, the tortoises, the *Galapaganus* weevils, *Scalesia*, *Opuntia*, and *Tropidurus* (see Table 6). The monophyly of *Opuntia* is unknown (criterion #3), and two other groups, *Tropidurus* and *Galapaganus*, are not monophyletic when only Galápagos species are considered (criterion #3). Of the remaining three groups, the finches and tortoises are known to be monophyletic (if the Cocos Island Finch is included), and *Scalesia* is presumably monophyletic, since the genus is endemic to Galápagos.

Except for the lava lizards, the disparity of the groups (criterion #5) must be measured in qualitative terms only. Applying their own definition of adaptive radiation, Losos and Miles (2002) found that *Tropidurus* are not exceptionally disparate and dismissed them as a possible adaptive radiation. Because the disparity of the finches and tortoises is remarked upon frequently, I will count each as a disparate group. Based on the size differences among *Opuntia* and *Scalesia* species, I might conclude both are disparate. I regard the disparity of *Opuntia* much less certain than among *Scalesia*, since the disparity of the Galápagos *Opuntia* species is unlikely to be exceptional. I consider the classification of *Scalesia* species in a separate genus than their mainland relatives as weak evidence of exceptional disparity. Based on the published photographs and descriptions, I do not consider *Galapaganus* weevils to be exceptionally disparate.

Table 6. Adaptation and radiation criteria applied to six Galápagos groups.

| | | finches | tortoises | *Galapaganus* | *Scalesia* | *Opuntia* | *Tropidurus* |
|---|---|---|---|---|---|---|---|
| Adaptive | 1. Diverse habitats? | Yes | No | ? | ? | ? | ? |
| | 2. *In situ* evolution? | Yes | Yes | No? | Yes | ? | No? |
| Radiation | 3. Monophyletic? | Yes | Yes | with main-land forms | Yes | ? | with main-land forms |
| | 4. Diverse? | Yes | Yes | Yes | Yes | Yes | Yes |
| | 5. Disparate? | Yes | Yes | No | Yes? | ? | No |
| | Adaptative? | Yes | No | No | Yes? | ? | No |
| | Radiation? | Yes | Yes | Yes? | Yes | ? | Yes? |
| | Adaptive Radiation? | Yes | No | No | Yes? | ? | No |

The adaptive criteria are less certain. For criterion #1, the finches can be said to occupy diverse habitats by virtue of their food preference. As explained above, evidence of diverse habitat in tortoises is lacking, as Carlquist (1974, p. 201) noted. Additionally, evidence of adaptive significance to tortoise shell morphology is also lacking. Based on these issues, I would argue that the tortoises do not occupy diverse habitats. Diversity of habitat in the remaining four groups is unknown. As noted above, several traits of *Scalesia* have been suggested to be adaptive, including leaf margin (Eliasson 1974) and ray florets (Nielsen *et al.* 2002). The significance of these traits to the adaptation of *Scalesia* plants to their habitat is not clear, especially since many of them overlap significantly in habitats. The habitat overlap observed in *Scalesia* is similar to the overlap observed in *Robinsonia* of the Juan Fernandez Islands, which Sanders *et al.* (1987) argued is a limited example of adaptive radiation.

Evidence of *in situ* evolution (criterion #2) is strong for the finch species (Sato *et al.* 2001) and tortoises subspecies (Caccone *et al.* 2002). In the case of the finches, however, we must posit a single migration of one species to Cocos Island. Presumably *Scalesia* also evolved *in situ*, since the genus is entirely endemic. Since the monophyletic status of *Opuntia* is unknown, I cannot evaluate whether the endemic species evolved in the archipelago. The *Galapaganus* weevils and *Tropidurus* lava lizards present special problems, since the island species are not monophyletic. This raises the possibility that some of the species originated on the mainland and migrated to the archipelago. Taken as a whole, the evolution of *Galapaganus* and *Tropidurus* species in the environments they currently occupy seems doubtful, because at least some of the species have migrated.

Taken together then, most of these groups constitute true or probable radiations. Because little is known about Galápagos *Opuntia* species, I consider them to be a dubious example of radiation. The adaptation of these groups is much less certain. Only the finches exhibit both criteria of adaptation. *Scalesia* species could have originated by adaptation if it could be shown that their habitats differ in an important way. The tortoises, *Galapaganus* weevils and *Tropidurus* lava lizards each fail to meet the stated criteria for adaptation.

Considering all five criteria together (Table 6), the evidence for adaptive radiation in the finches is strong, and the *Scalesia* may also be an adaptive radiation, pending further investigation of the morphological variation and its adaptive significance. The tortoises would seem to be a strong case of non-adaptive radiation. *Tropidurus* and the weevils could also be examples of non-adaptive radiation, if the origins of each species were examined in more detail. There is too little data at present to make a judgment on the nature of the diversity of Galápagos *Opuntia* species. Thus, according to my summary of Carlquist's (1974), three groups of Galápagos organisms in this monograph represent possible non-adaptive radiations, and two represent potential cases of adaptive radiation.

What then does this mean to the creationist? First, we cannot properly claim that there is no evidence for selection and adaptive radiation in the Galápagos. There is evidence of both adaptation and radiation in the finches, and there may also be evidence in *Scalesia*. What is interesting, though, is that there appears to be evidence of non-adaptive radiations in the Galápagos. The fact that the non-adaptive radiations outnumber the adaptive radiations supports my suggestion that the phenomenon of radiation itself (*i.e.* the episodic production of diverse and disparate species) can be decoupled from adaptation. This conclusion would be consistent with Carlquist's (1974) observation that adaptive radiations are more frequent in evolutionarily plastic groups, such as insects or Compositae. If the propensity to radiation is related to an intrinsic property of the group in question and not to the environment, I would expect a non-random taxonomic distribution as Carlquist claims. In other words, the production of biological diversity is not dependent on environmental adaptation.

What is the relationship, if any, between radiation and diversification? Diversification refers to the period of rapid, intrabaraminic speciation that occurred immediately following the Flood. Diversification was followed by a period largely characterized by species stasis. Radiation is the episodic production of a diverse and disparate group of closely-related species from a common ancestor. Based on these results, I would now argue that the two concepts are directly related, in that radiation is a small-scale episode of diversification. As Wood (2002a) has argued, post-Flood diversification is not causally random but instead appears to be pre-designed (e.g. Wood and Cavanaugh 2001). Carlquist's observation of a higher frequency of adaptive radiation in evolutionarily plastic groups would confirm the idea that rapid speciation is a capability built into organisms. Thus, both radiation and diversification are a rapid production of biodiversity that appear to be pre-designed. I conclude that radiation is a small-scale form of diversification.

The lack of evidence for adaption in the majority of Galápagos species radiations discussed in this monograph adds an interesting twist to the phenomenon of diversification. Wood *et al.* (2003) argue that the potential for diversification increases a baramin's ability to survive new environments, thus preserving God's revelation in creation. While this explanation may be true, the fact that non-adaptive radiations outnumber adaptive radiations suggests that more than adaptation is at work in the generation of intrabaraminic diversity. Previously, the diversification has been interpreted as a means of preserving the revelation of God in His creations by allowing for adaptation (Wise 2002, p. 216-220; Wood *et al.* 2003). It is also possible that the diversity of baramins and of species within baramins is actually part of the revelation of God by reflecting the diversity of the Trinity.

Finally, in groups that show no evidence of radiation, what evidence is there of traditional neodarwinian speciation? The plants of Galápagos retain characteristics (*e.g.* self-compatibility and wind-dispersed seeds) that would have contributed to their dispersal to the islands, implying that they have undergone little change since their arrival. The Galápagos penguin is hardly modified from its close cousin the Humboldt penguin. The Galápagos hawk, while behaviorally different from other *Buteo* species, nevertheless retains a morphological similarity sufficient to allow Swarth (1931) to identify its closest relative correctly as the Swainson's hawk. The presence of salt glands in terrestrial iguanids implies a pre-adaptation that was exploited in *Amblyrhynchus*. Dispersal polymorphisms in weevils reveal a complex trait that is continually lost and possibly regained. The occurrence of gigantism in non-Galápagos *Geochelone* species and of arborescence in non-Galápagos *Opuntia* species support a source of variation that is non-random and capable of producing the same biological trait in multiple lineages. Finally, the variability of bill size in Tholospiza finches could be interpreted as support for a high rate of beneficial genetic or developmental change, potentially inconsistent with an origin by random mutation.

Overall, then, I conclude that the Galápagos organisms provide excellent evidence of diversification and only limited evidence of natural selection or adaptative radiation. Although there is definitely a correlation between the biology (morphology, behavior, biochemistry, etc.) of Galápagos species and the habitats and niches they occupy, evidence of natural selection as the cause of this correlation is mostly lacking. Even instances where natural selection has been directly observed (e.g. B.R. Grant 1985) do not nullify the problem of Haldane's dilemma, since there is no evidence for fixed alleles as a result of natural selection.

The strength of this conclusion is mitigated by lack of evidence, which always makes for a weak argument. For example, I conclude that diversification is supported by the paucity of observations of natural selection. It is certainly possible that natural selection could be observed in detailed studies of other Galápagos organisms, thus necessitating modification of my conclusion. In this case, however, since diversification can be supported by general evidence not associated with Galápagos (e.g. Wood 2003a), I would expect that any forthcoming data from the Galápagos would continue to support the concept of diversification. In addition, the failure of some groups to fulfill the adaptive criteria for adaptive radiation (Table 6) also suggests that these groups (e.g. *Tropidurus* and *Galapaganus* which did not diversify *in situ*) could not be examples of adaptive radiation, even if adaptation played a role in their diversification.

In addition to necessary baraminology studies of Galápagos and related organisms, future research in diversification might focus most fruitfully on the genetic origin of bill variation in Tholospiza finches and of the iguana salt gland. Bill variation would probably be most fruitful, considering the voluminous work already published on finch bills, in comparison to the sparse literature on iguana salt gland variation. Since diversification can only by-pass Haldane's dilemma by increasing the rate of beneficial or neutral genetic changes with respect to deleterious changes, I would expect that bill and salt gland variation could reveal specific, genomic mechanisms that contributed to the origin of these beneficial changes. Wood's (2002a; 2003b) altruistic genetic element (AGEing) and genomic modularity models provide a framework within which such changes may be sought. Alternatively, the actual source of variation in these instances might be something unrelated to AGEing or genomic modularity.

What of the common creationist model of degenerative

speciation from a complex ancestral gene pool (Wieland 1992, Scherer 1993b)? Wood and Murray (2003, p. 179) argued that the model is generally unlikely to account for the characteristics of diversification. In the Galápagos, degenerative speciation is usually incapable of explaining organismal diversity. The finch bill variability is greater than other emberizines. $C_4$ photosynthesis in *Mollugo* supports an origin by mediated design. The recurrence of gigantism in tortoises and arborescence in prickly pears supports a mechanism of biological change that allows the emergence of traits in multiple intrabaraminic lineages. None of these cases support biological change by degeneration. In dispersal polymorphisms of weevils, however, the evidence is somewhat ambiguous and warrants further detailed study. Even if dispersal polymorphisms do constitute an example of a degenerative change, such changes still cannot account generally for diversification. While it is possible (and perhaps even probable) that some biological changes are attributable to degeneration, the general characteristics of diversification still rule out degeneration as a significant causal factor.

**5.5. Conservation and Environmentalism.** Although this work is primarily one of science, it seems almost wrong to ignore the issue of environmental ethics, when Galápagos has become so closely identified with questions of conservation. From the long-range concerns of most Galápagos scientists (e.g. Curry-Lindahl 1981; Pritchard 1996) to the more pressing problems of the recent oil spill near San Cristóbal (Wikelski *et al.* 2002) and rioting fishermen in Puerto Ayora (Schrope 2000), environmentalism is inextricably linked to life in the Galápagos. I preface these remarks by reminding the reader that I am not an ethicist but that I believe that the baraminological perspective offers a unique position from which to inform a biblical ethic of environmental stewardship.

One self-evident feature of the environmentalist movement is its passionate, almost religious, fervor to protect living things. Sometimes this zeal can even lead to a veiled disdain for fellow humans. For example, after describing the CDRS tortoise breeding project, Pritchard (1996) commented, "perhaps it also signals that there is even hope for mankind." Occasionally, humans are blamed unfairly, as in the case of the disappearance of land iguanas from Isla Baltra, which had been wrongly blamed on the target practice of bored U.S. soldiers when the island was used as a military base during World War II (Woram 1991). As a Christian, I sympathize with those who decry unnecessary destruction of the environment, but I cannot condone nor even understand how human life can be viewed as equally or less important than the life of an animal or plant.

As is usually the case with societal trends, many Christians have produced their own theistic versions of environmentalism (e.g. Klotz 1984; DeWitt 1994; Berry 1995; Ball 1998). The typical emphasis is on the dominion mandate given in Genesis 1:28 and on caring for the environment that God has given us. The general philosophical questions raised by environmentalists are not my concern here. Instead, where baraminology differs from the usual Christian perspective is on the question of the preservation of individual species.

To a baraminologist, diversification can be attributed partly to God's desire to see His revelation in creation persist (Wood *et al.* 2003). A divine desire for persistence of revelation could form the foundation of an ethic to preserve baramins. At the same time, the diversification of baramins changes the species, allowing some to go extinct while new species appear. The species then is not the fundamental unit of God's creation but rather could be considered as a unit of baraminic manifestation. As Wise (1994b, p. 140) argued, the species are not of primary importance in a baraminologically-informed ethic, and I consequently find it difficult to justify extraordinary measures taken to preserve species or subspecies. As long as the baramin persists, the potential for producing new species probably also persists (Wood and Murray 2003, p. 178), ensuring that God's revelation will continue to exist.

**5.6. Conclusion.** When I began to work on this monograph more than two years ago, I intended to write a short review article that could be published in any of the currently-existing creationist journals. The work soon consumed much of my attention, as the importance of the Galápagos became apparent. It has long been my belief that God reveals Himself in creation (Ps. 19, Rom. 1) and that if I studied His work and His Word carefully, I would come to know Him better. As I studied the Galápagos Islands, I found abundant evidence of His compassion and care for even the smallest creatures. Indeed, as Jesus said, "Are not five sparrows sold for two farthings, and not one of them is forgotten before God? ... Fear not therefore: ye are of more value than many sparrows" (Luke 12:6-7). Even in the harsh environment of the Galápagos Islands, God still cares and provides for the things He has made.

Imagine my surprise then to read in a book review of Johnson's *Darwin on Trial* that "The God of the Galápagos is careless, wasteful, indifferent, almost diabolical. He is certainly not the sort of God to whom anyone would be inclined to pray" (Hull 1991). I could not disagree more. Based on the preliminary work I have presented here, I would say that just the opposite is true. The organisms of the Galápagos reveal a wise and caring Creator that endowed His creatures with amazing abilities to survive in hostile and unpredictable environments, despite the influence of sin and the Curse. This is *exactly* the kind of God to whom I would not only pray but also trust with my life.

A mural at the Loma Linda Academy in Puerto Ayora, Santa Cruz states, "Todo la creación exalta al creador," *All creation exalts the creator* (quoted in Larson 2001, p. 216). I can think of no more fitting close to this work. To God be the glory, great things He has done.

# Appendix. Multidimensional Scaling in Baraminology

Classical multidimensional scaling (MDS) was originally developed for classifying complex data in the social sciences (see Young and Householder 1938). The method converts a matrix of Euclidean distances between objects into a set of *k*-dimensional coordinates of the objects, where *k* is a predetermined dimensionality. For example, using classical MDS, driving distances between a set of cities can be converted to a geographical map of the cities (Cox and Cox 1994, p. 2). The method has been applied to ecological problems (e.g. Kenkel and Orlóci 1986), and Wood (2004) recently introduced the technique to baraminology. Wood recommended classical MDS as a supplement to baraminic distance correlation and a complement to Analysis of Patterns (Cavanaugh 2002).

For a full presentation of the calculations of classical MDS, see Cox and Cox (1994). Briefly, given a matrix **D** of dissimilarity measurement $\delta_{rs}$ between objects *r* and *s* of a set of *n* objects, classical MDS calculates a set of *k*-dimensional coordinates, each of which corresponds to one of the *n* objects. The Euclidean distance $d_{rs}$ between the *k*-dimensional points representing *r* and *s* is very close to the dissimilarity measurement $\delta_{rs}$. Given a Euclidean **D**, classical MDS will recover *k*-dimensional points such that $d_{rs} = \delta_{rs}$. I calculate MDS using the cmdscale function in R version 1.9.1 (www.r-project.org).

Even though baraminic distances are not necessarily Euclidean or metric, Wood (2004) argued that classical MDS can still be used on baraminic distances. Either the baraminic distance matrix can be rendered metric by addition of the largest baraminic distance value in the matrix, or classical MDS can be applied directly to the baraminic distance matrix with recognition of the possible errors inherent in the calculations. For a complete discussion of the application of classical MDS to baraminology, see Wood (2004).

Wood (2004) recommended a measurement of *stress* to evaluate the fit between the calculated baraminic distances and the distances inferred from the *k*-dimensional classical MDS. Stress is adapted from a statistic given in Venables and Ripley (1997, p. 385) and resembles Kruskal's stress function for nonmetric scaling (Cox & Cox 1994, pp. 44-50). Stress is defined as:

$$S = \sqrt{\frac{\sum (\delta_{rs} - d_{rs})^2}{\sum \delta_{rs}^2}}$$

The smaller the stress, the better the fit between the baraminic distances ($\delta_{rs}$) and the distances inferred from the classical MDS ($d_{rs}$). In practice, stress can be calculated for all possible *k*, which is limited by the number of positive eigenvectors of the baraminic distance matrix **D**. The dimensionality that yields the minimal stress gives an estimation of the number of dimensions required to best model the baraminic distances. In addition, since 3D MDS is the preferred dimensionality for simplicity of viewing, the dimensionality of the minimal stress can give additional insight into how well the 3D MDS pattern matches the best possible pattern. For example, Wood (2004) found a minimal stress of 0.049 at twenty dimensions for the Heliantheae *sensu lato* baraminic distance matrix from Cavanaugh and Wood (2002). The stress for the 3D MDS of the same distance matrix was 0.367. Thus, the 3D MDS pattern represents the 20D MDS pattern, and the original baraminic distances, very poorly.

Wood (2004) calculated MDS for three baraminic distance matrices, one on Heliantheae *sensu lato* from Cavanaugh and Wood (2002), one on Equidae from Cavanaugh *et al.* (2003), and one on Poaceae from Wood (2002b). Comparing the original distances matrices to matrices made metric by addition of the largest distance in each matrix, Wood (2004) found that the original distances produced substantially lower stress for 3D structures without exception. Though Wood (2004) recommended continuing to use both corrected and uncorrected baraminic distance matrices in classical MDS calculations, his results indicated that uncorrected distances worked best in 3D MDS.

Wood's (2004) 3D MDS results for the Equidae closely matched the ANOPA results on the same dataset from Cavanaugh *et al.* (2003). Three-dimensional MDS of the Poaceae dataset clarified the baraminic position of taxa that Wood (2002b) could not assign in his original analysis. The stress calculations for classical MDS of the Heliantheae distance matrix suggested that any 3D pattern would poorly represent the complex distance matrix. Thus, Wood (2004) concluded that classical MDS was a valuable method for use in baraminology.

In the present study, all 3D MDS results have been archived as kinemages in the Multivariate Analysis Repository of the Baraminology Study Group website (http://www.bryancore.org/bsg/mar/).

# References

Abbot, I. and L.K. Abbott. 1978. Multivariate study of morphological variation in Galápagos and Ecuadorean mockingbirds. *Condor* 80: 302-308.

Abbott, I., L.K. Abbott, and P.R. Grant. 1977. Comparative ecology of Galápagos ground finches (*Geospiza* Gould): evaluation of the importance of floristic diversity and interspecific competition. *Ecological Monographs* 47:151-184.

Adsersen, H. 1980. Revision of the Galápagos endemic genus *Lecocarpus* (Asteraceae). *Botanisk Tidsskrift* 75:63-76.

Agenbroad, L.D. 2001. Channel Islands (USA) pygmy mammoths (*Mammuthus exilis*) compared and contrasted with *M. columbi*, their continental ancestral stock. In: Cavarretta, G., P. Gioia, M. Mussi, and M.R. Palombo, eds. *The World of Elephants*. Consiglio Nazionale delle Ricerche, Rome, pp. 473-475.

Anderson, D.L. 2000. The thermal state of the upper mantle: no role for mantle plumes. *Geophysics Research Letters* 27:3623-3626.

Anonymous. 2001. Creation studies at Galapagos. *Acts & Facts* 29(1): 3.

Anonymous. 2003. Seeing what Darwin saw in the Galápagos. *Acts & Facts* 32(8):1-2.

Applequist, W.L. and R.S. Wallace. 2001. Phylogeny of the portulacaceous cohort based on *ndhF* sequence data. *Systematic Botany* 26(2):406-419.

Arnold, E.N. 1979. Indian Ocean giant tortoises: their systematics and island adaptations. *Philosophical Transactions of the Royal Society of London, Series B* 286:127-145.

Arp, G.K. 1973. The Galapagos opuntias: another interpretation. *Noticias de Galápagos* 21:33-37.

Asma, S.T. 1996. *Following Form and Function*. Northwestern University Press, Evanston, IL.

Auffenberg, W. 1974. Checklist of fossil land tortoises (Testudinidae). *Bulletin of the Florida State Museum Biological Sciences* 18:121-251.

Austin, J.J. and E.N. Arnold. 2001. Ancient mitochondrial DNA and morphology elucidate an extinct island radiation of Indian Ocean giant tortoises (*Cylindraspis*). *Proceedings of the Royal Society of London, Series B* 268:2515-2523.

Austin, S.A. 1984. Rapid erosion at Mount St. Helens. *Origins (GRI)* 11(2):90-98.

Austin, S.A. 1986. Mount St. Helens and catastrophism. In: Walsh, R.E., C.L. Brooks, and R.S. Crowell, eds. *Proceedings of the First International Conference on Creationism.* Creation Science Fellowship, Inc, Pittsburgh, pp. 3-9.

Austin, S.A. 1991. *Mt. St. Helens: A Slide Collection for Educators.* Geology Education Materials, El Cajon, CA.

Austin, S.A., ed. 1994. *Grand Canyon: Monument to Catastrophe.* Institute for Creation Research, Santee, CA.

Austin, S.A. 2003. Nautiloid mass kill and burial event, Redwall Limestone (Lower Mississippian), Grand Canyon Region, Arizona and Nevada. In: Ivey, R.L., ed. *Proceedings of the Fifth International Conference on Creationism.* Creation Science Fellowship, Pittsburgh, pp. 55-99.

Austin, S.A., J.R. Baumgardner, D.R. Humphreys, A.A. Snelling, L. Vardiman, and K.P. Wise. 1994. Catastrophic Plate Tectonics: a global flood model of earth history. In: Walsh, R.E., ed. *Proceedings of the Third International Conference on Creationism.* Creation Science Fellowship, Pittsburgh, pp. 609-621.

Austin, S.A. and K.P. Wise. 1994. The pre-Flood/Flood boundary: as defined in Grand Canyon, Arizona and eastern Mojave desert, California. In: Walsh, R.E., ed. *Proceedings of the Third International Conference on Creationism.* Creation Science Fellowship, Pittsburgh, pp. 37-47.

Baker, H.G. 1955. Self-compatibility and establishment after "long-distance" dispersal. *Evolution* 9:347-349.

Ball, J. 1998. Evangelical protestant response to the ecological crisis. *PSCF* 50(1):32-39.

Barlow, N. 1935. Charles Darwin and the Galapagos Islands. *Nature* 136:391.

Barnston, A.G., M.H. Glantz, and Y. He. 1999. Predictive skill of statistical and dynamical climate models in SST forecasts during the 1997-98 El Niño episode and the 1998 La Niña onset. *Bulleting of the American Meteorological Society* 80(2):217-244.

Barrett, P.H. and R.B. Freeman, eds. 1987. *The Works of Charles Darwin Volume 10. The Foundations of the Origin of Species: Two Essays Written in 1842 and 1844.* New York University Press, New York.

Batten, D., K. Ham, J. Sarfati, and C. Wieland. 2000. *The Revised & Expanded Answers Book.* Master Books, Green Forest, AR.

Baumgardner, J.R. 1986. Numerical simulation of the large-scale tectonic changes accompanying the Flood. In R.E. Walsh, C.L. Brooks, and

R.S. Crowell, eds. *Proceedings of the First International Conference on Creationism*. Creation Science Fellowship, Pittsburgh, Volume II, pp. 17-28.

Baumgardner, J.R. 1994. Runaway subduction as the driving mechanism for the Genesis Flood. In: Walsh, R.E., ed. *Proceedings of the Third International Conference on Creationism*. Creation Science Fellowship, Pittsburgh, pp. 63-75.

Baumgardner, J.R. 2002. Catastrophic plate tectonics: the geophysical context of the Genesis Flood. *TJ* 16(1):58-63.

Baumgardner, J.R. 2003. Catastrophic plate tectonics: the physics of the Genesis Flood. In: Ivey, R.L., ed. *Proceedings of the Fifth International Conference on Creationism*. Creation Science Fellowship, Pittsburgh, pp. 113-126.

Baumgardner, J.R., A.A. Snelling, D.R. Humphreys, and S.A. Austin. 2003. Measurable $^{14}C$ in fossilized organic materials: confirming the young earth creation-flood model. In: Ivey, R.L., ed. *Proceedings of the Fifth International Conference on Creationism*. Creation Science Fellowship, Pittsburgh, pp. 127-142.

Baur, G. 1891a. On the origin of the Galapagos Islands. *American Naturalist* 25:217-229.

Baur, G. 1891b. On the origin of the Galapagos Islands. *American Naturalist* 25:307-326.

Baur, G. 1897. New observations on the origin of the Galápagos Islands, with remarks on the geological age of the Pacific Ocean. *American Naturalist* 31:661-680.

Berry, R.J. 1984. Darwin was astonished. *Biological Journal of the Linnean Society* 21:1-4.

Berry, R.J. 1995. Creation and the environment. *Science and Christian Belief* 7(1):21-43.

Bingham, M. 2001. *Penguins of the Falkland Islands and South America*. Environmental Research Unit Publications, Stanley, Falkland Islands.

Boag, P.T. 1983. The heritability of external morphology in Darwin's ground finches (Geospiza) on Isla Daphne Major, Galápagos. *Evolution* 37(5):877-894.

Boag, P.T. and P.R. Grant. 1981. Intense natural selection in a population of Darwin's finches (Geospizinae) in the Galápagos. *Science* 214:82-85.

Boersma, D. 1979. Penguins in the Galapagos. *Noticias de Galápagos* 29:15-16.

Boersma, P.D. 1974. *The Galapagos Penguin: A Study of Adaptations for Life in an Unpredictable Environment*, unpublished dissertation. Ohio State University, Columbus, OH.

Bowman, R.I. 1961. Morphological differentiation and adaptation in the Galápagos finches. *University of California Publications in*

*Zoölogy* 58:1-326.

Bowman, R.I., ed. 1966. *The Galápagos: Proceedings of the Symposia of the Galápagos International Scientific Project.* University of California Press, Berkeley and Los Angeles.

Bowman, R.I. 1983. The evolution of song in Darwin's finches. In: Bowman, R.I., M. Berson, and A.E. Leviton, eds. *Patterns of Evolution in Galapagos Organisms.* Pacific Division, AAAS, San Francisco, pp. 237-537.

Bremer, K. 1994. *Asteraceae: Cladistics & Classification.* Timber Press, Portland, OR.

Brown, R.H. 1975. C-14 age profiles for ancient sediments and peat bogs. *Origins (GRI)* 2(1):6-18.

Brown, R.H. 1986. $^{14}C$ depth profiles as indicators of trends of climate and $^{14}C/^{12}C$ ratio. *Radiocarbon* 28(2A):350-357.

Brown, R.H. 1988. Implications of C-14 age vs. depth profile characteristics. *Origins (GRI)* 15(1):19-29.

Brown, R.H. 1990. Correlation of C-14 age with the biblical time scale. *Origins (GRI)* 17(2):56-65.

Brown, W. 1995. *In the Beginning: Compelling Evidence for Creation and the Flood.* Sixth edition. Center for Scientific Creation, Phoenix.

Burns, K.J., S.J. Hackett, and N.K. Klein. 2002. Phylogenetic relationships and morphological diversity in Darwin's finches and their relatives. *Evolution* 56(6):1240-1252.

Caccone, A., G. Gentile, C.E. Burns, E. Sezzi, W. Bergman, M. Ruelle, K. Saltonstall, and J.R. Powell. 2004. Extreme difference in rate of mitochondrial and nuclear DNA evolution in a large ectotherm, Galápagos tortoises. *Molecular Phylogenetics and Evolution* 31: 794-798.

Caccone, A., G. Gentile, J.P. Gibbs, T.H. Fritts, H.L. Snell, J. Betts, and J.R. Powell. 2002. Phylogeography and history of giant Galápagos Tortoises. *Evolution* 56:2052-2066.

Caccone, A., J.P. Gibbs, V. Ketmaier, E. Suatoni, and J.R. Powell. 1999. Origin and evolutionary relationships of giant Galápagos Tortoises. *Proceedings of the National Academy of Science, USA* 96:13223-13228.

Cane, M.A. 1983. Oceanographic events during El Niño. *Science* 222: 1189-1195.

Cao, Y., M.D. Sorenson, Y. Kumazawa, D.P. Mindell, and M. Hasegawa. 2000. Phylogenetic position of turtles among amniotes: evidence from mitochondrial and nuclear genes. *Gene* 259:139-148.

Carlquist, S. 1974. *Island Biology.* Columbia University Press, New York.

Carpenter, C.C. 1966. Comparative behavior of the Galápagos lava lizards (*Tropidurus*). In: Bowman, R.I., ed. *The Galápagos.*

University of California Press, Berkeley, pp. 269-273.

Carroll, R.L. 1988. *Vertebrate Paleontology and Evolution.* W.H. Freeman and Co., New York.

Case, T.J. 1978. A general explanation for insular body size trends in terrestrial vertebrates. *Ecology* 59:1-18.

Cavanaugh, D.P. 2002. Analysis of Patterns (ANOPA), a New Pattern Recognition Mathematical Procedure for Problems in Engineering and Science, unpublished manuscript.

Cavanaugh, D.P. and T.C. Wood. 2002. A Baraminological Analysis of the tribe Heliantheae *sensu lato* (Asteraceae) using Analysis of Pattern (ANOPA). *Occasional Papers of the Baraminology Study Group* 1:1-11.

Cavanaugh, D.P., T.C. Wood, and K.P. Wise. 2003. Fossil equidae: a monobaraminic, stratomorphic series. In: Ivey, R.L., ed. *Proceedings of the Fifth International Conference on Creationism.* Creation Science Fellowship, Pittsburgh, pp. 143-153.

Chen, D., M.A. Cane, A. Kaplan, S.E. Zebiak, and D. Huang. 2004. Predictability of El Niño over the past 148 years. *Nature* 428:733-736.

Christiansen, R.L., G.R. Foulger, and J.R. Evans. 2002. Upper-mantle origin of the Yellowstone hotspot. *Geological Society of America Bulletin* 114(10):1245-1256.

Christie, D.M., R.A. Duncan, A.R. McBirney, M.A. Richards, W.M. White, and C. Fox. 1990. Drowned islands and submarine volcanoes from the Galapagos hotspot. *EOS: Transactions of the American Geophysical Union* 71:1695.

Christie, D.M., R.A. Duncan, A.R. McBirney, M.A. Richards, W.W. White, K.S. Harpp, and C.G. Fox. 1992. Drowned islands downstream from the Galapagos hotspot imply extended speciation times. *Nature* 355:246-248.

Chubb, L.J. 1933. Geology of Galapagos, Cocos, and Easter Islands. *Bernice P. Bishop Museum Bulletin* 110:3-42.

Clark, H.W. 1940. *Genes and Genesis.* Pacific Press, Mountain View, CA.

Clark, H.W. 1947. *Creation Speaks.* Pacific Press, Mountain View, CA.

Clarke, J.A., E.B. Olivero, and P. Puerta. 2003. Description of the earliest fossil penguin from South America and first Paleogene vertebrate locality of Tierra del Fuego, Argentina. *American Museum Novitates* 3423:1-18.

Clifford, L.D. and D.J. Anderson. 2002. Clutch size variation in the Nazca booby: a test of the egg quality hypothesis. *Behavioral Ecology* 13:274-279.

Coffin, H.G. 1983a. Mount St. Helens and Spirit Lake. *Origins (GRI)* 10(2):9-17.

Coffin, H.G. 1983b. *Origin by Design*. Review and Herald Publishing, Hagerstown, MD.

Cohen, N. and R. Bowman. 1964. The Galapagos International Scientific Project. *Noticias de Galápagos* 3:4-12.

Coleman, S. 1986. Darwin's finches. *Biblical Creation* 8:3-21.

Coleman, W. 1964. *Georges Cuvier Zoologist*. Harvard University Press, 1964.

Colinvaux, P.A. 1972. Climate and the Galapagos Islands. *Nature* 240: 17-20.

Colinvaux, P.A. and E.K. Schofield. 1976. Historical ecology in the Galápagos Islands I. A Holocene pollen record from El Junco Lake, Isla San Cristóbal. *Journal of Ecology* 64:989-1012.

Colp, R. 1986. "Confessing a Murder" Darwin's first revelations about transmutation. *Isis* 77:8-32.

Connor, E.F. and D. Simberloff. 1978. Species number and compositional similarity of the Galapagos flora and avifauna. *Ecological Monographs* 48:120-149.

Cooper, A. and D. Penny. 1997. Mass survival of birds across the Cretaceous-Tertiary boundary: molecular evidence. *Science* 275: 1109-1113.

Corso, A. and D. Forsman. 1997. Hybrids between Black Kite and Common Buzzard. *Alula* 3:44-46.

Courtillot, V., A. Davaille, J. Besse, and J. Stock. 2003. Three distinct types of hotspots in earth's mantle. *Earth and Planetary Science Letters* 205:295-308.

Cox, A. 1983. Ages of the Galapagos Islands. In: Bowman, R.I., M. Berson, and A.E. Leviton, eds. *Patterns of Evolution in Galapagos Organisms*. Pacific Division, AAAS, San Francisco, pp. 11-23.

Cox, A. and G.B. Dalrymple. 1966. Palaeomagnetism and potassium-argon ages of some volcanic rocks from the Galapagos Islands. *Nature* 209:776-777.

Cox, T.F. and M.A.A. Cox. 1994. *Multidimensional Scaling*. Chapman & Hall, New York.

Cracraft, J. 1985. Monophyly and phylogenetic relationships of the Pelecaniformes: a numerical cladistic analysis. *Auk* 102:834-853.

Cruz, F. and T. Beach. 1983. Weather data, on Floreana, 1982-83. *Noticias de Galápagos* 38:28.

Cuénod, P., V. Savolainen, L.W. Chatrou, M. Powell, R.J. Grayer, and M.W. Chase. 2002. Molecular phylogenetics of Caryophyllales based on nuclear 18S rDNA and plastid *rbcL*, *atpB*, and *matK* DNA sequences. *American Journal of Botany* 89(1):132-144.

Culp, G.R. 1994. Do birds of prey demonstrate stability of species? In: Walsh, R.E., ed. *Proceedings of the Third International Conference on Creationism*. Creation Science Fellowship, Pittsburgh, pp. 169-174.

Cumming, K. 1997. Reticulate evolution. *Impact* 289:i-iv.

Curry-Lindahl, K. 1981. Twenty years of conservation in the Galapagos. Assessment, lessons annd future priorities. *Noticias de Galápagos* 34:8-9.

Darlington, P.J. 1943. Carabidae of mountains and islands: data on the evolution of isolated faunas, and on atrophy of wings. *Ecological Monographs* 13:37-61.

Darwin, C. 1839. *Journal of Researches into the Geology and Natural History of the Various Countries Visited by the H.M.S. Beagle, under the Command of Captain Fitzroy, R.N. from 1832 to 1836.* First edition. Henry Colburn, London.

Darwin, C. 1845 [1896]. *Journal of Researches into the Natural History and Geology of the Countries Visited During the Voyage of the H.M.S. Beagle Round the World, under the Command of Capt. Fitz Roy, R.N.* Second edition. Appleton and Company, New York.

Darwin, C. 1859 [1979]. *The Origin of Species.* A facsimile of the first edition. Gramercy Books, New York.

Darwin, F. 1909. Introduction. In P.H. Barrett and R.B. Freeman, eds. 1987. *The Works of Charles Darwin Volume 10. The Foundations of the Origin of Species: Two Essays Written in 1842 and 1844.* New York University Press, New York, pp. xi-xxiv.

Darwin, F., ed. 1958. *Selected Letters on Evolution and Origin of Species with an Autobiographical Chapter.* Dover Publications, New York.

Dawson, E.Y. 1966. Cacti in the Galápagos Islands, with special reference to their relations with tortoises. In: Bowman, R.I., ed. *The Galápagos: Proceedings of the Symposia of the Galápagos International Scientific Project.* University of California Press, Los Angeles, pp. 209-214.

Dawson, W.R., G.A. Bartholomew, and A.F. Bennett. 1977. A reappraisal of the aquatic specializations of the Galapagos marine iguana (*Amblyrhynchus cristatus*). *Evolution* 31:891-897.

Dawson, Y. 1964. Cacti in the Galapagos Islands. *Noticias de Galápagos* 4:12-13.

deBraga, M. and O. Rieppel. 1997. Reptile phylogeny and the interrelationships of turtles. *Zoological Journal of the Linnean Society* 120:281-354.

DePaolo, D.J. and M. Manga. 2003. Deep origin of hotspots - the mantle plume model. *Science* 300:920-921.

Desmond, A. 1982. *Archetypes and Ancestors: Palaeontology in Victorian London 1850-1875.* University of Chicago Press, Chicago.

Detrick, R.S., J.M. Sinton, G. Ito, J.P. Canales, M. Behn, T. Blacic, B. Cushman, J.E. Dixon, D.W. Graham, and J.J. Mahoney. 2002. Correlated geophysical, geochemical, and volcanological manifestations of plume-ridge interaction along the Galápagos Spreading Center. *Geochemistry Geophysics Geosystems* 3(10), doi 10.1029/2002GC000350.

DeVries, T. 1973. *The Galapagos Hawk: An eco-geographical study with special reference to its systematic position*, unpublished dissertation. Vrije Uninversiteit te Amsterdam.

DeVries, T. 1975. The Galapagos hawk. *Noticias de Galápagos* 23: 13-15.

DeWitt, C.B. 1994. Christian environmental stewardship: preparing the way for action. *Perspectives on Science and the Christian Faith* 46(2):80-89.

Dobzhansky, T. 1951. *Genetics and the Origin of Species*. Third edition. Columbia University Press, New York.

Doolan, R. 1992. Penguin puzzle. *Creation Ex Nihilo* 14(4):51.

Dunbar, R.B., G.M. Wellington, M.W. Colgan, and P.W. Glynn. 1994. Eastern Pacific sea surface temperature since 1600 A.D.: the δ18O record of climate variability in Galápagos corals. *Paleoceanography* 9(2):291-315.

Dunson, W.A. 1969. Electrolyte excretion by the salt gland of the Galápagos marine iguana. *American Journal of Physiology* 216(4): 995-1002.

Edwards, G. and D. Walker. 1983. *$C_3$, $C_4$: Mechanisms, and Cellular and Environmental Regulation, of Photosynthesis*. University of California Press, Los Angeles.

Ehleringer, J.R., T.E. Cerling, and B.R. Helliker. 1997. $C_4$ photosynthesis, atmospheric $CO_2$, and climate. *Oecologia* 112:285-299.

Eliasson, U. 1974. Studies in Galápagos plants XIV. The genus *Scalesia* Arn. *Opera Botanica* 36:1-117.

Ernst, C.H., R.G.M. Altenberg, and R.W. Barbour. 2000. *Turtles of the World*: CD-ROM edition, version 1.2. ETI Expert Center for Taxonomic Identification, Amsterdam, UNESCO Publishing, Paris, and Springer-Verlag, Heidelberg and New York.

Estes, G., K.T. Grant, P.R. Grant. 2000. Darwin in Galápagos: his footsteps through the archipelago. *Notes and Records of the Royal Society (London)* 54(3):343-368.

Evans, D. 1992. 25 more years!!! *Noticias de Galápagos* 51:4.

Fedorov, A.V., S.L. Harper, S.G. Philander, B. Winter, and A. Wittenberg. 2003. How predictable is El Niño? *Bulletin of the American Meteorological Society* 84(7):911-919.

Feduccia, A. 1999. *The Origin and Evolution of Birds*. Yale University Press, New Haven, CT.

Fehrer, J. 1993. Interspecific hybridization within Cardueline and Estrildid finches (Carduelinae, Estrildidae: Passeriformes). In: Scherer, S., ed. *Typen des lebens*. Pascal Verlag, Berlin, pp. 197-215.

Felsenstein, J. 1993. PHYLIP (Phylogeny Inference Package) version 3.5c. Distributed by the author. Department of Genetics, University of Washington, Seattle.

Ferguson-Lees, J. and D.A. Christie. 2001. *Raptors of the World.* Houghton Mifflin, New York.

Fichman, M. 1977. Wallace: Zoogeography and the problem of land bridges. *Journal of the History of Biology* 10(1):45-63.

Fitter, J., D. Fitter, and D. Hosking. 2000. *Wildlife of the Galápagos.* Princeton University Press, Princeton, NJ.

Ford, H.A., D.T. Parkin, P. Parkin, A.W. Ewing, and E. McIntosh. 1971. The biochemical diversity of the Darwin's finches. *Noticias de Galápagos* 18:18-19.

Foster, J.B. 1964. Evolution of mammals on islands. *Nature* 202:234-235.

Foulger, G.R. and J.H. Natland. 2003. Is "hotspot" volcanism a consequence of plate tectonics? *Science* 300:921-922.

Frair, W. 1984. Turtles: Now and Then. In: *Proceedings of the Northcoast Bible-Science Conference.* Bible Science Association, Seven Hills, Ohio, pp. 33-38.

Frair, W. 1985. The enigmatic plateless river turtle, *Carettochelys*, in serological survey. *Journal of Herpetology* 19(4):515-523.

Frair, W. 1991. Original kinds and turtle phylogeny. *Creation Research Society Quarterly* 28:21-24.

Freeland, J.R. and P.T. Boag. 1999a. The mitochondrial and nuclear genetic homogeneity of the phenotypically diverse Darwin's ground finches. *Evolution* 53(5):1553-1563.

Freeland, J.R. and P.T. Boag. 1999b. Phylogenetics of Darwin's finches: paraphyly in the tree-finches, and two divergent lineages in the Warbler finch. *Auk* 116(3):577-588.

Friesen, V.L. and D.J. Anderson. 1997. Phylogeny and evolution of the Sulidae (Aves: Pelecaniformes): a test of alternative modes of speciation. *Molecular Phylogenetics and Evolution* 7:252-260.

Fritts, T.H. 1983. Morphometrics of Galapagos Tortoises: evolutionary implications. In: Bowman, R.I., M. Berson, and A.E. Leviton, eds. *Patterns of Evolution in Galapagos Organisms.* Pacific Division, AAAS, San Francisco, pp. 107-122.

Fritts, T.H. 1984. Evolutionary divergence of giant tortoises in Galapagos. *Biological Journal of the Linnean Society* 21:165-176.

Froede, C.R. 2001. Hotspots and hotspot tracks: new issues for plate tectonics and catastrophic plate tectonics. *Creation Research Society Quarterly* 38(2):96-99.

Froede, C.R. 2002. Support for plate tectonics and catastrophic plate tectonics missing from Hawaiian hotspot track. *Creation Matters* 7(4):1,4.

Froede, C.R., G.F. Howe, J.K. Reed, and J.R. Meyer. 1998. An overview of various igneous rock outcrops near the Van Andel Creation Research Center interpreted within a young-earth Flood model. *Creation Research Society Quarterly* 35(3):126-133.

Frost, D.R. 1992. Phylogenetic analysis and taxonomy of the *Tropidurus* group of lizards (Iguania: Tropiduridae). *American Museum Novitates* 3033:1-68.

Frost, D.R. and R. Etheridge. 1989. A phylogenetic analysis and taxonomy of Iguanian lizards (Reptilia: Squamata). *University of Kansas Museum of Natural History Miscellaneous Publication* 81: 1-65.

Futuyma, D.J. 1986. *Evolutionary Biology.* Second edition. Sinauer Associates, Sunderland, MA.

Gaffney, E.S. and P.A. Meylan. 1988. A phylogeny of turtles. In: Benton, M.J., ed. *The Phylogeny and Classification of the Tetrapods, Volume 1: Amphibians, Reptiles, Birds.* Clarendon Press, Oxford, pp. 157-219.

Galbraith, D.A., A.M. Mills, and R.J. Brooks. 1984. A critical review of 'Speciation or irruption: the significance of the Darwin finches.' *Journal of Biology Education* 18(1):72-76.

García-Pozuelo-Ramos, C. 1998. Dental variability in the domestic dog (*Canis familiaris*) implications for the variability of primates. *Creation Research Society Quarterly* 35(2):66-75.

García-Pozuelo-Ramos, C. 1999. Craniodental variability in the domestic dog (*Canis familiaris*) and its implications for the variability in primates. *Creation Research Society Quarterly* 36(3):116-123.

García-Pozuelo-Ramos, C. 2002. Variability of skull shape in the domestic dog and its implications for variability in other mammals and humans since the Flood. *Creation Research Society Quarterly* 39(1):15-20.

Garner, P. 1996. Continental flood basalts indicate a pre-Mesozoic Flood/post-Flood boundary. *Creation Ex Nihilo Technical Journal* 10(1):114-127.

Geist, D. 1996. On the emergence and submergence of the Galápagos Islands. *Noticias de Galápagos* 56:5-9.

Geist, D., T. Naumann, and P. Larson. 1998. Evolution of Galápagos magmas: mantle and crustal fractionation without assimilation. *Journal of Petrology* 30(5):953-971.

Giannini, N.P. and S. Bertelli. 2004. Phylogeny of extant penguins based on integumentary and breeding characters. *The Auk* 121(2): 422-434.

Gibbs, H.L. and P.R. Grant. 1987. Oscillating selection on Darwin's finches. *Nature* 327:511-513.

Giem, P. 2001. Carbon-14 content of fossil carbon. *Origins (GRI)* 51: 6-30.

Gilbert, S.F., G.A. Loredo, A. Brukman, and A.C. Burke. 2001.

Morphogenesis of the turtle shell: the development of a novel structure in tetrapod evolution. *Evolution & Development* 3(2): 47-58.

Gish, D.T. 1995. *Evolution: The Fossils Still Say No!* Institute for Creation Research, El Cajon, CA.

Goldstein, M.I., P.H. Bloom, J.H. Sarasola, and T.E. Lacher. 1999. Post-migration weight gain of Swainson's hawks in Argentina. *Wilson Bulletin* 11:428-432.

Gould, S.J. 1994. Evolution as fact and theory. In. *Hen's Teeth and Horse's Toes*. W.W. Norton & Co., New York, pp. 253-262.

Gould, S.J. 1999. *Rocks of Ages*. Ballantine, New York.

Graham, D.W., D.M. Christie, K.S. Harpp, and J.E. Lupton. 1993. Mantle plume helium in submarine basalts from the Galápagos platform. *Science* 262:2023-2026.

Grant, B.R. 1985. Selection on bill characters in a population of Darwin's finches: *Geospiza conirostris* on Isla Genovesa, Galápagos. *Evolution* 39(3):523-532.

Grant, B.R. and P.R. Grant. 1982. Niche shifts and competition in Darwin's finches: *Geospiza conirostris* and congeners. *Evolution* 36:637-657.

Grant, B.R. and P.R. Grant. 1983. Fission and fusion in a population of Darwin's finches: an example of the value of studying individuals in ecology. *Oikos* 41:530-547.

Grant, B.R. and P.R. Grant. 1987. Mate choice in Darwin's finches. *Biological Journal of the Linnean Society* 32:247-270.

Grant, B.R. and P.R. Grant. 1989. Natural selection in a population of Darwin's finches. *American Naturalist* 113:377-393.

Grant, B.R. and P.R. Grant. 1993. Evolution of Darwin's finches caused by a rare climatic event. *Proceedings of the Royal Society of London, Series B* 251:111-117.

Grant, B.R. and P.R. Grant. 1996a. High survival of Darwin's finch hybrids: effects of beak morphology and diets. *Ecology* 72(2):500-509.

Grant, B.R. and P.R. Grant. 1996b. Cultural inheritance of song and its role in the evolution of Darwin's finches. *Evolution* 50(6):2471-2487.

Grant, P.R. 1983. The role of interspecific competition in the adaptive radiation of Darwin's finches. In: Bowman, R.I., M. Berson, and A.E. Leviton, eds. *Patterns of Evolution in Galapagos Organisms*. Pacific Division, AAAS, San Francisco, pp. 187-199.

Grant, P.R. 1984. Extraordinary rainfall during the El Nino event of 1982-83. *Noticias de Galápagos* 39:10-11.

Grant, P.R. 1993. Hybridization of Darwin's finches on Isla Daphne Major, Galápagos. *Philosophical Transactions of the Royal Society of London, Series B* 340:127-139.

Grant, P.R. 1999. *Ecology and Evolution of Darwin's Finches.* 2nd ed. Princeton University Press, Princeton, NJ.

Grant, P.R. 2001. Reconstructing the evolution of birds on islands: 100 years of research. *Oikos* 92:385-403.

Grant, P.R. and B.R. Grant. 1987. The extraordinary El Niño event of 1982-83: effects on Darwin's finches on Isla Genovesa, Galápagos. *Oikos* 49:55-66.

Grant, P.R. and B.R. Grant. 1992. Hybridization of bird species. *Science* 256:193-197.

Grant, P.R. and B.R. Grant. 1996. Speciation and hybridization in island birds. *Philosophical Transactions of the Royal Society of London, Series B* 351:765-772.

Grant, P.R. and B.R. Grant. 1997a. Mating patterns of Darwin's finch hybrids determined by song and morphology. *Biological Journal of the Linnean Society* 60:317-343.

Grant, P.R. and B.R. Grant. 1997b. Genetics and the origin of bird species. *Proceedings of the National Academy of Science, USA* 94: 7768-7775.

Grant, P.R. and B.R. Grant. 1999. Effects of the 1998 El Niño on Darwin's finches on Daphne. *Noticias de Galápagos* 60:29-30.

Grant, P.R. and B.R. Grant. 2002a. Unpredictable evolution in a 30-year study of Darwin's finches. *Science* 296:707-711.

Grant, P.R. and B.R. Grant. 2002b. Adaptive radiation of Darwin's finches. *American Scientist* 90:130-139.

Grant, P.R., B.R. Grant, and K. Petren. 2000. The allopatric phase of speciation: the sharp-beaked ground finch (*Geospiza difficilis*) on the Galápagos Islands. *Biological Journal of the Linnean Society* 69: 287-317.

Gray, A.P. 1958. *Bird Hybrids: A Check-List with Bibliography.* Commonwealth Agricultural Bureaux, Farnham Royal, Bucks, England.

Gruber, H.E. 1974. *Darwin on Man.* E.P. Dutton & Co., New York.

Gruber, H.E. and V. Gruber. 1962. The eye of reason: Darwin's development during the *Beagle* voyage. *Isis* 53:186-200.

Gutscher, M.-A., J. Malavieille, S. Lallemand, and J.Y. Collot. 1999. Tectonic segmentation of the North Andean margin: impact of the Carnegie Ridge collision. *Earth and Planetary Science Letters* 168: 255-270.

Hall, J.L. 1990. *History of Life,* 6th ed. Hall Publications, Lynchburg, VA.

Hall, M.L. 1983. Origin of Española Island and the age of terrestrial life on the Galápagos Islands. *Science* 221:545-547.

Halpern, D., S.P. Hayes, A. Leetmaa, D.V. Hansen, and S.G.H. Philander. 1983. Oceanographic observations of the 1982 warming of the tropical eastern Pacific. *Science* 221:1173-1175.

Ham, J.B. 1984. Birds: evolution or creation? *Biblical Creation* 5:109-111.

Hamann, O. 2001. Demographic studies of three indigenous stand-forming plant taxa (*Scalesia, Opuntia,* and *Bursera*) in the Galápagos Islands, Ecuador. *Biodiversity and Conservation* 10:233-250.

Hamann, O. and S.W. Andersen. 1986. *Scalesia gordilloi* sp. nov. (Asteraceae) from the Galápagos Islands, Ecuador. *Nordic Journal of Botany* 6:35-38.

Harper, G.H. 1980. Speciation or irruption: the significance of the Darwin finches. *Journal of Biology Education* 14(2):99-106, and reprinted in *Creation Research Society Quarterly* 18:171-175 (1981).

Harper, G.H. 1985. The irruption theory of the Darwin finches. *Journal of Biology Education* 19(4):317-321.

Harpp, K.S., D.J. Fornari, D.J. Geist, and M.D. Kurz. 2003. Genovesa Submarine Ridge: a manifestation of plume-ridge interaction in the northern Galápagos Islands. *Geochemistry Geophysics Geosystems* 4(9), doi 10.1029/2003GC000531.

Harpp, K.S. and W.M. White. 1990. Geochemistry of Galapagos seamounts. *EOS: Transactions of the American Geophysical Union* 71:1695.

Harris, L.E. 1976. *Galápagos: A Creationist Visits Darwin's Islands.* Southern Publishing Association, Nashville.

Harrison, R.G. 1980. Dispersal polymorphisms in insects. *Annual Review of Ecology and Systematics* 11:95-118.

Hauff, F., K. Hoernle, G. Tilton, D.W. Graham, and A.C. Kerr. 2000. Large volume recycling of oceanic lithosphere over short time scales: geochemical constraints from the Caribbean Large Igneous Province. *Earth and Planetary Science Letters* 174:247-263.

Hayes, F.E., K.R. Beaman, W.K. Hayes, and L.E. Harris. 1988. Defensive behavior in the Galapagos Tortoise (*Geochelone elephantopus*), with comments on the evolution of insular gigantism. *Herpetologica* 44: 11-17.

Hazard, L.C. 2001. Ion secretion by salt glands of desert iguanas (*Dipsosaurus dorsalis*). *Physiological and Biochemical Zoology* 74(1):22-31.

Hazard, L.C., V.H. Shoemaker, and L.L. Grismer. 1998. Salt gland secretion by an intertidal lizard, *Uta tumidarostra*. *Copeia* 1998(1): 231-234.

Hedges, S.B. and L.L. Poling. 1999. A molecular phylogeny of reptiles. *Science* 283:998-1001.

Hedges, S.B. and C.G. Sibley. 1994. Molecules vs. morphology in avian evolution: the case of the "pelecaniform" birds. *Proceedings of the National Academy of Science, USA* 91:9861-9865.

Heise, P.J. 1998. *Phylogeny and Biogeography of Galápagos Lava*

*Lizards (Microlophus) Inferred from Nucleotide Sequence Variation in Mitochondrial DNA*, unpublished dissertation. University of Tennessee, Knoxville, Knoxville.

Helder, M.J. 1996. Let's rewrite the book on the Galapagos Islands. *Creation Matters* 1(4):1-2.

Hemsley, W.B. 1895. The flora of the Galápagos Islands. *Nature* 52: 623.

Hendrickson, J.D. 1966. The Galápagos Tortoises, Geochelone Fitzinger 1835 (Testudo Linnaeus 1758 in part). In: Bowman, R.I., ed. *The Galápagos: Proceedings of the Symposia of the Galápagos International Scientific Project.* University of California Press, Berkeley, pp. 252-257.

Hendrickson, J.R. and W.A. Weber. 1964. Lichens on Galápagos giant tortoises. *Science* 144:1463.

Hergt, J.M., M. Storey, G. Marriner, and J. Tarney. 1994. The Curaçao lava formation: samples of the oldest and most primitive magmas from the Galapagos plume. *Mineralogical Magazine* 58A:414-415.

Herron, E.M. and J.R. Heirtzler. 1967. Sea-floor spreading near the Galapagos. *Science* 158:775-780.

Hershkovitz, M.A., and E.A. Zimmer. 2000. Ribosomal DNA evidence and disjunctions of western American Portulacaceae. *Molecular Phylogenetics and Evolution* 15(3):419-439.

Hey, R. 1977. Tectonic evolution of the Cocos-Nazca spreading center. *Geological Society of America Bulletin* 88:1404-1420.

Hey, R., G.L. Johnson, and A. Lowrie. 1977. Recent plate motions in the Galapagos area. *Geological Society of America Bulletin* 88: 1385-1403.

Hickman, C.S. and J.H. Lipps. 1985. Geologic youth of Galápagos Islands confirmed by marine stratigraphy and paleontology. *Science* 227:1578-1580.

Hicks, D.J. and A. Mauchamp. 2000. Population structure and growth patterns of *Opuntia echios* var. *gigantea* along an elevational gradient in the Galápagos Islands. *Biotropica* 32:235-253.

Hoernle, K., P. van den Bogaard, R. Werner, B. Lissinna, F. Hauff, G. Alvarado, and D. Garbe-Schönberg. 2002. Missing history (16-71 Ma) of the Galápagos hotspot: implications for the tectonic and biological evolution of the Americas. *Geology* 30(9):795-798.

Hoernle, K., R. Werner, J.P. Morgan, D. Garbe-Schönberg, J. Bryce, and J. Mrazek. 2000. Existence of complex spatial zonation in the Galápagos plume for at least 14 m.y. *Geology* 28(5):435-438.

Houvenaghel, G.T. 1974. Equatorial undercurrent and climate in the Galapagos Islands. *Nature* 250:565-566.

Howe, G.F. and S.B. Austin. 2002. The Saguaro: God's desert sentry a Van Andel Creation Research Center Report. *Creation Research Society Quarterly* 39(3):177-188.

Howell, J.T. 1933. The Cactaceae of the Galapagos Islands. *Proceedings of the California Academy of Sciences* 21:41-54.

Hull, D.L. 1991. The God of the Galápagos. *Nature* 352:485-486.

Humphreys, D.R. 1986. Reversals of the earth's magnetic field during the Genesis Flood. In: Walsh, R.E., C.L. Brooks, and R.S. Crowell, eds. *Proceedings of the First International Conference on Creationism.* Creation Science Fellowship, Inc, Pittsburgh, pp. 113-126.

Humphreys, D.R., S.A. Austin, J.R. Baumgardner, and A.A. Snelling. 2003. Helium diffusion rates support accelerated nuclear decay. In: Ivey, R.L., ed. *Proceedings of the Fifth International Conference on Creationism.* Creation Science Fellowship, Pittsburgh, pp. 175-195.

Husen, S., E. Kissling, and R. Quintero. 2002. Tomographic evidence for a subducted seamount beneath the Gulf of Nicoya, Costa Rica: the cause of the 1990 Mw = 7.0 Gulf of Nicoya earthquake. *Geophysical Research Letters* 29(8), doi 10.1029/2001GL014045.

Huxley, J. 1953. *Evolution in Action.* New American Library, New York.

Huxley, J. 1964. *Evolution: The Modern Synthesis.* John Wiley & Sons, New York.

Huxley, J. 1966. Charles Darwin: Galápagos and After. In: Bowman, R.I., ed. *The Galápagos: Proceedings of the Symposia of the Galápagos International Scientific Project.* University of California Press, Berkeley, pp. 3-9.

Jackson, D.J. 1928. The inheritance of long and short wings in the weevil, *Sitona hispidula*, with a discussion of wing reduction among beetles. *Transactions of the Royal Society of Edinburgh* 45(27):665-735.

Jenkins, R.J.F. 1974. A new giant penguin from the Eocene of Australia. *Palaeontology* 17:291-310.

Johnsgard, P.A. 1993. *Cormorants, Darters, and Pelicans of the World.* Smithsonian Institution Press, Washington.

Junker, R. 2003. Primitiv oder fortschrittlich? *Studium Integrale Journal* 10(1):30-32.

Karis, P.O. and Ryding, O. 1994. Tribe Helenieae. In: Bremer, K., ed. *Asteraceae: Cladistics and Classification.* Timber Press, Portland, OR, pp. 521-558.

Kenkel, N.C. and L. Orlóci. 1986. Applying metric and nonmetric multidimensional scaling to ecological studies: some new results. *Ecology* 67:919-928.

Kennedy, M. and H.G. Spencer. 2004. Phylogenies of the frigatebirds (Fregatidae) and tropicbirds (Phaethonidae), two divergent groups of the traditional order Pelecaniformes, inferred from mitochondrial DNA sequences. *Molecular Phylogenetics and Evolution* 31:31-38.

Kennedy, R.A., J.L. Eastburn, and K.G. Jensen. 1980. $C_3$-$C_4$ photosynthesis in the genus *Mollugo*: structure, physiology and evolution of intermediate characteristics. *American Journal of Botany* 67:1207-1217.

Kennedy, R.A. and W.M. Laetsch. 1974. Plant species intermediate for $C_3$, $C_4$ photosynthesis. *Science* 184:1087-1089.

Kerr, R.A. 2002. Signs of success in forecasting El Niño. *Science* 297: 497-499.

Kizirian, D., A. Trager, M.A. Donnelly, and J.W. Wright. 2004. Evolution of Galapagos Island lava lizards (Iguania: Tropiduridae: *Microlophus*). *Molecular Phylogenetics and Evolution* 32:761-769.

Klotz, J.W. 1972. Flora and fauna of the Galapagos Islands. *Creation Research Society Quarterly* 9:14-22.

Klotz, J.W. 1984. A creationist environmental ethic. *Creation Research Society Quarterly* 21(1):6-8.

Kooyman, G.L. 2002. Evolutionary and ecological aspects of some Antarctic and sub-Antarctic penguin distributions. *Oecologia* 130: 485-495.

Köster, F. and H. Köster. 1983. Twelve days among the "Vampire Finches" of Wolf Island. *Noticias de Galápagos* 38:4-10.

Kumuzawa, Y. and M. Nishida. 1999. Complete mitochondrial DNA sequences of the green turtle and blue-tailed mole skink: statistical evidence for archosaurian affinity of turtles. *Molecular Biology and Evolution* 16(6):784-792.

Lack, D. 1940. Evolution of Galapagos finches. *Nature* 146:324-327.

Lack, D. 1947. *Darwin's Finches*. Harper & Brothers, New York.

Lack, D. 1961. *Evolutionary Theory & Christian Belief*, revised edition. Methuen & Co., London.

Lack, D.L. 1973. My life as an amateur ornithologist. *Ibis* 115:421-431.

Lalomov, A.V. and S.E. Tabolitch. 2000. Age determination of coastal submarine placer, Val'cumey, northern Siberia. *Creation Ex Nihilo Technical Journal* 14(3):83-90.

Lammerts, W.E. 1966. The Galapagos Island Finches. *Creation Research Society Quarterly* 3:73-79.

Lammerts, W.E. 1982. Effect of drought on the finches of a Galapagos island. *Creation Research Society Quarterly* 19:70-71.

Lanteri, A.A. 1992. Systematics, cladistics and biogeography of a new weevil genus, *Galapaganus* (Coleoptera: Curculionidae) from the Galápagos Islands, and coasts of Ecuador and Peru. *Transactions of the American Entomological Society* 118:227-267.

Lanteri, A.A. and B.B. Normark. 1995. Parthenogenesis in the tribe Naupactini (Coleoptera: Curculionidae). *Annals of the Entomological Society of America* 88(6):722-731.

Larson, E.J. 2001. *Evolution's Workshop*. Basic Books, New York.

Laurie, A. 1983a. Santa Fe in an El Nino year. *Noticias de Galápagos* 37:20-22.

Laurie, A. 1983b. Marine iguanas suffer as El Nino breaks all records. *Noticias de Galápagos* 38:11.

Laurin, M. and R.R. Reisz. 1995. A reevaluation of early amniote phylogeny. *Zoological Journal of the Linnean Society* 113:165-223.

Lawesson, J.E., H. Adsersen, and P. Bentley. 1987. An updated and annotated check list of the vascular plants of the Galápagos Islands. *Reports from the Botanical Institute, University of Aarhus* 16:1-74.

Lee, M.S.Y. 1993. The origin of the turtle body plan: bridging a famous morphological gap. *Science* 261:1716-1720.

Lee, M.S.Y. 1996. Correlated progression and the origin of the turtles. *Nature* 379:812-815.

Lee, M.S.Y. 1997. Reptile relationships turn turtle.... *Nature* 389:245-246.

Lee, M.S.Y. 2001. Molecules, morphology, and the monophyly of diapsid reptiles. *Contributions to Zoology* 70(1): http://dpc.uba.uva.nl/ctz/vol70/nr01/a01.

Lemire, M., R. Vernet, and C. Grenot. 1980. Electrolyte excretion by the nasal gland of an herbivorous Saharan lizard, *Uromastix acanthinurus* (Agamidae). Effects of single NaCl and KCl loads. *Journal of Arid Environments* 3:325-330.

Lester, L.P. and R.G. Bohlin. 1989. *The Natural Limits to Biological Change*. Probe Books, Dallas.

Lewis, R.W. 1987-1988. Theory and fact of evolution. *Creation/Evolution* XXII:34-37.

Linsley, E.G. 1977. Insects of the Galápagos (Supplement). *Occasional Papers of the California Academy of Sciences* 125:1-50.

Linsley, E.G. and R.L. Usinger. 1966. Insects of the Galápagos Islands. *Proceedings of the California Academy of Sciences, Fourth Series* 33(7):113-196.

Lipka, B., K. Steinmüller, E. Rosche, D. Börsch, and P. Westhoff. 1994. The $C_3$ plant *Flaveria pringlei* contains a plastidic NADP-malic enzyme which is orthologous to the $C_4$ isoform of the $C_4$ plant *F. trinervia*. *Plant Molecular Biology* 26:1775-1783.

Livezey, B.C. 1992. Flightlessness in the Galápagos cormorant (*Compsohalieus* [*Nannopterum*] *harrisi*): heterochrony, giantism and specialization. *Biological Journal of the Linnean Society* 105: 155-224.

Livingstone, D.N. 1984. Natural theology and neo-Lamarckism: the changing context of nineteenth-century geography in the United States and Great Britain. *Annals of the Association of American Geographers* 74(1):9-28.

Lopez, T.J., E.D. Hauselman, L.J. Maxson, and J.W. Wright. 1992.

Preliminary analysis of phylogenetic relationships among Galapagos Islands lizards of the genus *Tropidurus*. *Amphibia-Reptilia* 13:327-339.

Losos, J.B. and D.B. Miles. 2002. Testing the hypothesis that a clade has adaptively radiated: iguanid lizard clades as a case study. *American Naturalist* 160(2):147-157.

Lyell, C. 1832. *Principles of Geology*. John Murray, London.

Mace, S.R., B.A. Sims, and T.C. Wood. 2003. Fellowship, creation, and schistosomes. *Impact* 357:i-iv.

Macey, J.R., A. Larson, N.B. Ananjeva, and T.J. Papenfuss. 1997. Evolutionary shifts in three major structural features of the mitochondrial genome among iguanian lizards. *Journal of Molecular Evolution* 44:660-674.

MacFadden, B.J. 1992. *Fossil Horses*. Cambridge University Press, New York.

MacFarland, C.G., J. Villa, and B. Toro. 1974. The Galápagos giant tortoises (*Geochelone elephantopus*) part I: status of the surviving populations. *Biological Conservation* 6(2):118-133.

Mannen, H., S.C. Tsoi, J.S. Krushkal, W.H. Li, and S.S. Li. 1997. The cDNA cloning and molecular evolution of reptile and pigeon lactate dehydrogenase isozymes. *Molecular Biology and Evolution* 14(11): 1081-1087.

Markham, C.R. 1892. Discovery of the Galapagos Islands. *Proceedings of the Royal Geographic Society and Monthly Record of Geography* 14:314-316.

Márquez, C., G. Morillo, and L.J. Cayot. 1991. A 25-year management program pays off: repatriated tortoises on Española reproduce. *Noticias de Galápagos* 50:17-18.

Márquez, C., M. Wilson, S. Rea, F. Cepeda, and F. Llerena. 1987. The giant tortoise conservation program. *Noticias de Galápagos* 45:17-18.

Marsh, F.L. 1941. *Fundamental Biology*. Published by the author, Lincoln, NE.

Marsh, F.L. 1944. *Evolution, Creation, and Science*. First edition. Review and Herald Publishing Association, Washington, D.C.

Marsh, F.L. 1945. The present status of genetics and the origin of species. *Bulletin of Creation, the Deluge and Related Sciences* V(1):1-9.

Marsh, F.L. 1947. *Evolution, Creation, and Science*. Second edition. Review and Herald Publishing Association, Washington, D.C.

Marsh, F.L. 1950. *Studies in Creationism*. Review and Herald Publishing, Washington, DC.

Marsh, F.L. 1976. *Variation and Fixity in Nature*. Pacific Press Publishing Association, Omaha, Nebraska.

Martin, R.L. 1996. The phantom bridge exposed: the latest turtle attack.

*Creation Research Society Quarterly* 33(1):15-17.

Marvaldi, A.E., A.S. Sequeira, C.W. O'Brien, and B.D. Farrell. 2002. Molecular and morphological phylogenetics of Weevils (Coleoptera, Curculionoidea): Do niche shifts accompany diversification? *Systematic Biology* 51(5):761-785.

Mayr, E. 2001. *What Evolution Is*. Basic Books, New York.

Mayr, G. 2003. The phylogenetic affinities of the shoebill (*Balaeniceps rex*). *Journal für Ornithologie* 144:157-175.

Mauchamp, A. 1996. *Scalesia atractyloides*: one bite from extinction. *Noticias de Galápagos* 57:24-25.

Mauchamp, A. 1997. Monoecy in the dioecious *Croton scouleri*, endemic to Galápagos. *Noticias de Galápagos* 58:15-17.

Mauchamp, A., I. Aldaz, E. Ortiz, and H. Valdebenito. 1998. Threatened species, a re-evaluation of the status of eight endemic plants of the Galápagos. *Biodiversity and Conservation* 7:97-107.

McBirney, A.R. and K. Aoki. 1966. Petrology of the Galápagos Islands. In Bowman, R.I., ed. *The Galápagos*. University of California Press, Berkeley, pp. 71-77.

McBirney, A.R. and H. Williams. 1969. Geology and Petrology of the Galápagos Islands. *Geological Society of America Memoir* 118:1-197.

McCoy, D.L. 1992. Evidence against the evolutionary superiority of plant pathogenesis. In: *Proceedings of the 1992 Twin-Cities Creation Conference*. Twin Cities Creation Science Association, Roseville, MN, pp. 186-191.

McEwen, A. 1988. The English place-names of the Galápagos. *Geographical Journal* 154:234-242.

McFarland, C. and M. Cifuentes. 1996. Case study: Galápagos, Ecuador. In Dompka, V., ed. *Human Population, Biodiversity and Protected Areas: Science and Policy Issues*. American Association for the Advancement of Science, Washington, pp. 135-188.

McMullen, C.K. 1987. Breeding systems of selected Galápagos Islands angiosperms. *American Journal of Botany* 74:1694-1705.

McMullen, C.K. 1999. *Flowering plants of the Galápagos*. Comstock Publishing Associates, Ithaca, NY.

McPhaden, M.J. 1999. Genesis and evolution of the 1997-98 El Niño. *Science* 283:950-954.

McPhaden, M.J. 2004. Evolution of the 2002/03 El Niño. *Bulletin of the American Meteorological Society* 85(5):677-695.

Meiborn, A., D.L. Anderson, N.H. Sleep, R. Frei, C.P. Chamberlain, M.T. Hren, and J.L. Wooden. 2003. Are high $^3He/^4He$ ratios in oceanic basalts an indicator of deep-mantle plume components? *Earth and Planetary Science Letters* 208(3-4):197-204.

Merlen, G. 1985. The 1982-83 El Nino: some of its consequences for Galapagos wildlife. *Noticias de Galápagos* 41:8-15.

Merlen, G. and G. Davis-Merlen. 2000. Whish: more than a tool-using finch. *Noticias de Galápagos* 61:2-9.

Meschede, M. and U. Barckhausen. 2000. Plate tectonic evolution of the Cocos-Nazca spreading center. *Proceedings of the Ocean Drilling Program, Scientific Results* 170:1-10.

Monson, R.K. 1989. On the evolutionary pathways resulting in $C_4$ photosynthesis and Crassulacean acid metabolism (CAM). *Advances in Ecological Research* 19:57-110.

Monson, R.K., G.E. Edwards, and M.S.B. Ku. 1984. $C_3$-$C_4$ intermediate photosynthesis in plants. *BioScience* 34:563-574.

Monson, R.K. and B.D. Moore. 1989. On the significance of $C_3$-$C_4$ intermediate photosynthesis in the evolution of $C_4$ photosynthesis. *Plant, Cell and Environment* 12:689-699.

Montelli, R., G. Nolet, F.A. Dahlen, G. Masters, E.R. Engdahl, and S.-H. Hung. 2004. Finite-frequency tomography reveals a variety of plumes in the mantle. *Science* 303:338-343.

Morgan, W.J. 1971. Convection plumes in the lower mantle. *Nature* 230:42-43.

Morris, H.M. and J.D. Morris. 1996. *The Modern Creation Trilogy Volume Two Science and Creation.* Master Books, Green Forest, AR.

Morris, H.M. and G.E. Parker. 1987. *What is Creation Science?* Revised edition. Master Books, Green Forest, AK.

Motani, R., N. Minoura, and T. Ando. 1998. Ichthyosaurian relationships illuminated by new primitive skeletons from Japan. *Nature* 393: 255-257.

Moxie [Helder, M.]. 1996. Job sharing among Emperors. *Creation Science Dialogue* 23(4):6.

Murphy, O.C. and G.F. Howe. 1975. Desert survival and four-carbon photosynthesis. *Creation Research Society Quarterly* 12(2):113-114.

Myrcha, A., P. Jadwiszczak, C.P. Tambussi, J.I. Noriega, A. Gaździcki, and A. Tatur. 2002. Taxonomic revision of Eocene Antarctic penguins based on tarsometatarsal morphology. *Polish Polar Research* 23(1):5-46.

Nelson, B.C. 1927. *"After Its Kind" The First and Last Word on Evolution.* Augsburg Publishing House, Minneapolis.

Nelson, G. 1978. From Candolle to Croizat: comments on the history of biogeography. *Journal of the History of Biology* 11(2):269-305.

Nelson, J.B. 1978. *The Sulidae.* Oxford University Press, Oxford.

Nevins, S.E. 1974. Post-Flood strata of the John Day Country, northeastern Oregon. *Creation Research Society Quarterly* 10(4): 191-204.

Nielsen, L.R., M. Philipp, and H.R. Siegismund. 2002. Selective advantage of ray florets in *Scalesia affinis* and *S. pedunculata*

(Asteraceae), two endemic species from the Galápagos. *Evolutionary Ecology* 16:139-153.

Nobel, P.S. 1981. Influences of photosynthetically active radiation on cladode orientation, stem tilting, and height of cacti. *Ecology* 62: 982-990.

Norell, M.A. and K. de Queiroz. 1991. The earliest iguanine lizard (Reptilia: Squamata) and its bearing on iguanine phylogeny. *American Museum Novitates* 2997:1-16.

Numbers, R.L. 1992. *The Creationists.* University of California Press, Los Angeles.

Nyffeler, R. 2002. Phylogenetic relationships in the cactus family (Cactaceae) based on evidence from *trnK/matK* and *trnL-trnF* sequences. *American Journal of Botany* 89(2):312-326.

Oard, M.J. 2002. Is catastrophic plate tectonics part of earth history? *TJ* 16(1):64-68.

O'Daniel, D. 2002. Water, water everywhere ... and not a drop to drink? *Impact* 348:i-iv.

O'Hara, R.J. 1989. An estimate of the phylogeny of the living penguins (Aves: Spheniscidae). *American Zoologist* 29:11A.

Orr, R.T. 1966. Evolutionary aspects of the mammalian fauna of the Galápagos. In Bowman, R.I., ed. *The Galápagos.* University of California Press, Berkeley, pp. 276-281.

Ospovat, D. 1981. *The Development of Darwin's Theory: Natural History, Natural Theology, and Natural Selection, 1838-1859.* Cambridge University Press, New York.

Padian, K. 1991. The origin of turtles: one fewer problem for creationists? *NCSE Reports* 11(2):18-19.

Palmer, C.E. and R.L. Pyle. 1966. The climatological setting of the Galápagos. In Bowman, R.I., ed. *The Galápagos.* University of California Press, Berkeley, pp. 93-99.

Panero, J.L., R.K. Jansen, and J.A. Clevinger. 1999. Phylogenetic relationships of subtribe Ecliptinae (Asteraceae: Heliantheae) based on chloroplast DNA restriction site data. *American Journal of Botany* 86:413-427.

Peaker, M. and J.L. Linzell. 1975. *Salt Glands in Birds and Reptiles.* Cambridge University Press, Cambridge.

Peterson, R.T. 1967. The Galapagos eerie cradle of new species. *National Geographic* 131(4):541-585.

Petren, K. 1998. Microsatellite primers from *Geospiza fortis* and cross-species amplification in Darwin's finches. *Molecular Ecology* 7: 1771-1788.

Petren, K., B.R. Grant, and P.R. Grant. 1999. A phylogeny of Darwin's finches based on microsatellite DNA length variation. *Proceedings of the Royal Society of London, Series B* 266:321-329.

Petto, A.J. 1983. The turtle: evolutionary dilemma or creationist shell game? *Creation/Evolution* 3:20-29.

Pielke, R.A. and C.N. Landsea. 1999. La Niña, El Niño and Atlantic hurricane damages in the United States. *Bulletin of the American Meteorological Society* 80(10):2027-2033.

Pitman, R.L. and J.R. Jehl. 1998. Geographic variation and reassessment of species limits in the "masked" boobies of the eastern Pacific Ocean. *Wilson Bulletin* 110:155-170.

Platz, J.E. and J.M. Conlon. 1997. ...And turn back again. *Nature* 389: 246.

Podos, J. 2001. Correlated evolution of morphology and vocal signal structure in Darwin's finches. *Nature* 409:185-188.

Polans, N.O. 1983. Enzyme polymorphisms in Galapagos finches. In: Bowman, R.I., M. Berson, and A.E. Leviton, eds. *Patterns of Evolution in Galapagos Organisms*. Pacific Division, AAAS, San Francisco, pp. 219-236.

Porter, D.M. 1980. Charles Darwin's plant collections from the voyage of the *Beagle*. *Journal of the Society for the Bibliography of Natural History* 9:515-525.

Porter, D.M. 1983. Vascular plants of the Galapagos: origins and dispersal. In: Bowman, R.I., M. Berson, and A.E. Leviton, eds. *Patterns of Evolution in Galapagos Organisms*. Pacific Division, AAAS, San Francisco, pp. 33-96.

Price, G.M. 1945. An unregimented biologist. *Bulletin of Creation, the Deluge and Related Sciences* V(1):9-11.

Pritchard, P.C.H. 1996. The Galápagos Tortoises: nomenclatural and survival status. *Chelonian Research Monographs* 1:1-85.

Raghavendra, A.S., G. Rajendrudu, and V.S.R. Das. 1978. Simultaneous occurrence of $C_3$ and $C_4$ photosynthesis in relation to leaf position in *Mollugo nudicaulis*. *Nature* 273:143-144.

Rassmann, K. 1997. Evolutionary age of the Galápagos iguanas predates the age of the present Galápagos islands. *Molecular Phylogenetics and Evolution* 7:158-172.

Rassmann, K., F. Trillmich, and D. Tautz. 1997. Hybridization between the Galápagos land and marine iguanas (*Conolophus subcristatus* and *Amblyrhynchus cristatus*) on Plaza Sur. *Journal of Zoology, London* 242:729-739.

Reed, J.K., ed. 2001. *Plate Tectonics: A Different View*. Creation Research Society, St. Joseph, MO.

Reed, J.K. 2002. Reinventing stratigraphy at the Palo Duro basin. *Creation Research Society Quarterly* 39:25-39.

Reilly, P. 1994. *Penguins of the World*. Oxford University Press, New York.

Reiss, M. 1986. Correspondence. *Biblical Creation* 8:67-68.

Reisz, R.R. and M. Laurin. 1991. *Owenetta* and the origin of turtles. *Nature* 349:324-326.

ReMine, W.J. 1990. Discontinuity systematics: A new methodology of biosystematics relevant to the creation model. In: Walsh, R.E. and C.L. Brooks, eds. *Proceedings of the Second International Conference on Creationism.* Creation Science Fellowship, Pittsburgh, pp. 207-213.

ReMine, W.J. 1993. *The Biotic Message.* St. Paul Science, St. Paul, MN.

Rest, J.S., J.C. Ast, C.C. Austin, P.J. Waddell, E.A. Tibbetts, J.M. Hay, and D.P. Mindell. 2003. Molecular systematics of primary reptilian lineages and the tuatara mitochondrial genome. *Molecular Phylogenetics and Evolution* 29:289-297.

Richards, M.A., R.A. Duncan, and V.E. Courtillot. 1989. Flood basalts and hot-spot tracks: plume heads and tails. *Science* 246:103-107.

Richards, M.A., D.L. Jones, R.A. Duncan, D.J. DePaolo. 1991. A mantle plume initiation model for the Wrangelia Flood Basalt and other oceanic plateaus. *Science* 254:263-267.

Richardson, R.A. 1981. Biogeography and the genesis of Darwin's ideas on transmutation. *Journal of the History of Biology* 14(1):1-41.

Riedinger, M.A., M. Steinitz-Kannan, W.M. Last, and M. Brenner. 2002. A ~6100 $^{14}$C year record of El Niño activity from the Galápagos Islands. *Journal of Paleolimnology* 27:1-7.

Rieppel, O. 2001. Turtles as hopeful monsters. *BioEssays* 23(11):987-991.

Rieppel, O. and M. deBraga. 1996. Turtles as diapsid reptiles. *Nature* 384:453-455.

Rieppel, O. and R.R. Reisz. 1999. The origin and early evolution of turtles. *Annual Review of Ecology and Systematics* 30:1-22.

Riesing, M.J., L. Kruckenhauser, A. Gamauf, and E. Haring. 2003. Molecular phylogeny of the genus *Buteo* (Aves: Accipitridae) based on mitochondrial marker sequences. *Molecular Phylogenetics and Evolution* 27:328-342.

Robinson, D.A. 1997. A mitochondrial DNA analysis of the Testudine apobaramin. *Creation Research Society Quarterly* 33:262-272.

Robinson, D.A. and D.P. Cavanaugh. 1998a. A quantative approach to baraminology with examples from Catarrhine primates. *Creation Research Society Quarterly* 34:196-208.

Robinson, D.A. and D.P. Cavanaugh. 1998b. Evidence for a holobaraminic origin of the cats. *Creation Research Society Quarterly* 35:2-14.

Robinson, H. 1981. A revision of the tribal and subtribal limits of the Heliantheae (Asteraceae). *Smithsonian Contributions to Botany* 51: 1-102.

Roff, D.A. 1990. The evolution of flightlessness in insects. *Ecological Monographs* 60:389-421.

Romer, A.S. 1945. *Vertebrate Paleontology.* University of Chicago

Press, Chicago.

Rosenberg, D.K. and S.A. Harcourt. 1987. Population sizes and potential conservation problems of the endemic Galapagos penguin and flightless cormorant. *Noticias de Galápagos* 42:24-25.

Ross, H. 2004. *A Matter of Days*. NavPress, Colorado Springs.

Roth, A.A. 1985. Are millions of years required to produce biogenic sediments in the deep oceans. *Origins (GRI)* 12(1):48-56.

Roth, A.A. 1998. *Origins: Linking Science and Scripture*. Review and Herald Publishing Association, Hagerstown, MD.

Roth, V.L. 2001. Ecology and evolution of dwarfing in insular elephants. In: Cavarretta, G., P. Gioia, M. Mussi, and M.R. Palombo, eds. *The World of Elephants*. Consiglio Nazionale delle Ricerche, Rome, pp. 507-509.

Ruse, M. 1982. Creation science is not science. *Science, Technology, and Human Values* 7:72-78.

Sage, R.F. and R.K. Monson. 1999. *$C_4$ Plant Biology*. Academic Press, San Diego.

Sanders, R.W., T.F. Stuessy, C. Marticorena, and M. Silva O. 1987. Phytogeography and evolution of Dendroseris and Robinsonia, tree-Compositae of the Juan Fernandez Islands. *Opera Botanica* 92: 195-215.

Sarfati, J. 2002. *Refuting Evolution 2*. MasterBooks, Green Forest, Arkansas.

Sato, A., C. O'hUigin, F. Figueroa, P.R. Grant, B.R. Grant, H. Tichy, and J. Klein. 1999. Phylogeny of Darwin's finches as revealed by mtDNA sequences. *Proceedings of the National Academy of Science, USA* 96:5101-5106.

Sato, A., H. Tichy, C. O'hUigin, P.R. Grant, B.R. Grant, and J. Klein. 2001. On the origin of Darwin's finches. *Molecular Biology and Evolution* 18(3):299-311.

Sayre, R.T. and R.A. Kennedy. 1977. Ecotypic differences in the $C_3$ and $C_4$ photosynthetic activity in *Mollugo verticillata*, a $C_3$-$C_4$ intermediate. *Planta* 134:257-262.

Scherer, S., ed. 1993a. *Typen des Lebens*. Pascal-Verlag, Berlin.

Scherer, S. 1993b. Basic Types of Life. In: Scherer, S., ed. *Typen des Lebens*. Pascal-Verlag, Berlin, pp. 11-30.

Scherer, S. 1998. Basic types of life: evidence of design from taxonomy? In Dembski, W.A., ed. *Mere Creation*. InterVarsity Press, Downers Grove, IL.

Schilling, E.E., J.L. Panero, and U.H. Eliasson. 1994. Evidence from chloroplast DNA restriction site analysis on the relationships of *Scalesia* (Asteraceae: Heliantheae). *American Journal of Botany* 81: 248-254.

Schloss, J.P. 1998. Evolutionary accounts of altruism and the problem of goodness by design. In: Dembski, W.A., ed. *Mere Creation*.

InterVarsity, Downers Grove, IL, pp. 236-261.

Schluter, D., T.D. Price, and P.R. Grant. 1985. Ecological character displacement in Darwin's finches. *Science* 227:1056-1059.

Schneider, R.A. and J.A. Helms. 2003. The cellular and molecular origins of beak morphology. *Science* 299:565-568.

Schreiber, A., M. Stubbe, and A. Stubbe. 2000. Red kite (*Milvus milvus*) and black kite (*M. migrans*): minute genetic interspecies distance of two raptors breeding in a mixed community (Falconiformes: Accipitridae). *Biological Journal of the Linnean Society* 69(3):351-365.

Schrope, M. 2000. Galapagos ecologists under threat from violent protests. *Nature* 408:761.

Schulte, J.A., J.R. Macey, A. Larson, and T.J. Papenfuss. 1998. Molecular tests of phylogenetic taxonomies: a general procedure and example using four subfamilies of the lizard family Iguanidae. *Molecular Phylogenetics and Evolution* 10:367-376.

Sequeira, A.S., A.A. Lanteri, M.A. Scataglini, V.A. Confalonieri, and B.D. Farrell. 2000. Are flightless *Galapaganus* weevils older than the Galápagos Islands they inhabit? *Heredity* 85:20-29.

Shaffer, H.B., P. Meylan, and M.L. McKnight. 1997. Tests of turtle phylogeny: molecular, morphological, and paleontological approaches. *Systematic Biology* 46:235-268.

Shumway, G. 1954. Carnegie Ridge and Cocos Ridge in the east equatorial Pacific. *Journal of Geology* 62:573-586.

Sibley, C.G. and B.L. Monroe, Jr. 1990. *Distribution and Taxonomy of Birds of the World.* Yale University Press, New Haven, CT.

Siegel-Causey, D. 1988. Phylogeny of the Phalacrocoracidae. *Condor* 90:885-905.

Simkin, T. 1977. Another eruption of the Fernandina volcano. *Noticias de Galápagos* 26:25.

Sites, J.W., S.K. Davis, T. Guerra, J.B. Iverson, and H.L. Snell. 1996. Character congruence and phylogenetic signal in molecular and morphological data sets: a case study in the living Iguanas (Squamata, Iguanidae). *Molecular Biology and Evolution* 13:1087-1105.

Slevin J.R. 1959. The Galápagos islands: a history of their exploration. *Occasional Papers of the California Academy of Sciences* 25:1-150.

Smith, A.D. 2003. Intraplate volcanism: concepts, problems and proofs. *Astronomy & Geophysics* 44:2.8-2.9.

Smith, A.G. 1966. Land snails of the Galápagos. In Bowman, R.I., ed. *The Galápagos.* University of California Press, Berkeley, pp. 240-251.

Smith, G.T.C. 1990. A brief history of the Charles Darwin Foundation for the Galapagos Islands 1959-1988. *Noticias de Galápagos* 49: 1-36.

Smith, J.M. 1958. *The Theory of Evolution*. Pelican Books, Baltimore.

Smith, T.B. 1993. Disruptive selection and the genetic basis of bill size polymorphism in the African finch *Pyrenestes*. *Nature* 363: 618-620.

Smith, W.H.F. and D.T. Sandwell. 1997. Global sea floor topography from satellite altimetry and ship depth soundings. *Science* 277: 1956-1962.

Snell, H. and S. Rea. 1999. The 1997-98 El Niño in Galápagos: Can 34 years of data estimate 120 years of pattern? *Noticias de Galápagos* 60:11-20.

Snell, H.M., P.A. Stone, and H.L. Snell. 1995. Geographical characteristics of the Galápagos Islands. *Noticias de Galápagos* 55: 18-24.

Snelling, A.A. 1996. Where should we place the Flood/post-Flood boundary in the geological record? *Creation Ex Nihilo Technical Journal* 10:29-31.

Snelling, A.A. 2000. Conflicting 'ages' of Tertiary basalt and contained fossilized wood, Crinum, central Queensland, Australia. *Creation Ex Nihilo Technical Journal* 14(2):99-122.

Snelling, A.A. 2003. The relevance of Rb-Sr, Sm-Nd, and Pb-Pb isotope systematics to elucidation of the genesis and history of recent andesite flows at Mt Ngauruhoe, New Zealand, and the implications for radioisotopic dating. In: Ivey, R.L., ed. *Proceedings of the Fifth International Conference on Creationism*. Creation Science Fellowship, Pittsburgh, pp. 285-303.

Snelling, A.A., J. Scheven, P. Garner, M. Ernst, S.A. Austin, M. Garton, E. Scheven, K.P. Wise, and D. Tyler. 1996. The geological record. *Creation Ex Nihilo Technical Journal* 10(3):333-334.

Spring, O., N. Heil, and U. Eliasson. 1999. Chemosystematic studies on the genus *Scalesia* (Asteraceae). *Biochemical Systematics and Ecology* 27:277-288.

Spring, O., N. Heil, and B. Vogler. 1997. Sesquiterpene lactones and flavanones in *Scalesia* species. *Phytochemistry* 46:1369-1373.

Stambaugh, J. 1991. Creation's original diet and the changes at the Fall. *Creation Ex Nihilo Technical Journal* 5:130-138.

Stauffer, R.C. 1959. "On the Origin of Species": an unpublished version. *Science* 130:1449-1452.

Stauffer, R.C., ed. 1975a. *Charles Darwin's Natural Selection, Being the Second Part of His Big Species Book Written from 1856 to 1858*. Cambridge University Press, New York.

Stauffer, R.C. 1975b. General introduction. In R.C. Stauffer, ed. *Charles Darwin's Natural Selection, Being the Second Part of His Big Species Book Written from 1856 to 1858*. Cambridge University Press, New York.

Steadman, D.W. 1986. Holocene vertebrate fossils from Isla Floreana,

Galápagos. *Smithsonian Contributions to Zoology* 413:1-103.

Stebbins, G.L. 1966. Variation and adaptation in Galápagos plants. In: Bowman, R.I., ed. *The Galápagos: Proceedings of the Symposia of the Galápagos International Scientific Project.* University of California Press, Los Angeles, pp. 46-54.

Steinberger, B., R. Sutherland, and R.J. O'Connell. 2004. Prediction of Emperor-Hawaii seamount locations from a revised model of global plate motion and mantle flow. *Nature* 430:167-173.

Stephens, S.G. 1958. Salt water tolerance of seeds of *Gossypium* species as a possible factor in seed dispersal. *American Naturalist* 92:83-92.

Stephens, S.G. 1966. The potentiality for long range oceanic dispersal of cotton seeds. *American Naturalist* 100:199-210.

Stephens, S.G. and Rick, C. M. 1966. Problems on the origin, dispersal, and establishment of the Galápagos cottons. In: Bowman, R.I., ed. *The Galápagos: Proceedings of the Symposia of the Galápagos International Scientific Project.* University of California Press, Los Angeles, pp. 201-208.

Storey, B.C. 1995. The role of mantle plumes in continental breakup: case histories from Gondwanaland. *Nature* 377:301-308.

Sulloway, F.J. 1982a. Darwin and his finches: the evolution of a legend. *Journal of the History of Biology* 15:1-53.

Sulloway, F.J. 1982b. Darwin's conversion: the *Beagle* voyage and its aftermath. *Journal of the History of Biology* 15:325-396.

Sulloway, F.J. 1983. The legend of Darwin's finches. *Nature* 303:372.

Sulloway, F.J. 1984. Darwin and the Galapagos. *Biological Journal of the Linnean Society* 21:29-59.

Sulloway, F.J. 1985. Darwin's "dogged" genius: his Galapagos visit in retrospect. *Noticias de Galápagos* 42:7-14.

Svenson, H.K. 1938. Pteridophyta of the Galapagos and Cocos Islands. *Bulletin of the Torrey Club* 65:303-333.

Swarth, H.S. 1929. A new bird family (Geospizidae) from the Galapagos Islands. *Proceedings of the California Academy of Sciences* XVIII(2): 29-43.

Swarth, H.S. 1931. The avifauna of the Galapagos Islands. *Occasional Papers of the California Academy of Sciences* 18:1-299.

Tarduno, J.A., R.A. Duncan, D.W. Scholl, R.D. Cottrell, B. Steinberger, T. Thordarson, B.C. Kerr, C.R. Neal, F.A. Frey, M. Torii, and C. Carvallo. 2003. The Emperor Seamounts: southward motion of the Hawaiian hotspot plume in earth's mantle. *Science* 301:1064-1069.

Tarlow, E.M., M. Wikelski, and D.J. Anderson. 2001. Hormonal correlates of siblicide in Galápagos Nazca boobies. *Hormones and Behavior* 40:14-20.

Thompson, J.D., D.G. Higgins, and T.J. Gibson. 1994. CLUSTAL W:

improving the sensitivity of progressive multiple sequence alignment through sequence weighting, position-specific gap penalties and weight matrix choice. *Nucleic Acids Research* 22:4673-4680.

Thornton, I. 1971. *Darwin's Islands: A Natural History of the Galápagos.* The Natural History Press, Garden City, NY.

Trenberth, K.E. 1997. The definition of El Niño. *Bulletin of the American Meteorological Society* 78(12):2771-2777.

Tyler, D.J. 1997. Adaptations within the bear family: a contribution to the debate about the limits of variation. *Creation Matters* 2(5):1-4.

Valle, C.A. 1986. Status of the Galapagos penguin and flightless cormorant populations in 1985. *Noticias de Galápagos* 43:16-17.

Valle, C.A., F. Cruz, J.B. Cruz, G. Merlen, and M.C. Coulter. 1987. The impact of the 1982-1983 El Niño-Southern Oscillation on seabirds in the Galapagos Islands, Ecuador. *Journal of Geophysical Research* 92(C13):14437-14444.

Van Dyke, E.C. 1953. The Coleoptera of the Galapagos Islands. *Occasional Papers of the California Academy of Sciences* 22:1-181.

van Tuinen, M., D.B. Butvill, J.A.W. Kirsch, and S.B. Hedges. 2001. Convergence and divergence in the evolution of aquatic birds. *Proceedings of the Royal Society of London Series B* 268:1345-1350.

van Tuinen, M. and S.B. Hedges. 2004. The effect of external and internal fossil calibrations on the avian evolutionary timescale. *Journal of Paleontology* 78(1):45-50.

Vardiman, L. 1994a. An analytical young-earth flow model of the ice sheet formation during the "Ice Age". In: Walsh, R.E., ed. *Proceedings of the Third International Conference on Creationism.* Creation Science Fellowship, Pittsburgh, pp. 561-568.

Vardiman, L. 1994b. A conceptual transition model of the atmospheric global circulation following the Genesis Flood. In: Walsh, R.E., ed. *Proceedings of the Third International Conference on Creationism.* Creation Science Fellowship, Pittsburgh, pp. 569-579.

Vardiman, L. 1996a. *Ice Cores and the Age of the Earth.* Institute for Creation Research, El Cajon, CA.

Vardiman, L. 1996b. *Sea-Floor Sediment and the Age of the Earth.* Institute for Creation Research, El Cajon, CA.

Vardiman, L. 1998. Numerical simulation of precipitation induced by hot mid-ocean ridges. In: Walsh, R.E., ed. *Proceedings of the Fourth International Conference on Creationism.* Creation Science Fellowship, Pittsburgh, pp. 595-605.

Vardiman, L. 2003. Hypercanes following the Genesis Flood. In: Ivey, R.L., ed. *Proceedings of the Fifth International Conference on Creationism.* Creation Science Fellowship, Pittsburgh, pp. 17-28.

Vardiman, L., S.A. Austin, J.R. Baumgardner, E.F. Chaffin, D.B. DeYoung,

D.R. Humphreys, and A.A. Snelling. 2003. Radioisotopes and the age of the earth. In: Ivey, R.L., ed. *Proceedings of the Fifth International Conference on Creationism.* Creation Science Fellowship, Pittsburgh, pp. 337-348.

Vardiman, L., A.A. Snelling, and E.F. Chaffin. 2000. *Radioisotopes and the Age of the Earth.* Institute for Creation Research & Creation Research Society, El Cajon, CA.

Vargas, H., H.M. Snell, H.L. Snell, G. Miller, R. Miller, and H. Serrano. 1997. First report of penguins nesting on Isla Floreana. *Noticias de Galápagos* 58:30-32.

Venables, W.N. and B.D. Ripley. 1997. *Modern Applied Statistics with S-PLUS.* Springer-Verlag, New York.

Vincek, V., C. O'hUigin, Y. Satta, N. Takahata, P.T. Boag, P.R. Grant, B.R. Grant, and J. Klein. 1997. How large was the founding population of Darwin's finches? *Proceedings of the Royal Society of London, Series B* 264:111-118.

Voous, K.H. and T. de Vries. 1978. Systematic place and geographic history of the Galapagos hawk, *Buteo galapagoensis*. *Le Gerfaut* 68: 245-252.

Walker, T. 2001. Post-Flood volcanism on the Banks peninsula, New Zealand. *TJ* 15(1):96-104.

Walker, T. 2002. Devils Tower and Bible glasses. *Creation* 24(3):20-23.

Warheit, K.I. 1990. *The Phylogeny of the Sulidae (Aves: Pelecaniformes) and the Morphometry of Flight-related Structures in Seabirds: A Study of Adaptation*, unpublished dissertation. University of California at Berkeley, Berkeley.

Wells, J. 2000. *Icons of Evolution.* Regnery Publishing, Washington, D.C.

Werner, R., K. Hoernle, P. van den Bogaard, C. Ranero, R. von Huene, and D. Korich. 1999. Drowned 14-m.y.-old Galápagos archipelago off the coast of Costa Rica: implications for tectonic and evolutionary models. *Geology* 27(6):499-502.

Werner, T.K. and T.W. Sherry. 1987. Behavioral feeding specialization in *Pinarolaxias inornata*, the "Darwin's finch" of Cocos Island, Costa Rica. *Proceedings of the National Academy of Science, USA* 84: 5506-5510.

Weston, P. 1999. Turtles. *Creation* 21:28-31.

Whitcomb, J.C. and H.M. Morris. 1961. *The Genesis Flood.* Presbyterian and Reformed Publishing, Phillipsburg, NJ.

White, W.M., A.R McBirney, and R.A. Duncan. 1993. Petrology and geochemistry of the Galápagos Islands: portrait of a pathological mantle plume. *Journal of Geophysical Research* 98(B11):19533-19563.

Wieland, C. 1991. Variation, information, and the created kind.

*Creation Ex Nihilo Technical Journal* 5:42-47.

Wieland, C. 1992. Darwin's finches: evidence supporting rapid post-Flood 'adaptation'. *Creation Ex Nihilo* 14:22-23.

Wieland, C. 1995. The Beak of the Finch: Evolution in Real Time [Book Review]. *Creation Ex Nihilo Technical Journal* 9:21-24.

Wieland, C. 1997. Beetle bloopers. *Creation* 19(3):30.

Wiens, J.J. and B.D. Hollingsworth. 2000. War of the iguanas: conflicting molecular and morphological phylogenies and long-branch attraction in iguanid lizards. *Systematic Biology* 49:143-159.

Wiggins, I.L. 1966. Origins and relationships of the flora of the Galápagos Islands. In: Bowman, R.I., ed. *The Galápagos: Proceedings of the Symposia of the Galápagos International Scientific Project.* University of California Press, Los Angeles, pp. 175-182.

Wiggins, I.L. and D.M. Porter. 1971. *Flora of the Galápagos Islands.* Stanford University Press, Stanford.

Wikelski, M., V. Wong, B. Chevalier, N. Rattenborg, and H.L. Snell. 2002. Marine iguanas die from trace oil pollution. *Nature* 417: 607-608.

Wilkinson, M., J. Thorley, and M.J. Benton. 1997. Uncertain turtle relationships. *Nature* 387:466.

Williams, A. 2004. Baraminology, biology and the Bible. *TJ* 18(2): 53-54.

Williams, H. 1966. Geology of the Galápagos Islands. In: Bowman, R.I., ed. *The Galápagos: Proceedings of the Symposia of the Galápagos International Scientific Project.* University of California Press, Los Angeles, pp. 65-70.

Wink, M., Z. Mikes, J. Rheinheimer. 1997. Phylogenetic relationships in weevils (Coleoptera: Curculionoidea) inferred from nucleotide sequences of mitochondrial 16S rDNA. *Naturwissenschaften* 84: 318-321.

Wise, K.P. 1990. Baraminology: A young-earth creation biosystematic method. In: Walsh, R.E. and C.L. Brooks, eds. *Proceedings of the Second International Conference on Creationism.* Creation Science Fellowship, Pittsburgh, pp. 345-358.

Wise, K.P. 1992. Practical baraminology. *Creation Ex Nihilo Technical Journal* 6:122-137.

Wise, K.P. 1994a. *Australopithecus ramidus* and the fossil record. *Creation Ex Nihilo Technical Journal* 8:160-165.

Wise, K.P. 1994b. It matters where you start. In R.D. Land and L.A. Moore, eds. *Life at Risk.* Broadman & Holman, Nashville, TN, pp. 130-143.

Wise, K.P. 2002. *Faith, Form, and Time.* Broadman & Holman, Nashville.

Wise, K.P. and M. Croxton. 2003. Rafting: A post-Flood biogeographic dispersal mechanism. In: Ivey, R.L., ed. *Proceedings of the Fifth International Conference on Creationism.* Creation Science Fellowship, Pittsburgh, pp. 465-477.

Wood, R.C. 1976. *Stupendemys geographicus*, the world's largest turtle. *Breviora* 436:1-31.

Wood, T.C. 2001. Genome decay in the mycoplasmas. *Impact* 340: i-iv.

Wood, T.C. 2002a. The AGEing process: Post-Flood intrabaraminic diversification caused by Altruistic Genetic Elements (AGEs). *Origins (GRI)* 54:5-34.

Wood, T.C. 2002b. A baraminology tutorial with examples from the grasses (Poaceae). *TJ* 16:15-25.

Wood, T.C. 2002c. The terror of anthrax in a degrading creation. *Impact* 345:i-iv.

Wood, T.C. 2003a. Mediated design. *Impact* 363:i-iv.

Wood, T.C. 2003b. Perspectives on AGEing, a young-earth creation diversification model. In: Ivey, R.L., ed. *Proceedings of the Fifth International Conference on Creationism.* Creation Science Fellowship, Pittsburgh, pp. 479-489.

Wood, T.C. 2005. Visualizing baraminic distances using classical multidimensional scaling. *Origins (GRI)* 57:9-29.

Wood, T.C. and D.P. Cavanaugh. 2001. A baraminological analysis of subtribe Flaveriinae (Asteraceae: Helenieae) and the origin of biological complexity. *Origins (GRI)* 52:7-27.

Wood, T.C. and D.P. Cavanaugh. 2003. An evaluation of lineages and trajectories as baraminological membership criteria. *Occasional Papers of the Baraminology Study Group* 2:1-6.

Wood, T.C. and M.J. Murray. 2003. *Understanding the Pattern of Life.* Broadman & Holman, Nashville.

Wood, T.C., P.J. Williams, K.P. Wise, and D.A. Robinson. 1999. Summaries on camel baraminology. In D.A. Robinson and P.J. Williams, eds. *Baraminology'99.* Baraminology Study Group, Lynchburg, VA, pp. 9-18.

Wood, T.C., K.P. Wise, R. Sanders, and N. Doran. 2003. A refined baramin concept. *Occasional Papers of the Baraminology Study Group* 3:1-14.

Woodmorappe, J. 1981. The essential nonexistence of the evolutionary-uniformitarian geologic column: a quantitative assessment. *Creation Research Society Quarterly* 18(1):46-71.

Woodmorappe, J. 1996. *Noah's Ark: A Feasibility Study.* Institute for Creation Research, El Cajon, CA.

Woodmorappe, J. 2001. Mammal-like reptiles: major trait reversals and discontinuities. *TJ* 15(1):44-52.

Woodmorappe, J. 2002. Walking whales, nested hierarchies, and chimeras: do they exist? *TJ* 16(1):111-119.

Woodmorappe, J. 2003. Bird evolution: discontinuities and reversals. *TJ* 17(1):88-94.

Woodmorappe, J. and M.J. Oard. 2002. Field studies in the Columbia River basalt, north-west USA. *TJ* 16(1):103-110.

Wooster, W.S. and J.W. Hedgpeth. 1966. The oceanographic setting of the Galápagos. In: Bowman, R.I., ed. *The Galápagos: Proceedings of the Symposia of the Galápagos International Scientific Project.* University of California Press, Berkeley, pp. 100-107.

Woram, J.M. 1989. Galapagos Island names. *Noticias de Galápagos* 48:22-32.

Woram, J.M. 1991. Who killed the iguanas? *Noticias de Galápagos* 50:12-17.

Wright, J.W. 1983. The evolution and biogeography of the lizards of the Galapagos Archipelago: Evolutionary genetics of *Phyllodactylus* and *Tropidurus* populations. In: Bowman, R.I., M. Berson, and A.E. Leviton, eds. *Patterns of Evolution in Galapagos Organisms.* Pacific Division, AAAS, San Francisco, pp. 123-155.

Wyles, J.S. and V.M. Sarich. 1983. Are the Galapagos iguanas older than the Galapagos? Molecular evolution and colonization models for the archipelago. In: Bowman, R.I., M. Berson, and A.E. Leviton, eds. *Patterns of Evolution in Galapagos Organisms.* Pacific Division, AAAS, San Francisco, pp. 177-186.

Wysong, R.L. 1976. *The Creation-Evolution Controversy.* Inquiry Press, Midland, MI.

Xiaoping, Z. and K. Bremer. 1993. A cladistic analysis of the tribe Astereae (Asteraceae) with notes on their evolution and subtribal classification. *Plant Systematics and Evolution* 184:259-283.

Xu, X., Z. Zhou, X. Wang, X. Kuang, F. Zhang, and X. Du. 2003. Four-winged dinosaurs from China. *Nature* 421:335-340.

Young, G. and A.S. Householder. 1938. Discussion of a set of points in terms of their mutual distances. *Psychometrika* 3(1):19-22.

Young, P.H. 2003. Whales still have no ancestor. *Creation Research Society Quarterly* 39:213-218.

Zardoya, R. and A. Meyer. 1998. Complete mitochondrial genome suggests diapsid affinities of turtles. *Proceedings of the National Academy of Science USA* 95:14226-14231.

Zera, A.J. and R.F. Denno. 1997. Physiology and ecology of dispersal polymorphism in insects. *Annual Review of Entomology* 42:207-230.

Zimbelmann, F. 1993. Grundtypen bei Greifvögeln (Falconiformes). In: Scherer, S., ed. *Typen des Lebens.* Pascal-Verlag, Berlin, pp. 185-195.

Zug, G.R. 1997. Galápagos Tortoise nomenclature: still unresolved. *Chelonian Conservation and Biology* 2(4):618-619.

# Index

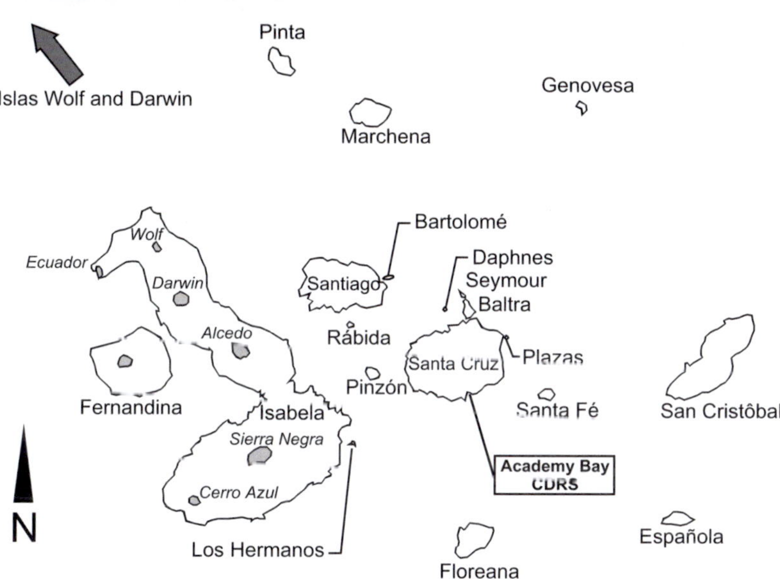


Plate 1. Satellite photograph of the Galápagos Islands (top) and map of the islands (bottom). Calderas on Isabela and Fernandina are indicated in gray. Photo courtesy NASA.

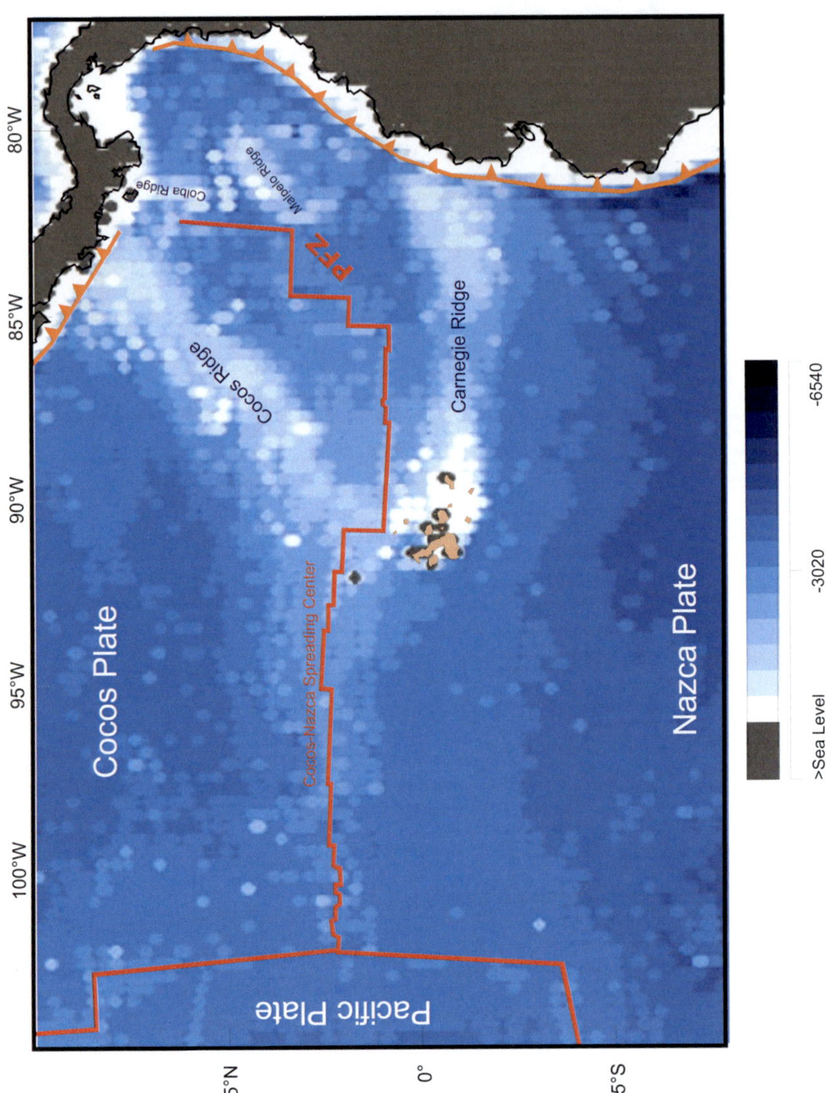


Plate 2. Sea floor around Galápagos, with significant ridges labeled and spreading centers and fracture zones (red lines) and subduction zones (orange) indicated. PFZ = Panama Fracture Zone. Depth key is in meters. Data from Smith and Sandwell (1997).

Plate 3. A barren landscape on Isla Santiago. Note people for scale. Photo courtesy Corel Corporation.

Plate 4. Vegetation coverage on Isla Santa Cruz. Photo courtesy Roger Sanders.

Plate 5. Marine (*Amblyrhynchus*, right) and land (*Conolophus*, left) iguanas. Photos courtesy Corel Corporation.

Plate 6. Marine iguana (*Amblyrhynchus*) grazing on algae on an exposed rock. Photo courtesy Corel Corporation.

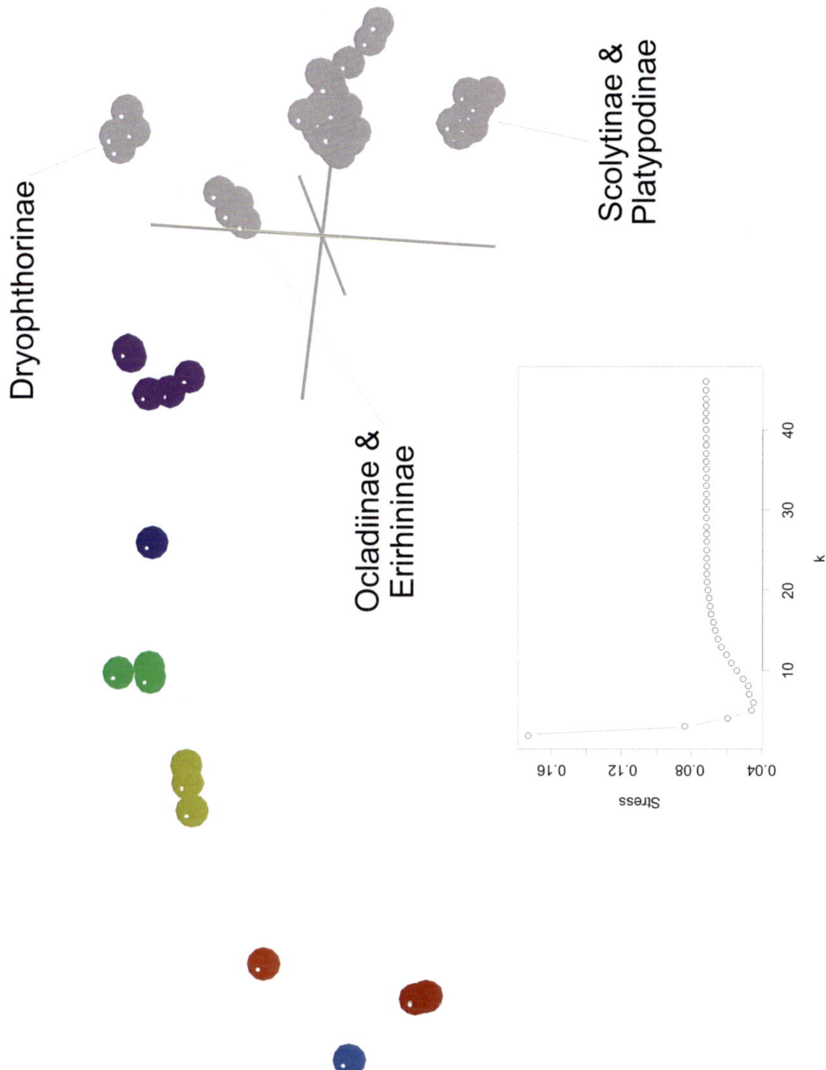


Plate 7. Three-dimensional classical MDS applied to uncorrected weevil baraminic distances (top) and the stress of *k*-dimensional MDS on the same baraminic distance matrix plotted as a function of the number of dimensions (*k*). Taxa shown are from left to right Chrysomeloidea (light blue, consisting of families Megalopodidae and Cerambycidae), Nemonychidae (red), Anthribidae (orange), Belidae (yellow), Attelabidae (green), Caridae (dark blue), Brentidae (purple), and Curculionidae (grey).

Plate 8. Variety of growth habits in *Scalesia*:: shrubby *S. affinis*, I. Isabela (top left), bushy *S. helleri* , I. Santa Cruz (bottom left), and arborescent *S. pedunculata*, I. Santa Cruz (right). Photos courtesy Roger Sanders.